W9-COS-560

In Search of
Security

IN SEARCH OF
SECURITY

A Socio-Psychological Portrait of Today's Germany

GERD LANGGUTH

Translated by Dirk Johnson

PRAEGER

**Westport, Connecticut
London**

Library of Congress Cataloging-in-Publication Data

Langguth, Gerd.
In search of security : a socio-psychological portrait of today's
Germany / Gerd Langguth; translated by Dirk Johnson.
p.   cm.
Includes bibliographical references and index.
ISBN 0–275–95231–2 (hc : alk. paper).—ISBN 0–275–95380–7 (pb)
1. Germany—Economic conditions—1990– 2. Germany—Economic
policy—1990– 3. Germany—Social conditions—1990– 4. Germany—
Politics and government—1990– 5. Germany—History—Unification,
1990. I. Title.
HC286.8.L35   1995
306′.0943′ 09049—dc20   95–31398

British Library Cataloguing in Publication Data is available.

Library of Congress Catalog Card Number: 95–31398
ISBN: 0–275–95231–2
0–275–95380–7 (pbk.)

First published in 1995

Praeger Publishers, 88 Post Road West, Westport, CT 06881
An imprint of Greenwood Publishing Group, Inc.

Printed in the United States of America

The paper used in this book complies with the
Permanent Paper Standard issued by the National
Information Standards Organization (Z39.48–1984).

10 9 8 7 6 5 4 3 2 1

Contents

1. In Lieu of an Introduction: Change and Transformation—
    The Search for Security   1

    Normalcy and Society: The Search for Identity   3

    *The End of the Postwar Era: Wrestling with New
    Responsibility*   5

    The Age of Fast Motion: Wrestling with Reality   8

2. Youth and the Change in Values   11

    Changes in Social Norms and the Pluralism in Lifestyles   11

    *Youth as Sociological Barometer: Satisfaction with
    Democracy—Impatience with Political Parties*   19

    Normal Youth and Spectacular Minorities   20

    *Historical Fragment: The First Signs of Protest and the
    Beginnings of the Youth Rebellion*   21

    *Historical Turning Point: The 1968 Rebellion and the
    "Double-Service Economy"*   22

    Contemporary Fragment: Today's Protests   26

    Today's Situation: Cultural Skepticism   27

    Forms of Protest: Violent Minorities   29

    *The Consequence of Protest: Decision Makers Prepared
    to Take Action*   35

3. The Germans' View of Politics   39

The Unity of the Germans   40

Changes in the East since Reunification   48

The Elections of 1994: Who Voted for Whom and Why?   53

*With a Firm View to the Past: PDS—The Party with a
Janus Face*   62

4. The Germans and Their Nation   73

*The Joy of Unification: The Euphoria of Harmony Rather
Than National Euphoria*   73

*A Common History: Outward Unity Rather Than Inner
Unity*   76

*A Divided History: Dictated Identity Rather Than Lived
Identity*   77

*The Liquidation of History: Against the Suppression of
Memory*   82

The Role of Intellectuals: Against a Feeling of Lethargy?   85

Nation and Democracy: A Process, Not a Condition   89

5. The Economic Challenges of a Reunified Germany   93

The Divided Economy   93

Germany's Economic Situation   97

The Starting Point   98

An Assessment of Germany's Economic Situation   100

Weaknesses of the German Economy   101

Strengths of the German Economy   103

The Social Market Economy as an Economic Factor   105

Measures to Improve Economic Competitiveness   107

Economic Challenges of German Reunification   111

6. Germany's International Role   113

Foreign and Security Policy   113

European Policy   151

Development Policy   163

7. In Lieu of a Conclusion: The Germans in Search of
Security—Ten Theses   181

Contents

Notes   213

Selected Bibliography   235

Index   243

In Lieu of an Introduction: Change and Transformation— The Search for Security

Germany is the only country in the world where two major transformations are taking place simultaneously: the process of modernization that is needed during a period of worldwide recession; and the transformation in the east from a command economy into a free-market economy.

These two processes should not be allowed to run in isolation from each other. Rather, both together (combined with a massive financial transfer of approximately DM 160 billion a year from west to east) must help contribute to the political, social and economic unification of Germany—both internally and externally.

It is a multifaceted and complex process, requiring both sides to merge and become one nation. No one could have expected this process, affecting both east *and* west, to proceed without friction. Reunification came as a surprise—even to the Germans themselves!

A blueprint that shows how to merge two completely different societies did not exist. After all, the collapse of communism and German unification came all too unexpectedly. Thousands of books have described the transformation of capitalism into socialism, but none have laid out the reverse process. In that sense, it is unfair to charge the political leadership with a failure of vision in the reunification of Germany. After all, what have academics, for instance, contributed? In Germany, academics continue to be predominantly theoretical, and they have remained aloof from these specific issues.

An observer of all this is confronted with a host of complex problems. For one, the social processes at work in present-day Germany are not only influenced by the more significant east-west conflict, but by the east-east conflict as well. In the new federal states (whose population of 16 million comprises about one fifth of Germany's total), we are now beginning to witness major clashes between former "perpetrators" and "victims" of the old regime—that is, between those who for forty years took part in the communist dictatorship, and those who suffered under it. This is further exacerbated by the fact that perpetrators and victims are often one and the same.

Moreover, the reunification process and the social changes resulting from it are part of a radical historical transformation the world over—just *one* cog in the giant wheel of change. But it is the Germans in particular who feel affected by this situation. It is the end of old certainties: in west Germany, the certainty of integration into the EC (European Community) and NATO; in east Germany, the certainty of belonging to an "eternal" alliance with the Soviet Union and its socialist ideology. Now, the Germans are searching for a new orientation and a new sense of security.

Many Germans are beginning to wonder if the old frameworks will be able to withstand the "pressures of the moment"—if the old answers are really suitable for new questions. Disorientation and dissatisfaction have become widespread; there is a greater longing for security. But the demand for security is no longer just a military-political matter; it has become much more a demand directed at politics in general. All present debate must deal with the emotional and existential, the direct and the indirect, implications of security.

Will integration make west Germany more "eastern" and east Germany more "western"? What are "western" and "eastern" values in this context? In reunifying, the GDR officially joined the Federal Republic—but does that mean the "Bonn Republic" will now cease to exist? Will an important reference point disappear?

If the Germans are now searching for new certainties, how stable (or how vulnerable to crises) will German democracy become?

Germany is at the center of Europe, and it has the second largest population and a still very powerful economy. What will happen if (as foreign nations are now demanding) it increasingly takes on the role of a stabilizing power? One question that often arises at international conferences is "Do Germans want to become more 'European'?" Or—as some fear—"Do Germans want the Europeans to become more 'German'?" How do Germans perceive their own role?

Which of Germany's present political problems are "self-inflicted," that is, originate primarily in Germany? Or, isn't it a fact that many of the same social tensions are now beginning to appear in other Western industrial societies as well? Have the Germans, then, just been sucked into a vortex of worldwide developments they themselves are powerless to control?

NORMALCY AND SOCIETY: THE SEARCH FOR IDENTITY

These numerous questions from home and abroad must make Germans realize that the burden of history cannot simply be brushed aside—even if 60.9 percent of the German population were born after 1945 (29.9 percent are younger than twenty-five). That fact alone might make us ask if Germany is on its way to becoming a normal society. But what is "normal," considering Germany's historical development?

The founding fathers of the Federal Republic were witnesses to Hitler's dictatorship and the crimes of the Holocaust; even the East German regime derived its legitimacy from "antifascism." At the same time, they also witnessed the internal threat of a new totalitarianism arise in the Eastern part of their nation during the Cold War era. This generation of Germans is presently retiring from all aspects of social, economic and political life, and thus from responsibility.

In west Germany, top positions are now being filled by a generation primarily influenced by the 1968 student revolts—people who came to maturity within about the last twenty-five years. But those student revolts, marking a decisive historical break in West German society, are as far removed from the present student generation as the end of World War II was to the present generation of fifty-year-olds. This raises the question of history's function, particularly if it is no longer directly experienced or lived history.

Without a doubt, there is an inextricable link in most recent German history between memory, confession, forgiveness, reconciliation, and a sense of common identity and new security. Without memory, there can be no justice; and without historical reminiscence, no sense of confidence or identity. Identity is not something static; it grows, it forms itself anew, it must be put into question. This, too, is a sign of "normalcy": one must learn to tolerate questions and tensions.

But the political climate and national and international laws also prevented Germany from returning to a sense of normalcy for more than four decades. The focus of the East-West conflict was Germany, particularly Berlin; it was there that two great world powers faced off in direct, tangible confrontation. Germany's tie to the West was natural and instinctive for the majority of the West Germans, though Adenauer initially had to force the political opposition to accept a Western orientation. The latter was the only possible form of protection against an expansionist communism. A comparable "Eastern orientation" did not exist for the former East Germans.

For the majority of East Germans, West Germany remained the standard against which they measured themselves; it was their actual point of reference. This is reflected in the East German leadership's failure to establish a "socialist German nation." In more than a literal sense, East Germany's antennae were directed toward West Germany.

At the same time, the two Germanies were incorporated into a network of international organizations—the former GDR into the Warsaw Pact and COMECON, both of which were viewed as compulsory by the majority of East Germans. Of all the ruling elites in the states in the Warsaw Pact, the East German leadership was most serious in its dependence on Moscow and its ideological subordination to the Communist Party of the Soviet Union.

The GDR gained its formal "sovereignty" at about the same time as did the Federal Republic. The inner sovereignty that West Germany regained in 1955 was only relative, since the Federal Republic remained dependent on the three major victorious allies (particularly on the United States) in all important matters pertaining to her international status and security.

West Germany's admission to NATO in 1955 quite naturally led to the integration of the newly established Federal Armed Forces, or Bundeswehr, into a military pact system. The European integration process that had begun with the Montan Union, in 1952, and the Treaty of Rome, in 1957, further guaranteed the economic and political stabilization of West Germany—first through the Community of Six, presently through the fifteen-member European Union.

European integration has been seen as two sides of a coin: On the one side, the West Germans wanted, and received, protection against the communist threat. "Security *for* Germany" was the slogan. On the other side, Europe demanded security *from* Germany; it wanted to prevent Germany from going her own way. Europe achieved this by linking Germany to the European Community.

Whereas most East Germans felt that membership in the Warsaw Pact and in COMECON was forced upon them by Moscow, West Germans had intrinsically accepted their nation's integration into both European and international organizations. For many of the founding generation of Germans, Europe was a form of substitute nation—or at the very least, it became their major point of reference.

For some, this function was fulfilled by the United States. The positive image of America offered a sense of stability and identification, and it became a part of the general philosophy for the majority of the Germans and for many politicians. The Germans knew that the military power of the United States protected West Germany, and this knowledge remained a constant component of their political thinking.

It became difficult for many Germans to identify with the German nation in light of past experience with Hitler's dictatorship. "Patriotism" became a historically loaded term. The experience with Hitler had showed Germans how emotional ties to a nation could be brought to a feverish pitch and then be channeled toward brutal and murderous aims, which consequently burdened Germany with historical guilt. As a result, the opinion makers of the founding generation placed greater stress on the component of "reason," whereas the "emotional" component was played down—even though it has played a major role in the democratic and national political traditions of other nations.

But there can be little doubt that the national component offers man a greater sense of orientation. Today's generation of young people once again feels the need for this component and no longer seems to believe that "the national" only reflects misguided emotionalism.

Now is the time to combine once and for all national feeling with democracy in the search for identity. The aim would be to create national consciousness as part of a broad (democratic) identity. Had the symbols of a free German democracy—the black, red and gold colors of the federal flag—been nurtured more, then maybe the old imperial flag would not be so popular in certain German circles. Ignaz Bubis, chairman of the Council of Jews in Germany, was right in pointing this out.

It appears that for forty years the guiding political principle of the Federal Republic was to create the impression that it was in the German national interest *not* to have a national interest. Of course, this just kept the country from achieving political normalcy. Both European integration and member-ship in NATO were declared congruent to the national interest—but spe-cifically national interests were never really outlined. By ignoring these, the country has in the end potentially helped the rise of extremist factions.

THE END OF THE POSTWAR ERA: WRESTLING WITH NEW RESPONSIBILITY

Is Germany on the road to normalcy?

The postwar era ended on October 3, 1990. The political realities that arose from the war were incorporated into international treaties: primarily in the CSCE (Conference on Security and Cooperation in Europe) charter for a new Europe in Paris (November 24, 1990) as well as in the declaration of the four victorious powers and the intra-German agreements. Once again, Germany became a fully sovereign member of the international community.

The four victorious powers passed their responsibility for Germany—most clearly reflected in the unique legal status of Berlin—over to the Germans. This full sovereignty is a symbol for many non-Germans that Germany has significantly increased its power. This impression has been further reinforced by the "partnership in leadership," declared by former American President Bush, and by the more prominent role assumed by Chancellor Kohl at international summits.

Many Germans do not want to admit to this new and unaccustomed international standard that has resulted from reunification. They have yet to liberate themselves from the chains of their own (primarily self-imposed) political restrictions. They are still uncomfortable with their sudden power and greater potential influence, but also with increased international pressure and the calls for greater burden sharing. Germans are still too unaccustomed to their powerful voice in the political concert of Europe.

This is underscored by the way in which Germans have reacted to the growing demand that they participate in international engagements—particularly in connection with security and peacekeeping activities under United Nations auspices. Germans are continuing to struggle with their new role.

The much-discussed "German condition" (*deutsche Befindlichkeit*) clearly shows to what extent the former East-West conflict—despite its dangers—also served as protection. The Germans may have—almost inconspicuously—been involved in all tensions and crises, but at the same time, they also knew that they were integrated into a larger political framework in which they could play a subordinate role. The responsibility that Germans had at this time was kept to a level of passive solidarity with the West. Or more bluntly: Germans lived free from responsibility rather than trying to secure freedom as responsible partners.

Most Germans are well aware that they must assume this new responsibility, but many are still unclear about how this responsibility will eventually take shape. Like many other nations at the end of the Cold War, the Germans too are searching for new certainties and new security. But what will this new security mean?

The end of the Cold War—which could reemerge due to the unstable situation in Russia—has produced a new psychological climate in Germany. In moments of major East-West conflicts, West German society was internally secure. It was also relatively easy to build up a contrasting position to totalitarianism, dictatorship and the abuse of human rights. One knew in effect what one was *against*.

It is now, however, much more difficult to project one's own positive political philosophy—particularly in liberal Western societies, where it is not easy to define and establish a general consensus. For this reason, there is a greater need for political and civic education. It has to become an integral part of a responsible and legitimized political strategy.

Moreover, in contrast to the time of the student revolts, contemporary (west) German society is much more defined by pragmatically oriented political decisions than by ideological conflict. For many citizens, and for youth in particular, there are no clear, definable differences that distinguish the political philosophies of the major German parties.

Is there a danger, then, that German society—which is prone to secularizing influences, like many others—will suddenly give rise to new ideologies while it searches for new answers, and that this, in turn, could lead to new turmoil in society? Are we witnessing once again the powerful longing for a strong, authoritative leadership? The danger is there.

This also holds true for the new German states, where nostalgia for the old GDR is on the rise: this is often just a search for clear worldviews in an era of desecularization and the decline of Christianity. As much as the Germans long for harmony, they also want to be able to differentiate between political philosophies, parties and their representatives; they want them to have clear contours.

This is an understandable demand—but democratic tradition and forty years of experience should also serve as a bulwark against the search for new (old?) ideologies. The challenges of the present call for a reaffirmation of Adenauer's guiding political principles: the tie to the West, the Social Market Economy, the rule of law.

Freedom anchored in morality—neither the unfettered freedom of liberalism, nor the freedom of the individual subordinated to social ends: this should be the guiding principle at this moment of German unification. The principles of the political philosophy that Adenauer primarily helped to establish are historically timeless; but they also act as a flexible and defined framework that can adapt to the political exigencies of the moment. The German Constitution (*Grundgesetz*) is a further example of this.

People in the west are justifiably proud of forty years of constitutional law; just as the people in the east are of their successful peaceful revolution and their defeat of communist party rule. The memory of the uprising on June 17, 1953, should always be evoked in connection with this.

THE AGE OF FAST MOTION: WRESTLING
WITH REALITY

As Germany reunites, it is crucial that both sides as well as the nation as a whole once again begin to see beyond the present situation so that the Germans can live in partnership with their allies and neighbors. Not only is the individual called on to put an end to his "ego trip" and to become responsible again for the whole community; but the Germans as a whole are called on to give up their tendency toward self-pity, complaining and German self-preoccupation, to discover the situation in other countries in Europe as well as in the rest of the world, and to take on the responsibilities that accrue from that.

But one can only gain a perspective on others and on the whole if one is standing on a firm foundation, on a secure platform. And herewith, the circle is closed: the unique challenge for politics is to confront the insecurity of people by offering a clear sense of orientation.

All major industrial nations are being influenced by a phase of growing uncertainty. Economic transformations, social developments, secularizing influences, feelings of isolation, mechanization and necessary bursts of modernization: all these are contributing to man's insecurity. This is just intensified by the ever increasing speed with which these changes and encroachments are occurring.

Combined with this is the fact that the complexity of today's decision-making processes has raised doubts about the general governability of large modern organizations—nations, major cities, large corporations—along with the fact that the complexity of the issues alone creates obfuscation. The more difficult and complex the issues that need to be managed are, the more that individuals, particularly in wealthy societies, will tend to introduce their own very personal and egotistical view of things. This selfish defense mechanism can be seen as an emergency brake of last resort, and it naturally works against the interests of society as a whole.

Thus, one can say that the basic condition of man in all modern industrial societies is the search for security. In Germany, this search is not only influenced by the previously mentioned developments occurring in east and west; it is also influenced by the fact that Germany is situated in the heart of Europe, and is therefore particularly affected by the major challenges of the moment: the waves of migrants, asylum seekers, and the coexistence of diverse cultures in society.

Furthermore, there is also a wide array of domestic social developments: for example, the media's barrage on the senses and the direct confrontation with highly diverse, worldwide political and cultural conflicts via virtually live television coverage ("CNN factor"). In this age of fast motion, rapid technological and political changes are being broadcast at ever higher speed.

As a consequence, politics has to offer a sense of orientation in this age of growing uncertainty. Politics should not be just restricted to efficiently solving day-to-day problems. The role of political leadership has got to be that of governing rather than administering.

At the same time, politics in a secularized society must not be tempted into becoming a form of substitute religion. It cannot be stressed enough that the desire to experience politics as a substitute religion could give new wind to forms of socialist ideologies, and could increase the longing for simple solutions and charismatic leaders. The philosopher Karl Popper was right in pointing out that the desire of ideologues to realize heaven on earth has always produced hell.

The profound sense of insecurity many Germans feel has made it more difficult for the reunifying nation to establish a new common identity. The Germans are lacking a strong "national identity," one that can serve as an anchor in stormy times, one bound to the ideal of democracy and European integration—a national identity that is much more prevalent in other countries and can give people there more support in similar times of turmoil.

Because Germany's reunification and social transformation are part of a radical worldwide historical change, and because Germans in both east and west are particularly sensitive to this change and are looking for orientation, it is understandable (considering this dual situation) that Germans as well as foreigners are curious as to Germany's position and the role she will play at home and abroad.

The Germans have reached the very end of security. They are searching for new securities. In view of the manifold challenges in domestic politics and the new world order, it is important to develop a "survival strategy." Thus, this book poses the most essential questions in German politics:

- What is the position of Germans, particularly the young, toward democracy?

- Will the Germans unite to form a real nation? Will they become a stability anchor in Europe?

- How will the Germans master their economic role, both domestically and internationally?

- What kind of consequences will the Germans take with respect to their increased international responsibility in and outside of Europe?

This book will attempt to offer precise answers to questions presently being raised by both Germans and foreigners alike. It will not strive to be exhaustive. Rather, it will concentrate specifically on controversial topics of a "symptomatic" nature. It will state positions and present the reader with guideposts. As opposed to breaking down subjects into various political categories, the book will attempt to focus on the whole picture, and to give integrated answers to questions.

2

Youth and the Change in Values

In recent decades, social norms have lost much of their force in Germany, and it has become increasingly difficult to solve the problems of social consensus and public welfare. These are developments—particularly in west Germany—that can be found in other modern industrial societies as well. But what is unique about the German situation is that, due to the experiences of history, democratic traditions have not had as much time to take root here, whereas some other countries have had these traditions for centuries. These links to tradition are crucial in the development of a national self-consciousness, and they give the people a sense of stability in times of crisis. The second factor unique to Germany is the need to bring together two different societies, each with its own distinct experiences and value systems, within a short period of time.

CHANGES IN SOCIAL NORMS AND THE PLURALISM IN LIFESTYLES

West German society has clearly developed in the direction of greater individualization and pluralism. East German society, however, has undergone very different experiences. Its lifestyle has been different; it was not influenced by a 1968–style rebellion; and it now expects a lot from politicians and decision makers after decades of political oppression. Specifically, the following general trends can be found in present-day German society.

Individualization[1]

More and more Germans are creating their own personal lifestyles, and are no longer looking to social institutions for orientation. As a result, large organizations—such as churches, political parties, unions, but also clubs and social associations—are losing their power to integrate. This trend is underscored by the transformations in the social institutions of marriages and families: single households now make up 34.9 percent of the national population; in cities, that rate is as high as 50 percent. Smaller families have become the general trend: 22.4 percent of all marriages are now childless. Two million Germans live together as unmarried couples. Statistics show that "among certain age groups in large cities, marriage has become a minority lifestyle; single status has by and large taken its place."[2] Therefore, it might be better to "actually speak of a 'singularization' rather than an 'individualization,' "[3] since single status has become a typical lifestyle choice in urban areas for the age group of twenty-seven- to forty-five-year-olds.

Even in rural regions, there are signs that marriage has lost its appeal; here, families now barely make up a third of all households.[4] In general, studies have shown that single status exists now as a fully independent lifestyle alongside marriage, though the existence of a single household and the state of being single in no way mean the lack of a steady partnership: two thirds of the polled singles claimed to have a partner that they had known for over a year.[5] These studies further reveal that marriage is valued less highly by the younger than by the older generation. Whereas the older generation regarded marriage positively, giving it a ranking of 4.5 on a scale of 6, the younger generation only gave it a ranking of 2.9.[6]

The divorce rate has also increased. In Germany, almost every third marriage presently ends in divorce; in the United States, every second.[7] A study comparing children born in 1960 with those born in 1980 reveals that a child's risk of being affected by its parents' divorce has more than tripled.[8] Though individualization and lifestyle pluralism does not mean marriage and families are disappearing, new lifestyles are appearing on the scene.

This lifestyle pluralism, occurring at the same time that social institutions, parties and unions have been losing authority, means that politicians are now confronted with many more "target groups"; it has made it more difficult for political elites to formulate a unified message. Though it has directly affected the political communication of all parties, it has particularly hurt the large national parties.

Secularization

Ties to churches have weakened, and fewer people attend religious services. This pronounced trend toward secularization in society has continued with reunification. Only about a third of the east German population still have church bonds, though membership in confirmation classes has increased. The so-called ordination of youth (*Jugendweihe*), a practice once introduced as an alternative to the Protestant confirmation service by the East German SED (Socialist Unity Party), has survived the communist system and remains a widespread phenomenon—an indication of the extent of secularization in East German society. Before German reunification, in the spring of 1989, 170,000 boys and girls participated in the *Jugendweihe*—97 percent of all fourteen-year-olds. After a radical drop in participation in 1990–91, the numbers rose once again the following years.[9] In 1994, approximately 77,000 adolescents[10] between thirteen and fourteen went through the initiation; in East Berlin, it was even as high as half of all adolescents born in 1980.

Germans in east and west also have different opinions on Christianity: according to an Allensbach Institute poll, both east and west Germans are divided on the question whether the reference to God should be removed from the preamble of the German Constitution, the so-called Basic Law. Fifty-seven percent of the west German population are against its removal; a fifth (20 percent) would support it; and roughly a fourth (23 percent) remain undecided. In east Germany, on the other hand, 48 percent wish to see the reference to God eliminated from the Constitution; 22 percent are against the idea; and about a third remain indifferent.[11]

Table 2.1 indicates the denominational statistics for all of Germany. What this table reveals is that approximately 30 percent of the east German population have ties to a church, whereas in west Germany, 80 percent do. After years of East German dictatorship, the process of "de-Christianization" has had its effects. The different levels of religious feeling between east and west is revealed in a poll taken in December 1993, appearing in Table 2.2.

While 35 percent of West Germans still "regularly" visited church in the early 1970s, by the early 1990s, the figure had dropped to under 30 percent. (Twenty-eight percent go at least twice a month; and 40 percent claim to go "sometimes"—i.e., once or several times a year.) The proportion of west Germans who no longer claim any church affiliation has risen from 25 percent to 28 percent since 1971. This downward spiral is particularly dramatic among Catholics. In 1953, 60 percent of all Catholic voters

Table 2.1
Church Statistics

	Catholics[1)	Protestants[2)
Old States	41.9 %	38.9 %
New States	4.9 %	26.1 %
Church Service Goers		
Old States	20.0 %	4.8 %
New States	24.0 %	not available

Sources: 1. Office of the German Bishops Conference/Bonn, telephone survey of February 21, 1994. 2. Protestant Church of Germany, Hannover, Statistical Report TII 90/91, Hannover 1993; own calculations.

claimed to be committed Catholics, according to polls. By 1993, however, the figure had dropped to 23 percent in west Germany.[12]

The Higher Value of Leisure Time

In 1950 the standard workweek was 48 hours; in 1990 the standard workweek in reunified Germany averaged 38.5 hours. In 1950 there were, on average, twelve paid vacation days; in 1990 there were thirty-one days!

More Time Spent in the Educational System

In Germany, both the number of students and the time needed to educate them have risen. More high school graduates now get on the university track. Whereas in 1965 only 7.5 percent of high school graduates received the credentials required to enter a university (or technical school), that figure has since risen substantially: by 1970 it was 11.3 percent, by 1980 21.7 percent and by 1992 35.7 percent.[13] The large majority of high school graduates who can enter a university also plan to attend—even though their average age is as high as twenty-one (in France and the United Kingdom, the average age is nineteen). The average age of German university graduates is 28.7 (compared to 26.4 in 1984); at the technical schools, the average age is 27.1. In the United Kingdom, on the other hand, the average age for students with their first university diploma is 23 to 24; in France, it is 24. In Germany, therefore, the tendency is clearly toward more young people going to a university, and once there, studying longer. But the longer young people remain within the university system, the longer it will take them to become economically self-sufficient, and the more difficult the transition

Table 2.2
Level of Religiosity in an East-West Comparison

	West %	East %
Frequency of church visits		
at least 1 x per week	13	5
at least 1 x per month	15	4
several times a year	28	13
once a year	12	12
1 x per year/never	29	64
not available	3	3
Frequency of church visits by protestants		
at least 1 x per week	4	7
at least 1 x per month	13	11
several times a year	32	37
once a year	17	20
seldom/never	32	24
not available	3	1
Frequency of church visits by catholics		
at least 1 x per week	23	42
at least 1 x per month	20	7
several times a year	29	14
once a year	9	10
seldom/never	18	26
not available	2	2
Church solidarity		
strong solidarity	17	8
weaker solidarity	51	32
no solidarity	28	55
not available	4	4
Church solidarity of protestants		
strong solidarity	10	19
weaker solidarity	59	66
no solidarity	27	13
not available	4	2
Church solidarity of catholics		
strong solidarity	25	38
weaker solidarity	52	44
no solidarity	21	14
not available	2	14

Source: Konrad-Adenauer-Stiftung (KAS), December 1993, Archive-No. 9305/6.

will be from youth to financially autonomous adulthood. In the last decades, an intermediary stage of "postadolescence" has emerged in modern industrial societies, and this phase is particularly long in Germany.

A Nonuniform Change in Values

In west Germany, there has been a shift toward "postmaterial" values resulting from the 1968 rebellion—especially among the more affluent members of the population. But "traditional" values have become more important for young people than is generally assumed. What is meant by "postmaterialism" is the decline in traditional middle-class values among the young.[14] Ronald Inglehart believes that societies which have solved the problems of material and physical security develop "postmaterial" value systems; these systems are a trademark of affluent Western societies.[15] As a result of the Extraparliamentary opposition movement (APO) in the 1960s, the following shift in values occurred in Germany:

1. The demand for personal freedom and self-realization has become more important than traditional values such as duty, the acceptance of social norms and job motivation.
2. With traditional models of orientation losing their significance, fewer people are willing to take personal risks and more people are beginning to believe that government must satisfy their need for personal stability.
3. Attitudes toward education and upbringing have gone through a marked transformation. People now reject reform schools that use direct and repressive means of punishment; the new goal is to raise children to self-sufficiency as early as possible.
4. There has also been a clear shift in the relationship between men and women: traditional roles have been discarded; women have entered traditionally "male" professions. Men are now doing more chores in the home and are helping to raise the children.
5. Environmental questions have assumed a new and higher priority ever since an intense antitechnological mood arose in parts of the population.

But does this trend toward "postmaterial" values, which many theorists affirm, really have the same level of intensity after reunification? Though it might be a difficult claim to prove empirically, there is now a much greater support for traditional values among the younger generation than policy makers realize. Part of the reason for this is that traditional values are not purely material—a fact that gets lost in today's abbreviated accounts. The term "postmaterialism" itself gives an imperfect picture. After all, material security was never merely an end in itself, but was always simultaneously linked to intrinsically ideal values. Some of these traditional values can be found in today's environmental movement.

On the whole, people are more oriented to material values at times when economic prosperity seems seriously threatened. Thus, the shift in values that has been observed in west Germany's recent past (and the consequences of it) should not be given undue emphasis. People in politics and science are often tempted to concentrate solely on the new, the spectacular, while tending to ignore the traditional values that continue to influence a large part of the population, particularly the younger generation. Recent experience seems to show that "family"—or at least the willingness to engage in a serious relationship—is now judged more positively by a segment of today's younger generation. There is also a higher approval of job motivation and the idea of a strong nation, one that can secure freedom from within and without. Though the family is still held in high esteem, it is of course not immune from intense pressures; the trend toward greater individuality is hindered by the ties and the responsibilities of family. But polls of young people show that they judge a happy and fulfilled family life to be an important goal.[16] For many, the family symbolizes a stronghold that offers orientation and satisfies the need for security. Yet, a large proportion of the youth remain skeptical toward marriage and family.

Two parallel trends also exist in people's attitudes toward their professions. A large portion of the population are career-conscious and have a high level of job motivation. On the other hand, there continues to be a small, yet significant cross section of the younger generation that opt for very individual lifestyles (for example, as members of the extreme right or left or by exhibiting "unpolitical" behavior) that separate them from the established culture, especially from the adult world. But both the media and sociologists often treat this behavior as though it were representative of the entire younger generation.

The shift in values, therefore, does not conform to one pattern; the large majority of Germans continue to be oriented toward traditional values. There might have been a trend toward "postmaterial" values among many intellectuals and prosperous sectors of the population in recent decades, in which values such as hard work, punctuality, discipline, and so on were treated as "secondary virtues." Often there is skepticism toward traditional values in the media. The quest for higher ratings gives sensationalistic news items center stage in reports and analyses and results in an explosion of talk shows, on which the most nonconformist behavior gets rewarded a spot on a panel.

Therefore, it is important to have a differentiated picture of young people and their world. On the one hand, greater individuality is observable in the way people live and in the overall pluralism of lifestyles; this has led to changes in social commitments. Large organizations, as mentioned, are suffering as a result of this lack of commitment. On the other hand, there is a greater willingness to engage spontaneously in local movements and in environmental groups to achieve concrete goals. There are also other areas where young people continue to show a willingness to cooperate for a longer period of time.

Decline in the Power of "Milieus"

In west Germany, there has been a decline in the significance of traditional social milieus. Though changes in the character of milieus have occurred in other modern industrial societies as well, this phenomenon has been particularly pronounced in Germany due to the repercussions of World War II, mass migration and the intense rebuilding at the end of the war. Whereas people in earlier decades grew up in relatively homogeneous groupings (e.g., worker milieu, Protestant milieu, Catholic milieu, rural milieu, etc.), the impact of milieus has drastically diminished in the meantime. As a result, many people have lost the specific sense of protection and orientation that milieus once offered. The decline in the power of milieus is revealed by the changes in the workforce. Since 1950, the percentage of workers in the overall workforce has fallen from 50 percent to under 40 percent; the percentage of the self-employed, freelancers and farmers has fallen from over 20 percent to approximately 10 percent. The service sector has grown substantially. It now comprises over half the workforce (primarily office employees and civil servants; see Table 2.3).

The two largest political parties in Germany, the Christian Democratic Union/Christian Social Union (CDU/CSU) and the Social Democratic Party (SPD), have been affected by these transformations. Whereas committed Catholics made up 25 percent of all voters in 1965, by the mid-1990s only 10 percent of the entire German electorate consisted of practicing Catholics. About half of all CDU voters were practicing Catholics in the mid-1960s. Again, by the mid-1990s, that figure had dropped to a fifth of CDU voters. This decline was precipitated by reunification, since Catholics make up less than 5 percent in the new states (*Länder*) in eastern Germany. SPD electoral patterns have also been dramatically affected—through the erosion of traditional union-bound worker milieus. But what has also become apparent is that the electoral bases of both national parties have

Table 2.3
Employment according to Professional Position in Former West German Territory

	1950 %	1990 %
worker	50.9	37.4
employee	16.0	43.3
civil servant	4.0	8.5
self-employed	14.8	8.8
co-workers	}29.2	}10.8
family members	14.4	2.0

Source: 1950: Statistisches Bundesamt (ed.), *Statistisches Jahrbuch für die Bundesrepublik Deutschland 1954*, p. 112 (Diagram 2). Percent figures according to own calculations. 1990: Statistisches Bundesamt (ed.), *Datenreport 1992* (Bonn 1992), p. 99.

gradually converged from a sociological perspective since the end of the 1960s.[17]

The unions too have lost prestige. This can be seen as a sign of the increased reluctance on the part of Germans to join large organizations as well as the result of a change in social structures, as mentioned above. According to a poll taken in July 1994, very few people in the workforce wish to join a union. Only 2 percent of nonmembers would join a union if they were asked; two years earlier, the percentage was still 5 percent. Even more vehement are those who would never want to be associated with a union. Whereas two years ago 45 percent of respondents categorically denied interest in union membership, by 1994 that figure had risen to 72 percent. Forty percent of all union members are even considering dropping out, and in east Germany the figure is as high as 54 percent.[18]

YOUTH AS SOCIOLOGICAL BAROMETER: SATISFACTION WITH DEMOCRACY—IMPATIENCE WITH POLITICAL PARTIES

The issues I have addressed concerning a shift in values are expressed most clearly in the developments affecting younger Germans. A closer look at this generation reveals that German youth see themselves as part of a burgeoning international "youth culture." Here, as everywhere else, there are signs of social disintegration, which can be a cause for concern; but the majority of the younger generation are integrating into the society at large—a society only gradually overcoming political division. According to studies, it is the youth in east and west who, of all generations, reveal the least differences in respect to their value systems.

NORMAL YOUTH AND SPECTACULAR MINORITIES

When politics, the social sciences or the media focus their attention on youth, they risk concentrating on the spectacular individual cases—for example, on the violence of youth against foreigners or the problem of drug addiction. This might be understandable from the perspective of the media and their need for interesting material; it also helps to spotlight areas where decisive political action might be necessary. But it most certainly does not present an "objective" picture of youth. Today, the word "normal" has almost become a stigmatized term. Unnoticed are the great majority of young people, "normal" in the best sense of the word, that is, adolescents and young men and women who are clearly motivated in their jobs and professions, who lend support to others in various ways and for whom family is a high priority.[19]

In 1990, a poll of high school students from all over Germany revealed that 53 percent of west German and 55 percent of east German students said they would do anything they could to graduate with high honors from school.[20] This display of "Prussian" virtues by east German students was even more pronounced in the 1992 "Shell Study." According to this study, 64 percent of young women and 56 percent of young men in the new states see life as a responsibility to which they would like to "devote all their energies." They want "to achieve something in life, even if at times life becomes difficult and strenuous."[21]

If one looks at the motivation of young people more closely, one notices it is not only directed toward individual advancement but also toward helping others. Between 1985 and 1992, for example, 49,520 young adults did a year's worth of volunteer services[22]—in hospitals, old age homes, homes for the handicapped, social service institutions, kindergartens, youth homes and psychiatric institutions. In 1987, a voluntary "year of ecology"— a type of experimental project—was instituted; by 1993, 802 young people had participated.[23] In fact, there were many more volunteers than openings. These voluntary efforts helped to do jobs that were necessary for communities, and the people involved were highly dedicated. But in this age of "reality television," these kinds of efforts go unnoticed; however, blockades of military barracks and nuclear power plants by a small handful of protesters are certain to get media attention. Here again, the public is presented with a sensationalistic and distorted picture of "youth"; but it is unfair to those youths who are truly committed to their jobs.

It is not only their sense of commitment that goes largely unnoticed; often, their outlook on the future is also misrepresented. Contrary to pessimistic projections, a general feeling of optimism prevails—more than in 1981, for example. At that time, according to a Shell Study, 60 percent of fifteen- to twenty-four-year-olds in West Germany were "rather gloomy" about "society's future"; only 30 percent were "relatively optimistic." Ten years later, however, 71 percent of west German youth considered themselves "relatively optimistic." In March 1993, 95 percent[24] of west German and 83 percent of east German adolescents and young people between the ages of fourteen and twenty-seven were satisfied with their lives.[25] Among those people who were satisfied with their lives, 90 percent supported the idea of democracy.[26] Despite this high level of satisfaction with democracy, one cannot overlook the high level of dissatisfaction with politicians. According to the Shell Study of 1992, 82 percent of the people surveyed agreed with the statement that the population was being "deceived" by politicians.[27] The high percentage of youthful nonvoters, more than in the general population, shows that many are fed up with politics. The percentage of nonvoters between the ages of eighteen and twenty-four, for example, rose from 15.5 percent in 1972 to 37.1 percent in the Bundestag elections of 1990.

HISTORICAL FRAGMENT: THE FIRST SIGNS OF PROTEST AND THE BEGINNINGS OF THE YOUTH REBELLION

Youth protest is not a recent phenomenon. Social history shows that there have been classical forms of generational conflict time and time again; these often involve disagreements over plans for the future and over attitudes toward traditional values and norms. The youth movement before and after World War I—frequently referred to as the *Wandervogelbewegung*—was an example along these lines. Despite its demands for alternative, avant-garde ways of living, this movement had a positive foundation: it wanted to reform the existing conditions of life. The National Socialists tried—and, unfortunately, were relatively successful—to adopt various elements of the youth movement and forms of youth protest. "Step aside, old people!" was the slogan used by Gregor Strasser, one of the leaders of the National Socialist Party. This had consequences for the postwar discussion. It explains why Reinhard Buchwald, a professor of German at the University of

Heidelberg, wrote the following in a publication after the war: "An entire young generation's worldview has collapsed. They have lost faith in moral values."[28]

After World War II, in America, there was talk of a "beat generation"; the beatniks also had an effect on Europe, particularly on Germany. Probably few people can now remember the clashes among hooligans in the big cities of West Germany. For many young people in the world, music helped form an identity. Increasingly, the mass media began to exert an influence and helped to develop a worldwide youth culture, centered predominantly in the United States and Great Britain.[29]

The most important catalyst for youth protest—in the form of the new social movements (NSB), for example—was the student unrest of the late 1960s, especially in 1968. This form of rebellion took place in all Western industrial nations and had a great impact on the United States, but also on countries like France and West Germany. The rebellion had two major consequences. For one, some members in the protest movement began to distinguish between violence against people and violence against objects— a very dubious relativization of the law. In fact, it mocked and ridiculed the law's function as a peaceful arbiter. On the other hand, an entire generation of university graduates, who began to enter careers in education and the media, were influenced by its antiauthoritarian ideals and its one-sided dismantling of traditional value systems.

HISTORICAL TURNING POINT: THE 1968 REBELLION AND THE "DOUBLE-SERVICE ECONOMY"

The voicing of protest and dissatisfaction, the presentation of alternative projects and public debate are all acceptable elements of a democratic society.[30] But for the first time in the Federal Republic's history, the leftist student protest movement tried to legitimize violence as a means of political protest. It is worth taking a closer look at two specific ideological strands of political protest, since they continue to influence the political thought of today's young people. One line of protest—in the tradition of the Neo-Marxist New Left of the late 1960s—aimed at the radical transformation of the entire political, social and economic system of the Federal Republic. The other line produced—in the early 1970s—the criticism of culture, technology and civilization that helped forge the ecological and citizens' initiative movements.

This was the starting point for the shift in values. Whereas the older generation of Germans still accepted the previously mentioned norms of duty and responsibility—reflected in the values of career, hard work, job motivation, respect for tradition, and law and order—the younger generation, having grown up in prosperous times, began to turn to "postmaterial" values. "Nineteen Sixty-Eight" is thus a highly complex nexus of events; it stands for a value shift that occurred in Germany as in other Western industrial societies. New paradigms developed that conflicted with the values that had held sway in the Germany of the "economic miracle." The traditional means of explaining conflict situations no longer applied. It was more than just a generational conflict or a protest against an imagined or real coming to terms with the Nazi past.

Ernst Fraenkel, a political scientist from Berlin, came closer than anyone else to grasping the complexity behind the problem. As early as 1963–64, in his essay "Strukturdefekte der Demokratie und deren Überwindung" (Structural Defects of Democracy and How to Overcome Them),[31] Fraenkel had already detected signs of this shift in values. His analysis is remarkable not only for picking up on these shifts so early on, but also because he described with great accuracy—and without overemphasizing causal relationships—the deeper reasons behind them. At the time, Fraenkel recognized that there was a close connection between the economic, political and social achievements of Western industrial societies and the state of mind of a population that had grown accustomed to these achievements. He diagnosed a discrepancy between, on the one hand, an "objective feeling of well-being" arising from material prosperity and the achievements of a market economy and parliamentary democracy, and, on the other hand, a "subjective feeling of uneasiness."

According to Fraenkel, people began to demand and expect more from the state as a result of the growth in state services and prosperity. Fraenkel noticed that the population was growing more apathetic toward politics and parliament. Thus he was one of the first social scientists in Germany to recognize the contradictions (of primarily socio-psychological origin) between the objective achievements of the German political order and the critical state of mind of many people; this he saw as one of the most consistent problems, one of the drawbacks, of the social welfare state.

In 1970, Richard Löwenthal, another political scientist from Berlin, was right to see the 1968 rebellion as "a profound crisis of Western civilization," that is, "a crisis in the society's ability to transmit its fundamental values to youth in times of tumultuous technological and social change."[32] Naturally, it affected the social structure in Germany. Since the 1968 rebellion, we have witnessed the emergence of a "double-service economy"—a phenomenon that has become manifest in our present age. The trends that have been described in German society show that more and more people are active in the service economy while traditional milieus (including professional ones) are disappearing. The principle of "service" has become a determinant in that more responsibility is being delegated to (governmental) institutions that are in themselves not responsible. There has been an increasing demand for political and social services that once lay in the personal domain, and this has brought about a change in the political structure. Political decision makers are confronted with expectations that they cannot fulfill. This "delegating away" of responsibility within a dual social service economy also influences the framework of values in a democratic society. Instead of freedom with responsibility, there has been a search for freedom from responsibility.

Today the 1968 rebellion is frequently cast in a heroic light. It is presented as a time when youth sought to break through to a new age and to fight against the "thousand-year-old dust" that had collected at universities. The generation was in the spotlight, making waves with its provocative slogans ("Don't trust anyone over thirty!") and sensationalistic methods, including go-ins and sit-ins. Of course, it is hard to deny that these young people gave West German society the charge to move forward; but a social movement should also be evaluated in terms of its intentions, its ideology, and not only on the basis of its results.

One should call to mind, for example, that the former "Socialist German Student Association" (SDS), one of the motivating forces behind the protest movement, evolved increasingly into an antipluralistic and totalitarian combat unit. People seem to forget that the former APO utilized methods such as intimidating teachers and students who held different political outlooks. Within the movement, they tried to exert antidemocratic absolute authority; their goal was not the tolerance of diversity, but to push through an ideology based on class conflict. Violence was considered an acceptable means of politics: by making a distinction between violence against people and objects, they tried to break through the taboo that had surrounded the issue of violence.

In the final analysis, this led to terrorism in the form of the Red Army Faction (RAF) as well as other terrorist organizations. The leading intellectuals of the 1968 rebellion supported an elitist ideology that made the intellectual into the political actor, the "revolutionary subject"; according to these intellectuals, the exploited "proletariat" was not capable of recognizing its own exploitation. This elitist concept was supposed to explain why intellectuals were in the best position to protect themselves from the "manipulation" of the media and the state—a state that was increasingly slipping under "fascist" control.

In retrospect it is often overlooked that many high school and university students (i.e., members of a "young intellectual cadre") actually sympathized with the goals of the SDS—at least in its early stages. Part of the reason for the success of this "antiauthoritarian" protest movement was that many of its adherents were united in their feeling of being "anti" something, that is, they were against the achievements of a liberal democracy and a social economy. The members of the protest movement were assured of support as long as they were unified against the postwar West German order. Herbert Marcuse, a role model of the antiauthoritarian movement, believed that "within a negative formulation, there already existed the core of something positive."[33] Though at first it had spread spontaneously throughout Germany and elsewhere, it soon began to lose its integrative force once the student protest movement felt the need to develop its own clear, positive vision.

The 1968 rebellion, which was initially an import from American universities (particularly from Berkeley), in the end had an impact on all Western industrial societies. But what is most remarkable about all this is that such a highly emotional mass movement, clearly directed against the principles of a liberal democracy, could sweep up so many young German intellectuals. Aside from asking the question as to what caused this shift in values and the late 1960s protest movement related to it, it is also relevant to ask what kind of effects these developments had on the politics, the culture and the society of those times and now.

These effects have been most prominent and influential in the realms of journalism, but also in education and child rearing. One should be careful, however, not to solely blame the 1968 generation for the current generation's (partially justified) dissatisfaction with educational institutions. After all, many of the things the public accuses this generation of doing—and some people even refer to a "cultural revolution"—are actually the result of changes in social structures brought about by economic, technological and scientific developments. When analzying the connections between the shift in values and the protest movements, the question arises: Was the protest movement more or less just a consequence of the shift in values? Or did the 1968 rebellion *in and of itself* transform political and social life in West Germany through its use of media-effective demonstrations, its slogans, its spirit of protest and its development of an alternative culture?

Clearly, many of the defining issues of the 1968 period—such as the emergency laws, a cause of heavy protests at the time, or the American military engagement in Vietnam—are no longer relevant today. But many other fundamental issues still remain: the distinction that was made between violence against objects and people; the rejection of the state's monopoly on the use of force; and, related to the latter, the overt and covert attempts to destabilize the legal order. Here, the effects of the student rebellion will have to be assessed critically; and one should not overlook the path that leads from the protest movements of that period, through the alternative movement, right on to the environmental and peace movements of today.

On the other hand, a critical appraisal of the 1968 period and its consequences cannot ignore asking whether (and to what extent) the movement was also beneficial in that it reacted against outdated conventions and privileges. Certainly, the 1968 rebellion helped to modernize West German society. The problem is that positive and negative aspects lie so close together. There is a very fine line between acceptable demands for greater participation, personal responsibility and independence—slogans that can be found in today's management textbooks—and the danger that these same demands will slip into the realm of unrealistic and inhumane utopias or political ideologies.

CONTEMPORARY FRAGMENT: TODAY'S PROTESTS

The kind of topics that incite today's youth protests are clearly different from those that once motivated the Extraparliamentary Opposition (APO). Moreover, youth-oriented concerns are not the only issues that interest youth. But youth in general react differently to problems we all face—often with greater sensitivity, with greater spontaneity, but also more narrowly and radically. Sensitivity and radicalness, partiality and impatience are the privileges of youth; and they will constantly force the political establishment to rethink and reinterpret its policies.

Several issues of particular concern to young people can be brought into focus:

Young people are often more concerned with the overexploitation of the earth's natural resources than older people; they identify strongly with environmental protection. With the rise of the protest movement, the political leadership and the population at large had to begin to take this topic seriously. Young people now consider environmental protection one of the most important political issues.[34] Sixty-two percent of youth have a positive impression of people who are active in the service of environmental protection.

With their strong sense of social justice, young people are very sensitive toward the severe economic divisions separating rich and poor nations in the industrial world and Third World. As a result, North-South issues are one of the ten most important problems that concern youth.[35]

Young people are less able to comprehend the reasons behind the brutal war in former Yugoslavia and why European nations find it so difficult to agree on a course of action to help end this war.

Seeing that Germany is ranked as one of the leading industrial nations, young people demand greater state support for the "weaker" members of society—for senior citizens, the disabled, single parents and families with children.

Young people are generally more impatient with fossilized party structures; they are more easily irritated with bureaucraticization, inflexibility and with what they see as the "arrogance of power." They also reject political slogans. In a survey by the Konrad Adenauer Foundation, 51 percent agreed that "often politics is so complicated that people like me can't understand what's going on."[36]

Young people are also more impatient with the lengthy process of political decision making. For that reason, they are more enthusiastic about spontaneous, action-oriented forms of political participation. Their willingness to engage in large organizations such as parties and unions is decreasing.

TODAY'S SITUATION: CULTURAL SKEPTICISM

Young people find there are fewer possibilities to participate in society, and this critique seems to be combined with an overall skepticism toward our technological, economically prosperous civilization. This astounds in particular the older generation, which views this attitude as ungrateful. In 1957, Arnold Gehlen published a critical and highly disconcerting appraisal of modern society. In his socio-psychological study *Die Seele im technischen Zeitalter* (The Mind in the Technical Age), Gehlen wrote:

As everyone knows, modern, thoroughly rationalized communal societies are to a very high degree just pieces of equipment. A piece of equipment expects work that is limited, that is easily divided and acceptable; it demands and produces intersection types and functionaries, those whose work ethic, though not consisting of total self-abnegation, reflects a certain degree of depersonalization. The effects of automatization and rationalization can be such that man's behavior toward his "environment" can split off and take on a life independent of himself; that behavior will also include his related ideologies, his habits, opinions, and self-image."[37]

If Gehlen was accurate in his analysis of the effects of modern society on the minds and judgmental capacities (in both senses of the word) of its decision makers, then maybe it isn't all that suprising that youth react so sensitively to this very issue. Youth may not necessarily want role models, but they do at least want people who can talk to them while they discover and make their own ways in the world. What they do not want are intersection types, functionaries or depersonalized individuals as counterparts—people who, when asked, can no longer answer their questions because their inner nature stands in no relationship to a set of values or to their own personal opinions and attitudes.

Youth are so sensitive because their basic prevailing mood is one of heightened loneliness. This was very perceptively understood by the Polish doctor and pedagogue Janucz Korczak in his "The Loneliness of Childhood" and "The Loneliness of Youth."[38] Maybe it is the key to understanding the growing skepticism that youth have toward all types of large organizations. In any case, we will never be able to understand young people or engage in a conversation with them if we do not recognize or take seriously their sense of loneliness, or if we do not show understanding for their actions, which to a large degree stem from a spirit of loneliness.

If young people are honest with themselves, they will recognize that they are caught between a triangle of competing pressures: the pressures of loneliness, the machine of communal society and an all-pervasive moral impulse. These pressures can only lead youth to question the standards and conventions of society. If we are not willing to respond to their disorientation as a result of these threefold pressures—and as people, not as functionaries—then we are relegating them (and children) to their loneliness, instead of directing them on their way to responsible participation in a problematic, yet still promising society. At the same time, we would be depriving ourselves of the opportunity of giving youth helpful advice in a world that has become highly functional and economically oriented; the danger would be that, in the process, we ourselves would become victims of a reductionist economic mind-set.

All in all, with their hopes, dreams and lifestyles, German youth are not much different from any other young generation in the Western world. This is a reflection of the increasingly international youth culture, unified throughout the world by the mass media.[39] Often, this culture develops its own type of "underground" lingo and its own symbols that only initiates can understand. English has become the "cool" language to speak. The young live in their own "scenes," isolated and at a distance from the rest of civilization.

FORMS OF PROTEST: VIOLENT MINORITIES

The desire to question the established order is also reflected in the various forms in which youth engage in protest: it extends from the use of flyers and demonstrations to sit-ins or just simple "refusal." Young people strongly believe in the efficacy of direct political activities, either organized or unorganized. Yet, very few people believe in the efficacy of illegal or violent actions. Only a handful resort to such violent activities, for example, vandalizing political placards and destroying property by spray-painting walls. Statistics reveal that fewer than 5 percent engage in open signs of violent behavior; and fewer than 10 percent declared a desire to do so. Squatting seems to be the only exception: more than 20 percent of Germans in east and west stated they would be willing to engage in squatting in certain circumstances.[40] Squatting in general seems to be considered more acceptable by youth than other infringements.

Young members of right- and left-wing fringe groups, including followers, make up the majority of those willing to resort to violence. It is estimated that there are about 6,000 young adherents of left- and right-wing radicalism—mostly neofascist skinheads and leftist punks and so-called autonomous groups. According to the Federal Agency for the Defense of the Constitution, there are about 30,000–40,000 sympathizers of extremist groups. A relatively high percentage of youthful activists exist among the ranks of leftist and neofascist extremists. According to a 1993 report by the Federal Agency for the Defense of the Constitution, there are about thirty-six left-extremist core organizations with about 21,800 members; another six peripheral organizations with about 800 members; another thirty-eight organizations with 16,300 members influenced by the former; and beyond that, a further 6,700 anarchists and other "social revolutionaries," generally referred to as "autonomous groups."

This so-called scene can potentially mobilize more than several thousand additional people. This figure, however, does not include the Party of Democratic Socialism (PDS), the successor party to the (communist) Socialist Unity Party (SED) in former East Germany—particularly the several thousand members of the Communist Platform (KPF) within the PDS. Presently, the PDS lists a membership of about 130,000.[41] In 1993, there were more than forty publishers and outlets linked to left-extremist groups, publishing left-extremist newspapers, magazines and books.[42] Approximately 1,357 legal infringements with left-extremist motives were recorded in 1993.

Seventy-seven right-extremist organizations and other such groupings existed in Germany by late 1993 (in 1992, eighty-two); if one excludes double memberships, that leaves a total of 41,500 (in 1992, 41,900) right-extremist members, of which 5,600 (in 1992, 6,400) were militant—above all skinheads in loosely organized groups at the local and regional levels. There were about 950 neo-Nazis (in 1992, 800) who did not belong to any organization. All in all, then, there are about 42,400 right-radicals in Germany.

In 1993, there were about thirty-three independent right-radical publishers and outlets in service; the number of publications with a right-radical agenda increased to eighty-six in 1993 (in 1992, seventy-five). At least sixty-two publications appear quarterly, registering a total circulation of about 6.5 million.[43] In 1993, records show 2,232 acts of violence and 8,329 other legal infringements (such as threats, propaganda crimes, insults) that can be entirely or at least partially attributed to right-extremist sources; of these, 1,609 acts of violence and 5,112 further infringements can be classified as antiforeigner.[44]

In 1993, the Federal Agency for the Defense of the Constitution had information on 763 offenders who were either suspects or actual perpetrators of violent actions with right-extremist motivations. Of those, approximately 55 percent were under twenty—or more specifically: 16.8 percent were under eighteen; 39.1 percent were eighteen to twenty; 36.5 percent were twenty-one to thirty; only 4.9 percent were thirty-one to forty, and 2.7 percent were forty-one and up. Women made up only 3.6 percent of the total.[45]

The large majority of youth, however, rejects extremist groups. They reject right-radical skinheads (87 percent) even more than left-leaning punks (65 percent).[46] The chances are slim that these groups will become socially acceptable or develop into mass movements. Moreover, violence from right-radicals has consistently incited violence from the left. On the sidelines of peaceful civil demonstrations in protest of the Solingen murders, violent riots erupted among extreme-left autonomous groups, and rival Turkish gangs fought among each other. There is a real danger that violence on the far right will lead to escalations on the far left.

Violent youth make up but a small percentage of the total population, and they are rejected by the majority. Nevertheless, it cannot be denied that right-radical violence has poisoned the climate in Germany and has unsettled foreigners living in the country—even though a resounding majority of Germans continue to hold a favorable view of coexistence.[47] Often, right-radicalism does not have a "political" motivation in the strict sense of the word; rather, it can be seen as a type of unpolitical protest of "last resort." This, however, makes it political once again.

What is often expressed through right-extremist actions is frustration, hatred against all things foreign and hatred against the system itself. The widespread use of neo-Nazi symbols is often just a reflex action; it occurs without a deeper understanding of their historical and political significance. The desire to provoke, to break through "deep-seated taboos" (Hermann Lübbe), is frequently the primary motivation for the use of these symbols. The victim of the aggressor is the weaker individual, the one whose position of inferiority is clearly defined from the very beginning.

The brutality of right-extremist violence is part of a general trend toward brutality among violent youth, observable in today's schoolyards.[48] "Several years ago, a fight between hooligans was generally considered over when one of the two lay helpless on the ground. Now it is said that the victors continue to beat up on the helpless victim until he can no longer move."[49] What has risen dramatically between 1990 and 1993 is the number of crimes against foreigners. Under its listing of "antiforeigner crimes" in the period between January 1, 1991, and March 31, 1993, the Federal Criminal Police Office records 10 deaths, 29 attempted murders, 963 cases of bodily injury, 1,002 cases of arson, 13 bomb attacks, and 8,096 further crimes against foreigners—a total of 10,113 crimes.

What is striking is that, according to the Federal Office for the Defense of the Constitution, the number of right-extremist crimes is twice as high in east Germany (5.5 per 100,000 inhabitants) as it is in west Germany (2.4). In 1992, of the 2,584 violent crimes with right-extremist motives, 1,719 occurred in west Germany and 865 in east Germany—though only a fifth of the population lives in the eastern half.[50] For the same year, it is estimated that there were 6,400 militant right-extremists, of which 3,800 came from the east.[51]

Since violent extremists are highly mobile, one cannot place too much emphasis on this kind of statistic. Yet, there are certain circumstances that can explain this incongruity. After years of repression from the old regime, right-radical violence in today's east Germany can be seen as a reaction against the "Antifascism dictated from above." Among less-educated people, the protest developed into a form of "anti-antifascism." Moreover, the GDR could never develop a democratic culture of conflict. Contact with foreigners or outsiders was well-nigh impossible. After the collapse of communism, new police structures had to be set up from scratch. Many policemen who were previously members of the East German National Police were taken up by the new forces, though they were insufficiently trained for duty in an open society. Many of them are also uneasy because of their ties to the earlier regime.

More than 70 percent of the suspects in antiforeigner crimes are between the ages of fifteen and twenty;[52] only 5 percent are older than thirty. Nearly all suspects are men; just 4 percent are women! The large majority of suspects has a low to medium level of education. Eighteen percent of them are unemployed (20 percent of the eighteen- to twenty-four-year-olds, 30 percent of the twenty-one- to twenty-four-year-olds)—a higher rate than the average for that age group, but still a minority of the total. Only a small percentage have a history of broken homes or are dropouts from school or come from marginalized social groups. Roughly half of the suspects have had run-ins with the police; and a quarter have actually broken the law, but mostly for activities unrelated to violence against foreigners or other forms of extremist violence.

Among the smaller percentage of older suspects, the percentage of unemployment, criminality and membership in right-extremist organizations is particularly high. What becomes apparent when one compares suspects from east and west Germany is the higher number of unemployed in the former (26 percent to 12 percent) and a higher percentage of membership in right-extremist groups (37 percent to 19 percent). In east Germany, more criminal actions are carried out in large groups (64 percent) than in west Germany (21 percent), where violent acts are carried out more frequently by individuals or by small groups of less than ten. More than 90 percent of the cases were group actions; only a small portion (6 percent) were registered as individual acts. The statistics reveal four different types of suspects:

1. *The follower*: he normally has no criminal history. He is frequently drawn into violence by the group dynamics.
2. *The adolescent with criminal record (rowdy)*: he has a history of violence and uses violence as his normal means of resolving conflict—but initially without an antiforeigner or extremist political agenda.
3. *The antiforeigner/ethnocentrist*: he comes mostly from a socially disadvantaged class; he hates and fears foreigners because they compete with him for scarce resources, such as jobs.
4. *The right-extremist activist*: he often has a higher level of education, has contact to right-extremist organizations and plays the role of agitator and instigator.

It is interesting to note that most acts of violence are not planned in advance, but usually result spontaneously out of group dynamics, particularly as a result of alcohol abuse. Antiforeign motivations and the need to engage in violence often drive such behavior. This partially explains why it has been difficult for the police to get a handle on this sort of violence early on. These acts are predominantly instigated by antiforeigner motives and an inherent need for violence.

Right-extremist action and violent gangs cannot only be found in Western countries; recently, they have appeared in the developing democracies of East Central Europe as well. Outbreaks of hooligan violence during soccer matches—the term "hooligan" showed up in English newspapers as early as 1898!—have become commonplace in Western Europe. It is difficult to contain outbreaks of violence in open societies. In the suburbs of cities like Paris, Lyon and Marseille, there have been series of regular, quite spectacular riots. Particularly in the larger cities, the incidents of vandalism are alarming. One indicator of this is the increase in the number of vandalized telephone booths. For individuals with weak personalities, gangs give a sense of support, which they do not normally find in the society at large; and violence against people and objects gives them a feeling of strength.

What is very important for the cohesiveness of these groups is the use of symbols—hairstyles, tattoos, jewelry, clothing—which produces a feeling of identity. Many violent individuals prefer to let out their aggression on foreigners, outsiders and minorities. The question of violence, however, cannot only be assessed in political categories; it must also be seen from its psychological perspective. One psychotherapist writes:

A person who hates foreigners hates what is foreign in himself that he can't learn to accept. He hates his own wishes and desires, for they have either been knocked out of him or have been made to appear evil. He fights against a sense of weakness and inferiority that he must suppress because of pressures to produce, to succeed or to improve himself. His anger is justified, but he lets it out on unrelated objects; his pain turns into vicious vituperation to gain a feeling of security and ease. The foreigners aren't the threat; it's his life of alienation.[53]

Media reports, particularly on television, have only led to an increase in the rates of violence. The right-extremist agitator Michael Kühnen, who died several years ago, made this very point when he discussed the role of the media: "The secret of our success has been the involvement of the mass media." He and his supporters "need only to touch on a taboo subject, and reporters will sniff a good headline. Dozens of taboos can be found lying in the streets of Germany: the problem of the Jews, the lies of the Holocaust and war guilt, the historical greatness of Adolf Hitler, the illegal Nazi party."[54] Right-extremist activities have received a lot of attention in

Germany: "The reason why rightist groups have assumed a prominent role in Germany—both in membership and in the public imagination—is that the public reacts more sensitively to ghosts from the past. If people were to laugh at those balding men in their jackboots, then that would be the end of them. But who wants to laugh at these people when they are automatically reminded of the past?"[55]

Anti-Semitic remarks and activities are one of the absolute taboos in Germany; reports of them have led to impassioned protests by the population (in the form of candlelit demonstrations). The more that adolescents try to cause provocation and try to engage in anti-Semitic rabble-rousing, the more that people protest. Moreover, scientific studies have shown that the present German leadership has reacted positively to questions concerning its relationship to the Jewish people, whereas a large part of the elite in the Weimar Republic had a characteristically standoffish attitude to Jews. In the annual report of the London Institute of Jewish Affairs, published in July 1994, anti-Semitic incidents were compared in seventy different countries. The 250–page report includes a relatively long list of Western democracies where anti-Semitic symptoms are apparently on the rise. The list includes countries such as Australia, Canada, France, Germany, Great Britain, the United States, and even Sweden.[56] According to a report from the office of the Federal Ministry of the Interior, the number of crimes with an anti-Semitic bias increased from 562 in 1992 to 656 in 1993.[57] But the results from these demographic studies of anti-Semitism can also be seen as working against the assumption that there has been a general rise in the level of anti-Semitism in Germany.[58]

With a new generation's coming-of-age in Germany, anti-Semitism has declined. The kind of anti-Semitism that supports discriminatory measures against Jews can only be found among 5 percent of the west German population. Of those born in 1922 and earlier, about 25 percent can be considered anti-Semites; only 6 percent can be found among the younger generation (those born between 1940 and 1970).[59] Many people are surprised at the results of social studies that show anti-Semitism is less widespread in east Germany than it is in the former Federal Republic. On the other hand, new youth studies are beginning to expose a problematic trend in the new states as well.

The skepticism toward the way in which the former GDR condemned "fascism" has led many young people to conclude that something must have been good about Nazism. In studies carried out among east German youth, one can recognize a trivialization or relativization of National Socialism by students and apprentices. Between 1990 and 1992, the number of students who agreed with the statement, "The Jews are Germany's misfortune," rose from 9 to 11 percent; the proportion rose from 17 to 19 percent among apprentices. Among male apprentices, the figure was even higher: from 19 to 29 percent. The most anti-Semitic age group was the fourteen- to eighteen-year-olds. Fourteen percent of this group agreed with the statement, whereas only 5 percent of the twenty- to twenty-five-year-olds did, and only 1 percent of the twenty-five- to twenty-six-year-olds. Young men in particular appear to be susceptible.[60] The results from an Allensbach Institute study reveal that 7 percent of west Germans would not like to have Jewish neighbors, while 77 percent of west Germans would be against right-extremist neighbors.

Of course, schools and general political education—through the Federal Center for Political and Civic Education, for example—are doing their share to inform people about the crimes of the Holocaust. The conclusion of a study carried out by Konrad Brendler, a Wuppertal pedagogue, was that one of the reasons adolescents adopted right-extremist attitudes was the negative way in which the Holocaust was presented in families and schools. Frequently, these two social institutions were destructive of the self-image of many adolescents over the long term. What families and schools failed to provide in their dealings with the Holocaust was emotional support; without this, adolescents developed a "stubborn resistance." Just showing horrific documentary films as a way of educating was counterproductive: "Instead of closely observing how children react to these images and responding to their reactions accordingly, most teachers just repeat the same mistakes of their parents, who ignored their children's questions or who tried to hide behind noncommittal objective explanations."[61]

The author of the study has critical words for what he considers the overly scientific approach of current school curricula. On the whole, teachers presented facts without responding to the emotional and moral sensibilities of the students. Moreover, there was little thematic discussion after the presentation of such films; and there was little effort to bring the contemporary issue of antiforeigner violence into the discussion. His conclusion is that the use of documentaries in this fashion was often "inhuman and counterproductive."

THE CONSEQUENCE OF PROTEST: DECISION MAKERS PREPARED TO TAKE ACTION

Political decision makers will have to act with decisiveness to counter the increasing brutality in society, be it in the forms of left- or right-extrem-

ism or in the simple cases of random violence.[62] There has to be a tireless
effort to track down criminals and bring them to justice. Social problems—
for example, in the housing and employment markets—will have to be
tackled with great energy, for these are the problems that make people
susceptible to antiforeigner tirades.

If we look more closely at the causes of right-radicalism and antiforeigner agitation, we notice that much of it is an unpolitical form of
protest; it derives from frustration and is expressed in a general willingness
to use violence and brutality. These are fundamental concerns of educational
and youth policy, and they demand a political response.

The Courage to Educate

We must have the "courage to educate." A convention was held under
that name in 1978,[63] and among the participants were Golo Mann, Hermann
Lübbe and Wilhelm Hahn. One of the nine theses they signed declared: "We
object to the fallacy that treats the virtues of hard work, discipline and order
as obsolete just because they have been politically mistreated. The truth is
that these virtues are needed in all political circumstances: the need for them
is not connected to any specific system but is rooted in man" (Thesis 3). A
further thesis stated: "We object to the fallacy that believes an increasingly
scientific curriculum is the correct pedagogical response to the challenges
posed by our scientific civilization" (Thesis 8).

At the time, these appeals fell on deaf ears; they were stigmatized as
"backward" and "reactionary" by both politicians and respected peda-
gogues. It comes as a surprise, then, that Beate Scheffler, a representative
in the state assembly of North Rhine–Westphalia and member of the Green
Party, would be the one to criticize antiauthoritarian education: "We didn't
achieve our educational objectives. Instead of producing young people who
are mature, socially and ecologically committed, and politically motivated,
our education has turned out a type that is for the most part egocentric and
consumption-oriented and, in the worst case, violent and antiforeign."[64]

The undermining of authority left a vacuum. Peter König, who was born
in 1971, expresses this feeling well in an article he wrote for a leftist
alternative quarterly:

There's something wrong with our democracy. The democracy that we live in was
presented to us in school, and it was always used as an argument against our
interests. We learn a lot more in school than is in our curriculum, and a lot more

than negative educational statistics will make you believe. We are learning today's normal form of living together.

The responsibility of our education is constantly being shoved back and forth between parents who have no time and teachers who have too much work. In this chaos, we have lots of freedom, and we like that. We can run wild in this vacuum whose walls are made of cotton and whose limits we determine. That there might actually be other limits, this we only begin to realize when we're standing in front of a burning house that we've set on fire, and three policemen come up from behind and grab us. The rules of our game aren't logical and are difficult to understand, but a punch in the face, that's a buzz, and it gives you a clear feeling. Democracy's the opposite. It doesn't give you a buzz, it's complicated and it's much too strenuous. It's no fun, too sterile, and there's not enough pleasure. And pleasure—that's our highest goal.[65]

Media Restraint

Society must reach a consensus on the issue of television violence. One media study has shown that German viewers with the time, the inclination and a cable connection could watch up to seventy murders a day on television.[66] The report concluded that scenes of violence make up between 7 and 13 percent of all television broadcasting. According to statistics provided by the State Institute of Broadcasting in North Rhine–Westphalia, German television aired over 2,700 scenes of violence a week—with about 4,000 bodies appearing on screen—in the period under review. The major concentration of violence was in the two-hour time slot before prime time, between 6 and 8 P.M.

Of course, uncritical portrayals of violence in the media alone will not lead anyone to aggressive or criminal behavior; there are many causes for violence in society. But what is difficult to deny is that media violence can reinforce aggressive behavior. For example, specialists in the field refer to a "double-dose theory" when a child experiences family violence. As a victim of violence, he gets the impression through watching daily doses of television violence that the world is a violent place and that aggressive behavior is the way to achieve one's goals. The danger of such scenes of violence is not that they will be potentially imitated, but rather that norms, values and attitudes toward violence are subtly changed by them; they numb people to the effects of violence and brutality, particularly when violence is presented as the means of conflict resolution.

Few people deny nowadays that these portrayals have short-term physiological, emotional, cognitive and social effects on young children and adolescents.[67] The courage to educate in schools and a greater sense of responsibility from "hidden educators" in broadcast stations—for example, by installing a voluntary television self-censorship panel—will help protect young people from the false prophets of hate and violence.

A Foundation of Values

The younger generation must be taught that democracy and the Constitution are not value-free institutions.[68] Young people are often looking for narrow worldviews or ideologies that will offer them ultimate security; youth sects are an expression of this yearning. Young people must be taught that progress in society can only occur if differing worldviews compete openly; but a position claiming absolute authority won't lead to mutual tolerance or respect.

"Young people should not only be supported; they must also be challenged. Adults can only harm young people if they do not take on a leadership role. Young people want to be challenged, but they also want their opinions to be taken seriously. Young people need to be contradicted. What we're unfortunately lacking is a spirit of tolerant contradiction."[69]

3

The Germans' View of Politics

These trends in German society—certainly not the only ones—have had an effect, of course, on the political attitudes of Germans. The percentage of floating voters (voters with changing party preferences) has risen; presumably, this will be even more the case after reunification. These voters are primarily of the new middle class (the well-educated class of office workers, civil servants, highly skilled workers), younger than forty-five, who have grown out of their narrowly defined milieus.[1] In east Germany, on the other hand, a specific voting pattern has not had enough time to materialize yet, even though West German television once kept East Germans pretty well informed about political life in the West.

Until now, the independent has been the most conspicuous type of voter in east Germany; this should increase current floating vote trends. Eleven percent fewer east Germans than west Germans identified with a political party shortly after reunification. Whereas 49 percent of west Germans admitted to having "strong party ties" in mid-1991, only 38 percent of east Germans admitted to this in the same time period.[2] Except for a small, intact, church-oriented milieu, the SED regime succeeded in destroying traditional milieus in East Germany. About two thirds of east Germans are not linked to a church; a rural agricultural culture has been all but eliminated; and a middle class is only now beginning to form. As a result, the average east German voter bases his political decisions more on concrete political situations, on his day-to-day interests, than on a fundamental party preference.

Ever since the early 1980s, West Germany has seen a rise in voter abstention[3] as well as an increase in the number of floating voters. For many years, the large national political parties (CDU, CSU, SPD) picked up a 90 percent share of the total vote—with a voter participation rate, at times, of over 90 percent. The peak came in 1976: the large parties received 91.2 percent of the total vote. From then on, however, the large parties witnessed a steady decline in voter support. In 1990, for example, they only received 77.3 percent in the general national elections. The first prominent exception to this overall trend was the state election in Lower Saxony in March 1994; here, the two large parties (CDU and SPD) were still able to divide up 80.7 percent of the vote (with a slightly lower voter participation rate). And a greater percentage voted for the large political parties in the national elections of 1994.

One of the major reasons for Germany's political stability in the postwar era was the overwhelming political influence of the large national parties— CDU, CSU and SPD.[4] The type of social trends that I have discussed can, however, lead to a breakup of the German party landscape; this development is intensified by the German electoral system of proportional representation, which gives even smaller political movements a good chance to succeed.

In October 1994, an unprecedented number of small splinter parties were up for election. In March 1983, the Greens were the first protest party since the consolidation of the party system to receive the more than 5 percent of the vote needed to enter the Bundestag.[5] The right-extremist "Republikaner" Party, on the other hand, aside from smaller state elections and the European Parliament elections of 1989, failed to jump the 5 percent hurdle in the various state, national and European elections held in 1994.

But now, with the PDS (Party of Democratic Socialism), successor to the former East German SED (Socialist Unity Party), there is another party aside from the Greens that is to the left of the SPD in the new German states; it has a sizable voter potential. During the various elections of 1994 at the local, state, national and European levels, the PDS was able to pick up an impressive 15–20 percent of the total vote. (I will have more to say about the PDS in a subsequent section of this chapter: "With a Firm View to the Past: PDS—The Party with a Janus Face.") Despite the failure of communism, and because of dynamic political changes, the recent past has been suppressed; and after a grace period, the debate about socialism will enter a new phase in both East and West.

THE UNITY OF THE GERMANS

If one considers the complications and unforeseen problems of reunification and the integration of two highly diverse political cultures, it should not come as a surprise that there are two separate identities—east and west

German—that exist alongside a larger common German identity. On the other hand, the same value shift that the west has experienced has also taken place in the east, particularly among the youth. The younger generation in the east, for example, is even more inclined to exhibit "postmaterial" values than young west Germans. Scientific reports have shown that young east Germans are not much different than their counterparts in the west. The authors of one study conclude that "there is an increasing convergence between young east and west Germans, and this is beginning to affect other generations in the east as well."[6]

But clear differences arise over the question of how east and west Germans feel as Germans. The interesting conclusion of a September 1993 survey was that east Germans feel a much stronger common identity than west Germans. Only 15 percent of the people living in former West Germany see themselves "first and foremost as Germans," whereas 80 percent view themselves as "West German" (see Figure 3.1). One probable reason for this is that west Germans are beginning to fear the greater burdens and the major changes in their lives that will result from the massive transfer of funds to the east and the tax increases that will come from that. Moreover, many west Germans still emotionally associate "Germany" with West Germany; for them, the former GDR was just a big blank void on the map.

As for east Germans, a narrow majority of 51 percent consider themselves "first and foremost as Germans," 48 percent as "east Germans." Part

Figure 3.1
Identity as "German"

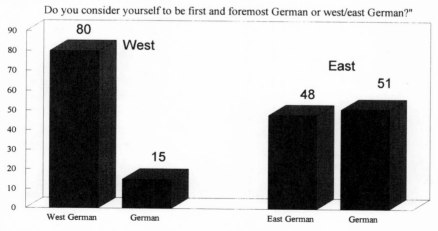

Do you consider yourself to be first and foremost German or west/east German?"

Source: Ipos, *Zusammenhalt in Deutschland*, September 1993 (West n = 2,007; East n = 1,056), published in October 1993.

of the reason for this is that German unity was a much more intense political goal for east Germans than for west Germans, because people in the east knew that reunification could only occur under free and open conditions. The former GDR always measured itself against the Federal Republic of (West) Germany; this was not the case the other way around.

Despite the political, social and economic problems associated with reunification, a majority of east and west Germans believe it was right to unify the two states in 1990. In September 1993, 81 percent of west Germans and 82 percent of east Germans thought that reunification was right. Only 16 percent in the west and 17 percent in the east thought it was a bad idea.[7]

Of course, the SED's decades of political indoctrination have left their mark; after all, no area was as infiltrated by communist ideology as the realms of education (including universities) and the media. Many east Germans claim that socialism isn't such a bad idea in principle but was just badly implemented by politicians. According to an Allensbach Institute survey conducted in April–May 1994, 36 percent of west Germans agreed with the question "Do you consider socialism a good idea that was just badly implemented?" On the other hand, 74 percent of east Germans answered "yes" to this same question (15 percent said "no," 11 percent were undecided).[8] These differences exist in the younger generation as well, not only in the general population. This is revealed in the following statistics from a Konrad Adenauer Foundation study (see Table 3.1).

Of the fifteen- to twenty-five-year-olds surveyed in west Germany, 56 percent thought that "socialism was destined to fail." In east Germany, the corresponding proportion was 30 percent. Sixty-nine percent of east Germans blamed incompetent politicians for the collapse of the socialist system, whereas only 41 percent of west Germans did. Thirty-two percent

Table 3.1
Attitude toward Socialism

What do you think caused the collpase of socialism in the former GDR?
1. Is the socialist system fundamentally destined to fail?
2. or were the politicians in power there incompetent?

	Answer 1			Answer 2		
	total %	west %	east %	total %	west %	east %
Total	51	56	30	47	41	69
Men	52	57	33	45	40	66
Women	49	55	26	48	42	72

Source: Konrad-Adenauer-Stiftung (KAS) Archive-No. 9104 (Youth Study).

of youth surveyed in east Germany still had a positive impression of socialism, whereas only 19 percent in west Germany did.[9] What these statistics show is that support for the idea of socialism rises with the general educational level. Also, the more that a young person sees himself as a "German," the less positive he is toward the idea of socialism.

There is also a divergence of attitudes toward democracy in east and west, and a decidedly lower satisfaction level with democracy in the east than in the west, though one would expect to find a high level of enthusiasm after decades of dictatorship. In the fall of 1993, 75 percent of west Germans were either "satisfied" or "somewhat satisfied" with democracy; in east Germany, only 57 percent expressed similar levels of satisfaction (Figure 3.2).

What is surprising is that these figures for east Germany were much more positive (72 percent) in the fall of 1991. This is most likely a natural reaction to the political and economic disappointments that have occurred since then, also in west Germany, where the percentage of people dissatisfied with democracy has risen in two years from 12 to 24 percent (in east Germany, the figure rose from 23 to 39 percent). Still, there remain significant differences in the two parts of Germany.

Though "political malaise" (*Politikverdrossenheit*) has developed into a catchword in Germany, the level of satisfaction with democracy—when compared to other countries in the European Union—is not at the very bottom of the scale, but lies somewhere in the middle, as can be seen in Figure 3.3 and Table 3.2. Again, what is important are the differences between east and west Germans.

East and west Germans' trust in government, authorities and parties has also fallen (Figure 3.4). This is probably a result of the unpopular political decisions that needed to be made. Indeed, it is disturbing to see that the east Germans' trust in democratic institutions is lower than in the West. With such a low level of trust in democratic institutions, political frustration can turn much more quickly and violently into forms of protest or rejection or into left- and right-extremism.

East and west German youth also revealed marked discrepancies in their level of satisfaction with democracy. Whereas only 9 percent of fifteen- to twenty-five-year-olds surveyed expressed themselves "unsatisfied" with democracy in west Germany, in east Germany 19 percent did.[10] Twenty-seven percent of west Germans are satisfied with democracy (in east Germany, 8 percent); 62 percent are relatively satisfied (in east Germany, 72 percent). This discrepancy between youth in east and west is further revealed in the question of trust. On the whole, east German youth trust

Figure 3.2
Level of Satisfaction with Democracy

%   in Western Germany

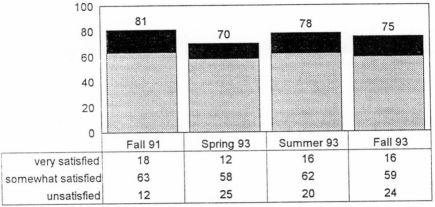

	Fall 91	Spring 93	Summer 93	Fall 93
very satisfied	18	12	16	16
somewhat satisfied	63	58	62	59
unsatisfied	12	25	20	24

▓ somewhat satisfied ■ very satisfied

%   in Eastern Germany

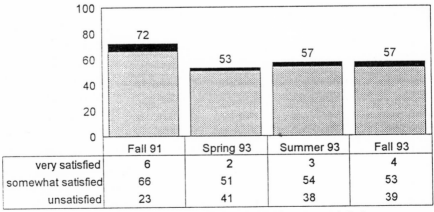

	Fall 91	Spring 93	Summer 93	Fall 93
very satisfied	6	2	3	4
somewhat satisfied	66	51	54	53
unsatisfied	23	41	38	39

▓ somewhat satisfied ■ very satisfied

Source: KAS-Archiv-Nr. 9105/6, 9301/2, 9303/4, 9305/6.

Figure 3.3
Level of Satisfaction with Democracy in European Union Member States, 1994

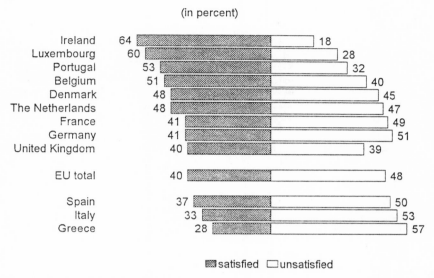

(in percent)

satisfied unsatisfied

Source: Eurobarometer 41, July 1994.

democratic institutions substantially less than their western counterparts (see Table 3.3). The only notable exception is the Bundeswehr (the German army), which more young east Germans claim to trust. In the east, there are also fewer conscientious objectors.[11]

As a result of growing economic problems, east Germans are less favorably disposed to the market economy. In early 1990, 77 percent still had a high opinion of the market economy; by early 1991, the figure had dropped to 53 percent; this fell even further to 44 percent by 1992.[12] It is also interesting to note the differences of opinion on society: whereas 28 percent of the people in the west viewed society as "largely unjust," in east Germany, 40 percent held that view. In east Germany, only 10 percent in the fall 1993 survey considered society "fairly just"; in west Germany, more than twice as many (21 percent) believed that to be the case (Figure 3.5).

In general, and exempting the period of national euphoria in 1990–91, Germans after reunification are less optimistic about the future (Table 3.4). A look at Germany at the end of 1993 revealed that there were considerable concerns and fears about job security; in east Germany, that ranked above all other concerns. On the other hand, surveys from early 1994 showed that more and more Germans (and after a delay, east Germans as well) believed

Table 3.2
Level of Satisfaction with Democracy in European Union Member States (in percent), 1976–92

Question: If you reflect on the way in which democracy (in your country) functions, are you very satisfied - fairly satisfied - fairly unsatisfied - totally unsatisfied?(1)

	1976	1977	1978	1979	1980	1981	1982	1983	1984	1985	1986	1987	1988	1989	1990	1991	1992
Belgium	53.2	53.4	48.6	45.5	33.9	36.5	42.1	48.0	46.1	54.7	48.4	49.6	54.6	60.6	60.4	58.8	55.8
Denmark	55.4	64.8	65.8	67.5	61.0	68.3	60.2	71.3	69.5	70.1	69.9	70.3	74.6	63.3	72.0	78.1	79.0
Germany - Old States	78.7	78.2	76.3	79.8	72.8	68.7	66.7	69.2	71.8	69.3	74.0	72.5	76.9	76.4	80.4	67.3	65.3
Germany - New States	-	-	-	-	-	-	-	-	-	-	-	-	-	-	49.4	39.1	43.3
France	42.0	45.8	44.2	40.4	35.3	53.4	42.3	41.7	39.5	41.7	49.8	48.2	53.2	54.8	48.4	51.8	40.7
Greece	-	-	-	-	52.9	52.1	58.6	60.0	58.7	55.0	56.7	55.1	51.4	49.2	38.5	36.0	35.6
Great Britain	43.9	60.8	57.2	52.8	51.9	48.5	52.4	63.8	60.5	51.9	51.8	58.2	57.3	55.5	49.5	60.6	59.3
Ireland	59.0	65.7	66.0	52.3	48.3	58.3	50.6	43.8	47.2	47.1	48.0	49.9	54.8	59.3	62.5	61.4	61.6
Italy	13.6	15.9	22.5	18.3	20.9	19.5	19.7	18.5	23.7	26.5	28.0	27.7	27.1	28.5	25.3	25.9	22.0
Luxembourg	54.6	69.3	65.1	67.1	76.3	75.2	60.3	60.9	65.6	69.3	70.7	72.2	70.0	79.1	72.2	75.6	73.8
The Netherlands	66.7	65.3	62.1	63.3	50.7	59.9	53.2	53.7	56.2	57.3	60.3	58.7	62.1	73.0	70.9	68.0	69.7
Portugal	-	-	-	-	-	-	-	-	-	34.5	55.8	63.2	52.9	59.4	68.0	73.3	71.8
Spain	-	-	-	-	-	-	-	-	-	51.4	53.7	52.0	47.4	58.4	56.1	58.7	55.0

(1) Original answer choices: 1 (very satisfied), 2 (fairly satisfied), 3 (fairly unsatisfied), 4 (totally unsatisfied), 0 (don't know/no response). The table includes those who chose either the answers 1 or 2.

Sources: Eurobarometer EB06, EB07, EB08, EB09, EB10, EB11, EB12, EB14, EB16, EB17, EB18, EB19, EB20, EB21, EB22, EB23, EB24, EB25, EB26, EB27, EB28, EB29, EB31, EB32, EB33, EB34, EB35, EB36, EB37; author's calculations numbers taken from: Oscar W. Gabriel and Frank Brettschneider (eds.), *Die EU-Staaten in Vergleich—Strukturen, Prozesse, Politikinhalte* (Opladen 1994), p. 549.

Figure 3.4
Trust in Governments, Authorities and Parties

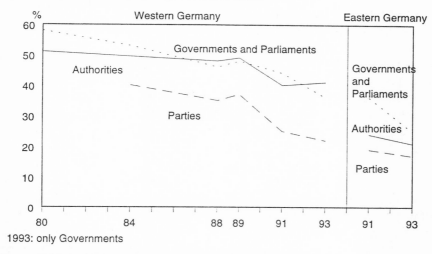

1993: only Governments

Source: KAS-Archiv-Nr. 8012, 8401, 8804, 8902, 9105/6.

Table 3.3
Trust in Institutions

How much trust do you have in the following institutions?

	Rank	Total		West		East	
		have trust	no trust	have trust	no trust	have trust	no trust
		%	%	%	%	%	%
Courts	1	54	16	56	15	44	22
Police	2	50	19	54	17	34	32
Army	2	40	30	40	31	40	25
Bundestag	4	39	18	41	17	29	24
Federal Government	5	31	27	32	26	27	30
Administration	6	28	38	31	30	18	45
Parties	7	17	32	18	31	12	37

Source: KAS Archive-No. 9104.

that the country's economy had improved; this helped the governing political parties (CDU, CSU and FDP) in the October 1994 elections.

Many Germans in both east and west, however, felt much more comfortable with their own situation than with the overall economic situation in

Germany. Marked differences still exist between opinions in west and east Germany on the general and personal economic situation (compare Figures 3.6 and 3.7).

The rapid economic, social and political changes occurring in east Germany have caused great insecurity. For some people, this has led to a form of nostalgia for the old order. It is a phenomenon that can be observed in other socialist societies that are going through similar transformation processes. On the whole, however, Germany's point of departure is much better, as the east was able to adopt the legal, economic and political framework from the west. On top of that, there has been an unprecedented financial transfusion.

Yet, Germans at the personal level are more optimistic about the future— 76 percent of west Germans, 70 percent of east Germans. Asked if they thought Germans on the whole were optimistic about the future, 37 percent of west Germans and, surprisingly, 49 percent of east Germans thought they were. Thirty-three percent of western youth and 38 percent of youth in the east thought this to be the case. That means that people were generally more optimistic about their personal futures than about either youth or society as a whole.

As for "satisfaction with one's life," 93 percent of west Germans are "largely satisfied" (7 percent "unsatisfied") and 76 percent of east Germans (as compared to 23 percent who are "largely unsatisfied"). But only 43 percent of all Germans thought that "most people in our society" were "largely satisfied" with their lives; 50 percent of west Germans and 56 percent of east Germans assumed that most people were "largely unsatisfied."[13] Figure 3.8 reveals the level of optimism in Germany.

CHANGES IN THE EAST SINCE REUNIFICATION

When east Germans compared the present situation with the time before reunification, 58 percent thought they were better off today, as compared to 15 percent who thought they were worse off. The greatest changes for the better have occurred in the realm of personal freedom; here, 75 percent saw an improvement and only 6 percent thought the situation was worse. In the economic sphere, 56 percent reported an improvement and 19 percent believed things were worse. East Germans saw a decline in two specific areas—in matters of social security (61 percent saw a decline, only 16 percent saw an improvement) and in interpersonal relationships, where 50 percent said that the situation had worsened, and just 6 percent thought their relationships to others had improved (see Figure 3.9).[14]

Figure 3.5
Attitudes toward Society

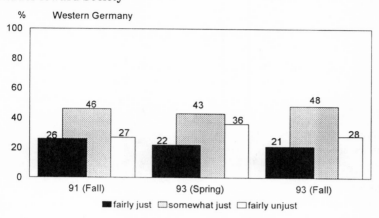

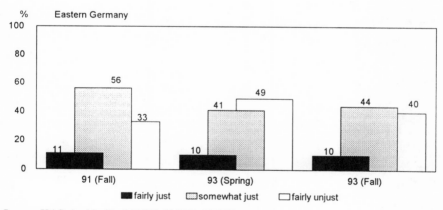

Source: KAS-Archiv-Nr. 9105/6, 9301/2, 9305/6.

An Allensbach study reveals that more needs to be done to improve the image of democracy in the new federal states. As Table 3.5 shows, there is a level of disillusionment with the idea of "the best governmental system." In November 1990, 41 percent of east Germans still believed that democracy was the best governmental system; but in February–March 1994, the figure had slipped to 31 percent. A comparison between the old Federal Republic and the eastern states shows that 76 percent of people in the west thought democracy was the best system; only 9 percent believed there were superior alternatives to democracy, whereas 28 percent believed that in east Germany (15 percent were undecided in west Germany, 41 percent in east Germany).[15]

Table 3.4
Concerns and Fears, Late 1993

	Germany as a whole		Western Germany		Eastern Germany	
	%	Rank	%	Rank	%	Rank
Great concern: That it will be increasingly difficult to find a job	61	1.	58	2.	74	1.
That we will not be able to afford our welfare system in the future	58	2.	60	1.	50	5.
That citizens will not be adequately protected against violence	53	3.	47	8.	73	2.
That pollution will destroy our natural resources	51	4.	51	4.	51	4.
That our economy will get worse	51	4.	53	3.	42	6.
That apartments will become scarce	48	6.	50	5.	41	8.
That citizens will face even greater burdens as a result of German unity	48	6.	49	7.	42	6.
That Germany will be exploited by refugees	47	8.	50	5.	35	9.
That social developments will lead to more people being left out in society	45	9.	43	9.	52	3.
That Germany will become oversaturated with foreigners	37	10.	39	10.	28	10.
That Germany's international responsibility will grow	34	11.	36	11.	27	11.
That Germany will just be exploited by the European Union	25	12.	27	12.	17	12.

Source: KAS Archive-No. 9305/6, December 1993. Approximately 4,100 surveyed.

Figure 3.6
West: Perception of Personal and General Economic Situation

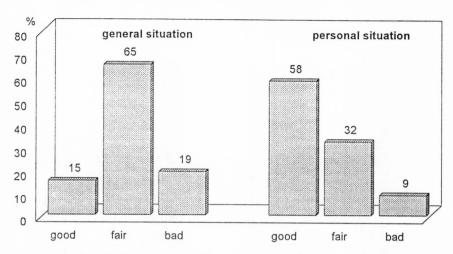

Source: Ipos, *Wirtschaftsstandort Deutschland*, May 1994, published in June 1994.

Figure 3.7
East: Perception of Personal and General Economic Situation

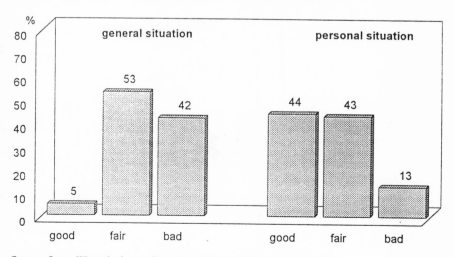

Source: Ipos, *Wirtschaftsstandort*, May 1994, published in June 1994.

Figure 3.8
Expectations for the Future

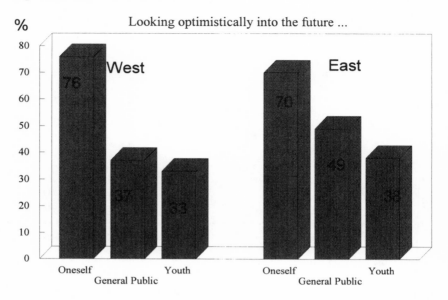

Source: Ipos, *Wirtschaftsstandort Deutschland*, May 1994, published in June 1994.

Figure 3.9
East: Compared to before Reunification, My Situation Today Is . . .

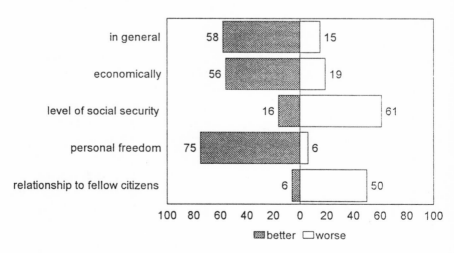

Source: Ipos, *Wirtschaftsstandort Deutschland*, May 1994, published in June 1994.

Table 3.5
Doubts about Democracy

Question: "Do you think that the form of democracy that we have in the Federal Republic is the best governmental system, or are there other systems that might be better?"

	Nov. 1990 %	April 1991 %	Sept. 1991 %	Dec. 1992 %	Dec. 1993 %	Febr./Mar. 1994 %
Democracy best form	41	31	34	41	32	31
Others that are better	19	26	29	20	30	28
Undecided	40	43	37	39	38	41
Total	100	100	100	100	100	100
n =	522	539	1080	1131	1145	1109

Source: Allensbacher Archive, IfD-Umfragen 9007/II, 5050, 5055, 5074, 5088, 5092.

Sixty-five percent in the west were willing to defend the political system of the Federal Republic when asked in December 1993 (24 percent had doubts, 11 percent were undecided); whereas only 36 percent of east Germans were willing to defend it (47 percent had doubts, 17 percent were undecided).[16]

THE ELECTIONS OF 1994: WHO VOTED FOR WHOM AND WHY?

The day Winston Churchill was voted out of office, he was assured of a grand departure: his victory over the German Reich had just occurred. His wife referred to this moment as his "hidden victory."

Though many people were convinced that the end of the Kohl era was just around the corner, the chancellor put himself up for election again just four years after his greatest triumph—the reunification of Germany. Despite having to make many unpopular decisions, Kohl was reelected on October 16, 1994, a great personal victory for the chancellor. He was reelected at the height of his popularity, both at home and abroad; and he was reconfirmed in his political course at a time when his policies were being challenged.

With victory in this, his fourth election (he was first elected in 1982), Kohl is on his way to serving longer than even Konrad Adenauer, chancellor of West Germany for the first fourteen years of the Federal Republic's history (from 1949 to 1963). On October 16, the day of the national elections and two further state elections (Thuringia and Mecklenburg–West Pomerania), the people once again voted Helmut Kohl into office. He was voted into office after a string of elections (eighteen in total) at all different levels, including state elections in Lower Saxony, Saxony-Anhalt, Brandenburg, Saxony and Bavaria. Though his coalition of CDU/CSU and FDP (Free Democratic Party) holds only a narrow margin of ten seats over the opposition parties (SPD, Bündnis 90/The Greens and PDS), this was more a result of the poor showings of his coalition partner, the FDP.

About a year prior to the elections, many media journalists began to herald "the end of an era"—so ran the cover story from a *Spiegel* magazine article of December 6, 1993—and there was talk about Kohl's decline in political fortunes. But then, more people started to recognize Kohl's international leadership role. When asked who would better represent German interests, half the people responded Kohl, and only one out of ten chose the SPD's candidate, Rudolf Scharping.[17] Germans have come to acknowledge Kohl's high international standing and his historical significance. When a prominent British journalist stated on the day of the elections that "all foreign countries are voting for Kohl," he only reconfirmed the chancellor's stature.[18]

In early 1994, however, very few observers in Germany and abroad thought it possible that Kohl could win another election. Even as late as May 1994, Kohl's political opponent, the SPD's Scharping, was receiving more support in opinion polls than Kohl was; this made the ultimate about-face even more dramatic for pollsters. They thought the government would pay the consequences of having to make unpopular decisions in connection with German reunification (for example, the drastic tax increase, the decision to transfer the capital from Bonn to Berlin, health care reform, etc.). Though it seemed that the polls were indicating a desire for change, in the end it was the desire for stability and continuity that won out. The national elections prove that Germans prefer to stick with tested models guaranteeing security in moments of great change.

The fact is the German electoral system makes it virtually impossible for one political party to obtain an absolute parliamentary majority. It has only occurred once: in the third legislative session (1957–61), when the CDU/CSU won an absolute majority of 50.2 percent. If Germany had a majority electoral system like Great Britain's, then the CDU and CSU would have taken two thirds of the legislative districts outright. Of the 328 legislative districts in total, the conservatives directly won 221 seats—or

67.4 percent in total (CDU 177; CSU 44). The SPD received 103 direct mandates, and the PDS 4.

Parties in countries with majority electoral systems, such as Great Britain, are in a much better position to win an absolute majority in parliament, even if their total number of votes falls below 50 percent. The British Conservatives, for example, were able to pick up 376 seats out of a total of 650 in the parliamentary elections of June 11, 1987, even though they had only won 42.3 percent of the nation's vote. Similarly, in the elections of April 10, 1992, the Conservatives won 336 seats out of a total of 651 seats after receiving 41.9 percent of the vote.

In the American presidential system, it is also possible to vote a president into office with far less than 50 percent of the national vote. This was the case in the November 3, 1992, election, when Bill Clinton won with just 43.2 percent of the vote. The German system is unique in that it combines elements of both a direct vote and a proportional representational system. The voter can cast two votes: with his first vote, he can vote directly for a candidate in his district; with his second vote, he votes according to his party preference. As a result, the second vote cast is much more important, because (according to the proportional principle) it has more effect on the majority outcome in parliament. Many voters still fail to realize this.

The German electoral system makes it much more difficult to establish a clear majority in the Bundestag. As long as there were only those parties included in the three-party system—the CDU and her sister party, the CSU; the SPD; and the FDP—the creation of a majority in the Bundestag was relatively simple. But in the 1980s, new parties emerged—most prominently, Bündnis 90/The Greens, but also the right-radical Republikaner Party, which won seats in several state parliaments and in the European Parliament (its 1989–94 session). Then the Party of Democratic Socialism (PDS), the successor to the former communist party (SED), emerged on the far left after reunification.

What makes it even more difficult to achieve a majority consensus in the Bundestag is the fact that the Bundesrat, the national assembly representing the federal states, is now controlled by the opposition party, the SPD. Since approximately 50 percent of all laws need to be approved by the Bundesrat, a form of Grand Coalition is, in a way, already in place: in important issues such as nursing insurance, for example, the government parties will need the votes of the opposition. The state governments, some of which are coalitions, must support both the interests of their national party and their specific state interests; therefore, parties and politicians will have a problem in projecting a clear political profile. After all, the interests of a state government are not always the same as those of a large parliamentary opposition party. In this kind of governmental system, compromise is crucial; and for all practical purposes, the Federal Republic is a consensus democracy.

There is another way in which the outcome of the recent national elections might have been dangerous for the ruling governmental coalition of CDU/CSU and FDP. If the states of Thuringia and Mecklenburg–West Pomerania had voted in a SPD government, then the SPD would have had a two-thirds majority in the Bundesrat. In this case, the SPD, through the states, would not only have been in the position to impede legislative initiatives from the ruling coalition, but it could also have forced its political will on the government. In the twelfth legislative period (1990–94), when the SPD held forty-one out of sixty-eight seats in the Bundesrat, they had enough votes to veto bills that demanded Bundesrat approval. The result was a laborious process of consensus building in the arbitration committee of the Bundestag and Bundesrat.

The second all-German election shows that the Germans, despite a vote for personal and political continuity, are living in a new republic whose political landscape has been changed for good. The party system within Germany as a whole is currently much more in flux than after the first election, which can be considered more a plebiscite. In that sense, it is surprising to see that the percentage of votes for the two large parties taken together has stabilized in relation to the last election. Whereas the two large parties received 77.3 percent of the vote in the 1990 elections, in 1994, they received 77.8 percent.

Table 3.6 reveals the trends underlying the German party system. It is necessary to point out that the twelfth and thirteenth national elections were the first all-German elections, which makes it impossible to compare them to earlier elections. The results from these elections show that it is difficult to analyze and evaluate the elections following German reunification in the same way as earlier elections. Making comparisons to electoral behavior and party voting patterns in the former Federal Republic will only confuse us, since the sociological makeup of the electorate has been thoroughly transformed.[19] One of Helmut Kohl's great achievements in this election was keeping right-radical parties out of the elections and out of the Bundestag: they only managed to pick up 2 percent of the vote. Democratic parties must try to bring back voters of radical parties into their fold, and force the parties themselves out of the party spectrum.

What the CDU was able to do with the Republikaner Party, the SPD failed to do with the PDS. That does not mean that Republikaner voters were

Table 3.6

Elections to the Bundestag of Germany (in percent)

	Turnout	CDU/CSU[1]	SPD	FDP	Greens	PDS	REP	Others
1949	78.5	31.0	29.2	11.9	-	-	-	27.8[2]
1953	85.8	45.2	28.8	9.5	-	-	-	16.5[3]
1957	87.8	50.2	31.8	7.7	-	-	-	10.3[4]
1961	87.7	45.3	36.2	12.8	-	-	-	5.7
1965	86.8	47.6	39.3	9.5	-	-	-	3.6
1969	86.7	46.1	42.7	5.8	-	-	-	5.5
1972	91.1	44.9	45.8	8.4	-	-	-	0.9
1976	90.7	48.6	42.6	7.9	-	-	-	0.9
1980	88.6	44.5	42.9	10.6	1.5	-	-	0.5
1983	89.1	48.8	38.2	7.0	5.6	-	-	0.5
1987	84.3	44.3	37.0	9.1	8.3	-	-	1.4
1990[5]	77.8	43.8	33.5	11.0	5.1[6]	2.4	2.1	2.1
1994[7]	79.1	41.4	36.4	6.9	7.3	4.4	1.9	1.7

1. CSU only in Bavaria.
2. Includes 5.7 percent for the Communist Party of Germany (KPD), 4.2 percent for the Bavarian Party (BP), 4 percent for the German Party (DP), 3.1 percent for the Center Party (ZP), 2.9 percent for the Economic Reconstruction Organization (WAV), 0.5 percent for the German Conservative Party/German Right Party (DKonP/DReP), 0.3 percent for Southern Schleswig Voter Association (SSW), and 4.8 percent for the Voter Groups / Individual Candidates (WGER/EZB).
3. Includes 5.9 percent for the Combined German Bloc/Bloc of the Refugees from the Homeland and the Legally Deprived (GB/BHE), 3.3 percent for the German Party (DP) and 0.8 percent for the German Center Party (Zentrum).
4. Includes 3.4 percent for the German Party (DP).
5. The first all-German election.
6. Of this total, 3.8 percent went to The Greens (Greens) in west German electoral territory and 1.2 percent to the combined ticket Bündnis 90/Greens–Citizens Movement (B90/Gr) in east German electoral territory. On the basis of a High Court ruling, there are two separate electoral territories:
    Electoral territory west (48,128,370 eligible voters): 78.6 percent voter participation; CDU/CSU 44.3 percent, SPD 35.7 percent, FDP 10.6 percent, The Greens 4.8 percent, PDS 0.3 percent, Republikaner 2.3 percent, others 2.0 percent.
    Electoral territory cast (12,308,190 eligible voters): 74.5 percent voter participation; CDU 41.8 percent, SPD 24.3 percent, FDP 12.9 percent, B90/Gr 6.1 percent, PDS 11.1 percent, Republickaner 1.3 percent, others 2.5 percent.
    In the previous (and first free) elections to the People's Chamber (March 18, 1990), in the former GDR, there was a voter participation rate of 93.4 percent: CDU 40.8 percent, SPD 21.9 percent, Liberals 5.3 percent, "Bündnis 90"–New Forum–Democracy Now–Initiative for Freedom and Human Rights (Bündnis 90) 2.9 percent, PDS 16.4 percent, and others 12.7 percent.
7. Preliminary returns.

drawn merely from the ranks of the CDU/CSU: some of the Republikaners' best showings came from worker strongholds with a long tradition of SPD support. But the Union parties firmly resisted all attempts to enter into a coalition—either direct or indirect—with the Republikaner. This was not the case with the SPD, who failed to distance themselves clearly from the PDS, particularly in the new *Länder*.

One of the changes in the party system is that the SPD now has more political competitors to its left. One of them is Bündnis 90/The Greens; the other, primarily in east Germany, is the PDS. The latter has good chances of increasing its membership within west Germany at the expense of the two other parties. In receiving four direct mandates, the PDS was able to circumvent the 5 percent hurdle needed to enter parliament; it received a considerable 4.4 percent of all votes cast. It will probably want to take advantage of this situation to extend its voter basis in west Germany, which it has a fair shot at doing.

Particularly in big cities with large student populations, the PDS was able to collect around 2 percent of the vote (in Bremen/Bremerhaven 2.7 percent; Hamburg 2.2 percent; Kiel 2 percent; in Frankfurt/Main, including suburbs of the Main-Taunus-Kreis 1.9 percent; and Hannover 1.9 percent). Five of thirty PDS mandates come from west Germany, a further four mandate holders were originally from the west. The four mandates that the PDS was able to pick up from the east came from districts with a high percentage of people who benefited from the SED regime. But, still, the PDS was successful in playing on specific east German interests: it went beyond mobilizing its highly supportive membership and succeeded in capitalizing on various forms of protest within the east German electorate as a whole. (For more on this, see the following section on the PDS.)

In its appeal for the voters' direct mandate, the PDS made the east Germans into informed users of their first and second vote options: in the four east Berlin electorate districts that went to the PDS, around a fifth of the second votes for the SPD (18 percent) and a fourth for the Bündnis 90/ The Greens (25 percent) went to the PDS.[20] The support for East Berlin's PDS candidates reflects a form of leftist alliance that desires political change.

Voting patterns were significantly different in east and west (including Berlin). For example, there was a lower voter participation rate in east Germany than in the west (73.6 percent versus 80.6 percent). On the national level, the most consolidated party was the CDU/CSU; it received 42.2 percent of the vote in west Germany, only slightly higher than the 38.5 percent for the east. The SPD was able to pick up a few more votes in east

Germany than in the first all-German election, but still only received 31.9 percent of the vote there, whereas it received 37.6 percent in west Germany. The FDP's poor performance also derives from the eastern states: it only received 4 percent of the vote there, while 7.7 percent in the west voted for the FDP.

Bündnis 90/The Greens—a fusion between the east German Bündnis 90 and the west German Green Party—received only 5.3 percent of the vote in the east (without Berlin, it would have been just 4.1 percent), while in west Germany, it received 7.8 percent. The most significant difference between east and west German voters is the varying support for the PDS: in east Germany (including west Berlin), it received 17.6 percent of the vote, whereas in the west only 0.9 percent. The Republikaner Party has become an insignificant political force in both parts of Germany: it received only 2 percent in the west and 1.4 in the east. Generally, the desire for political change came more from the eastern states: whereas the governing coalition received 49.9 percent of the vote in the west (42.2 percent for the CDU/CSU, 7.7 percent for the FDP), the CDU had to settle with 38.5 percent and the FDP with 4 percent in the east.

What are the reasons that led people to vote for continuity in Germany? One opinion poll that appeared shortly before the elections asked the following question: "If you could vote directly for the chancellor, who would receive your vote?" Forty-one percent chose Kohl and only 30 percent chose Scharping (for neither of the two, 26 percent; undecided, 3 percent).[21] The "Forschungsgruppe Wahlen," an election polling institute, interpreted the election results as a "personal victory for Helmut Kohl."[22] As the architect behind German unity, he assumed a historical prominence that even his political opponents were forced to recognize.

Another important explanation for the victory of the governmental parties is the dominance of economic problems. Opinion polls—taken in late spring 1994—show that people were expecting an economic recovery, which helped the Union parties'(CDU and CSU) political momentum: it looked as though the party had regained control of the economic situation in the west, and later, in the east as well. According to the "Forschungsgruppe Wahlen" institute, this was what contributed most to the CDU's respectable showing despite the difficult restructuring of the economy and a high level of unemployment in the east.

On the other hand, the SPD's problems were reflected in the electoral patterns of the workers in east Germany: 41 percent voted for the CDU, but only 35 percent voted for the SPD and 15 percent for the PDS (which is below average for this party).[23] The SPD was, however, able to mobilize its traditional bloc of supporters in the west: they gave the party 50 percent of their vote; among unionized workers, the SPD received as much as 60 percent.

The Union was likewise able to tap its traditional clientele: in rural regions in particular, it picked up almost every second vote; and among Catholic voters, it was equally successful, receiving 52 percent of the vote. The party's traditional followers—Catholic church-goers—gave the Union as much as 74 percent of their vote. The Union also did rather well with voters over sixty years old: in the west they supported the Union with 51 percent and in the east with 45 percent. The party's best results came from women over the age of sixty. Among voters under thirty-five, the SPD was the stronger party, receiving 38 percent to the CDU/CSU's 32 percent and the Greens' 13 percent. But among males under twenty-five, the Union fared better: 35 percent to the SPD's 33 percent. In the east, on the other hand, the PDS received 23 percent from those under thirty-five, an above average showing for this party.[24]

What was interesting about this election was that foreign policy played a negligible role in comparison to the elections of Clinton and Berlusconi. Only questions concerning European policy cropped up occasionally; but the election can hardly be considered a mandate on foreign policy. The election outcome was strongly influenced by the so-called "red socks" election campaign of the CDU. This campaign constantly reminded voters of the fact that the SPD-led government in Saxony-Anhalt could only be formed there through consent of the PDS after the state elections on June 26, 1994.

It was the CDU general secretary, Peter Hintze, who came up with this masterful political advertising ploy. Using stark imagery, it showed voters the problems associated with the political cooperation of the SPD and the PDS. This issue of the PDS must have had an impact on the SPD's final election results, since the thought that "the PDS could have an influence on the formation of the government" was rejected by three fourths of western voters (73 percent). Forty-six percent of eastern voters also rejected the option (though 53 percent, on the other hand, favored "a direct or indirect participation of the PDS in the formation of the government").[25] This campaign resulted in a polarization, since both parties reacted strongly to the campaign; but its goal was to intensify the overall debate of the issue.

The campaign also succeeded in upsetting the initial strategy of the SPD's candidate, who betted on the "Clinton effect," constantly emphasizing the slogan "jobs, jobs, jobs." The argument that a change at the top would rejuvenate government ultimately did not convince voters, though it seemed as though it was having an effect at the beginning of the year. In the final analysis, Kohl's victory to some extent derived from the weakness of the opposition and its challenger. Some pollsters at the end of 1993 were giving the Union less than 30 percent of the vote. Despite an improvement in its showing, the SPD could not have been content with the outcome, since it even fell a little short of the election results of 1987, when Johannes Rau was its candidate.[26]

For Bündnis 90/The Greens, the danger is that they might develop into a purely western party. The rise of the PDS has helped the Greens, since many voters now see them as slightly more right, and therefore politically more respectable. In the east, however, where ecological issues are less relevant, it was the PDS that had a greater pull among younger and more ideologically oriented voters. Five years after reunification, Bündnis 90/The Greens must begin to develop a new profile, for the Greens' competence in ecological questions doesn't seem to interest voters in the east.

A further reason for the party's poor showing in the east was that the former citizens' movement (Bündnis 90) was divided on the question of whether to ally with the PDS. The fact that Bündnis 90/The Greens made it into the Bundestag in this election, though it failed in the last one, was mostly a result of its better showing in the west, where it succeeded in mobilizing its core constituency.

In east Germany, on the other hand, the alliance of the citizens' movement with the western Greens obviously did not help to give the party a clear political profile and did not broaden its electoral base. Moreover, many of the former activists who had helped topple the old regime do not feel as though they have a political home in the party, nor do they feel adequately represented by the alliance of Bündnis 90/The Greens. The irony is that the people most responsible for the political changes in east Germany are being increasingly marginalized, despite integration with the western Greens. They feel that this western party, from the very beginning, was doing a poor job in representing their interests. Some of the members of the former citizens' movement have found a political home in the larger national parties; but there is no longer an independent political movement (such as the earlier "New Forum") to contain them.

Of all the parties, it is the FDP who must be the most unsatisfied with its performance. The Liberals have always played a significant role in the party history of the Federal Republic. Though the Liberals once again managed to win a place in the national government, they have consistently failed to make it into any of the state governments, nor were they elected into the European Parliament in the 1994 elections. Their showing has been equally disastrous at the local level. It now seems to be the FDP's sole function to secure parliamentary majorities—in this case, once again for the CDU/CSU. The FDP was only able to overcome the 5 percent hurdle because some CDU/CSU voters realized that their candidate, Helmut Kohl, would only be elected if the FDP made it into the Bundestag. The question is whether there is still room for an independent Liberal Party now that many of the Liberals' positions have been usurped by both the Union and the Social Democrats. Even the Greens, presently more established in the political landscape, have latched onto specific left-leaning Liberal policies. But the stability of Kohl's government will ultimately depend on the political stability of his FDP allies.

The reunification of Germany and the turmoil it has created in the party system will surely keep the issue of political alliances exciting in the future. All parties are confronted with difficult challenges, particularly the major opposition party, the SPD: it will have to start competing for votes with two other left-leaning parties, but without alienating its traditional conservative core constituents in the working class. It will be difficult for the SPD to stake out a leadership role, since the public will probably start turning to more radical movements and parties with a more defined oppositional profile, rather than a party that must continue to cater to a broad electoral base and to seek compromise solutions in state governments and the Bundesrat.

WITH A FIRM VIEW TO THE PAST: PDS—THE PARTY WITH A JANUS FACE

Although the PDS received only 4.4 percent of the total vote in the all-German election, it managed to send thirty members to the Bundestag. By winning four out of five of east Berlin's direct mandates, the PDS was able to bypass the 5 percent hurdle. According to German election laws, a political party can only cancel out the 5 percent requirement by winning at least three mandates direct. The results show that the successor party to the SED, the PDS,[27] no longer represents an isolated phenomenon but is now a party of national significance. Though it seemed at first to be a relatively insignificant factor, the party has brought momentum to politics in the Federal Republic ever since the state elections of Saxony-Anhalt on June 26, 1994. (In the first all-German elections, the PDS made it into the Bundestag because it only needed to fulfill the 5 percent requirement in the eastern states. In the recent national and European elections of 1994, however, the 5 percent hurdle applied for the first time to all of Germany.)

After the elections in Saxony-Anhalt, the CDU was kept from power with the help of the PDS. Although the CDU became the strongest party, it fell short of a majority, while the FDP did not make it into the state parliament; hence, only a Grand Coalition between SPD and CDU could have secured a stable majority.

Surprisingly, the SPD rejected this option. Though it didn't have enough to form a clear majority in the state parliament, even in alliance with the Greens (the SPD had received 34 percent of the vote, the Greens 5.1 percent), the SPD formed a minority government with the Greens that could only function through the implicit cooperation of the PDS, who had received 19.9 percent of the vote. Thus, after five years of German reunification, the political successor of the eastern communists was accepted by the Social Democrats—through a clever twist in the rules of procedure. According to the procedural rules governing the Saxony-Anhalt parliament, a relative majority is sufficient to elect a minister president after a third round of balloting. The PDS did not participate in the ballot on July 21, 1994, and thus became the actual "kingmakers." For the party system, this was a decisive political precedent, because until then, a partnership or some form of power sharing between the two parties did not seem likely at the state level; moreover, it was necessary for the national SPD to give its sanction.

The PDS on the left is a mirror image of what the Republikaner represent on the right-wing, radical spectrum. The distance with which the traditional parties have treated the Republikaner seems to have worked. But the attempt to isolate the PDS, which is a communist successor party, has been replaced by tolerance. This strategy has led to considerable controversies within the SPD hierarchy, because the PDS is now beginning "to establish its niche on the German left, which in the future will change the coordinates of political power within the Federal Republic."[28]

The PDS's toleration of the SPD-led government in Saxony-Anhalt has set a precedent, for the PDS might now tolerate future minority governments. Stefan Wolle, a member of the historical commission of the SPD, agrees with this assessment: "The PDS is a hypocritical party. Its voters and members are unified in their confused, deep-rooted and unpolitical hatred of the Federal Republic and its democratic and market-oriented political system. They combine this with a resentment of modernity and the West." The historian concludes that everything must be done "to prevent this party from growing in political stature."[29]

The new eastern states have experienced the same phenomenon as other former countries of the Warsaw Pact: previous communist organizations have received considerable support from the population at large. On average, the PDS managed to pick up about 20 percent of the east's votes in the European elections in June 1994, in the local elections held simultaneously, and in the state election of Saxony-Anhalt on June 26, 1994. They also made considerable gains in other 1994 state elections.

In the elections to the European Parliament on June 12, 1994, the PDS won 20.6 percent of the eastern vote (which includes east Berlin). It has picked up 500,000 more votes since the national elections of 1990, in which it received 11.1 percent in the east. In three of Berlin's electoral districts, the results were as high as 45 percent (in Hohenschönhausen, 46.3 percent; Marzahn, 45.7 percent; Mitte, 45 percent). At both the national and European levels, however, it failed to fulfill the 5 percent requirement, receiving but 4.7 percent of Germany's total votes. The PDS is still primarily an east German regional party.

In the elections to the European Parliament, the PDS benefited from the simultaneously held local elections: it picked up 24.3 percent in Mecklenburg–West Pomerania (up 5.3 percent from May 1990), 16.3 percent in Saxony (up 4.7 percent), 18.2 percent in Saxony-Anhalt (up 5.5 percent), and 15.7 percent in Thuringia (up 5.2 percent).

In the state elections in Saxony-Anhalt, held on June 26, 1994, the PDS received 19.9 percent of the vote, gaining 7.9 percent from the state elections of 1990 (an increase of 56,000 votes in total).

In the state elections in Brandenburg, held on September 11, 1994, the PDS received 18.7 percent of the vote, making it as strong as the CDU. This was a 5.3 percent increase from the state elections in 1990. And in Saxony the PDS won 16.5 percent, a 6.3 percent increase since the 1990 state elections.

In the state elections in Mecklenburg–West Pomerania, held parallel to the recent national elections, the PDS managed to pick up 22.7 percent, which was 7 percent more than four years previously; and in Thuringia, they received 16.6 percent, an increase of 6.9 percent.

In the recent national elections held on October 16, 1994, the PDS received 4.4 percent—an impressive 2,067,391 votes in total. In four out of five east Berlin electoral districts, the PDS was able to pick up a direct mandate, the so-called first vote. The results were 40.6 percent in Mitte-Prenzlauer Berg (Stefan Heym), 44.4 percent in Friedrichshain-Lichtenberg (Christa Luft), 48.9 percent in Hellersdorf-Marzahn (Gregor Gysi), and 36.8 percent in Hohenschönhausen-Pankow-Weissensee (Manfred Müller).

The PDS has a highly motivated core political constituency. Two thirds of PDS supporters say they have strong ideological ties to the party. Only a third admit this about the CDU and a fourth about the SPD and FDP. Eight out of ten of the party's followers will normally support the PDS in elections. Part of the PDS's core constituency are former functionaries of the SED regime who lost out as a result of reunification. Polls show that the average PDS voter is not any worse off financially than his other compatriots in the east. Yet, they are more clearly disenchanted with their situation. But this dissatisfaction doesn't necessarily derive from their actual economic status. Instead, these voters are mourning after their old privileges and their lost social status, and they vote PDS out of loyalty to communism/socialism.

It is not surprising that PDS supporters are least satisfied with the new social order in Germany. More than half of all PDS voters (58 percent) believe that the social order is "on the whole unjust"; and 39 percent of them claim they belong to a disadvantaged segment of the population. This is revealed by Table 3.7.

The PDS unquestionably draws on nostalgia for the former GDR. Only 14 percent of east Germans—but 35 percent of the maximum level of PDS supporters—believe that a revitalized socialism would be better for Germany's future than the present market economy. Fifty-seven percent of this latter group also think socialism is sensible and realizable "in principle"— that is, 34 percent of the entire east German population. Only 10 percent of west Germans are of this opinion (see Table 3.8).[30]

Only 56 percent of PDS voters think that the reunification of the two Germanies was "right"; 41 percent consider it "wrong." This separates PDS voters from the electorate as a whole: 82 percent of east Germans and 81 percent of west Germans consider reunification right.[31]

Table 3.7
Perceptions of Society

	PDS Voters %	Population East total %
...society is more or less just	3	10
more unjust	58	40
fairly just	35	45

I belong to a social group that is		
more disadvantaged	39	30
more favored	6	5
neither / nor	54	64

Source: KAS Archive-No. 9305.

Table 3.8
GDR Nostalgia

	East %	Approval Max. Level of PDS approval	Total %	West %
In one hundred years people will say socialism also had its good sides	56	72	24	16
The Bundestag should also have a true socialist party	48	70	21	14
Socialism only failed in the GDR because of its economics	40	52	28	29
In principle socialism is sensible and is also realizable	34	57	15	10
A real equality between all people is only possible in true socialism	29	51	15	11
The key sectors of the economy should be put under state control	28	41	12	8
A renewed socialism would be better for a future Germany than the present market economy	14	35	5	3

Approval: Scale Values +2 and +3 (Scale +3 to -3)

Source: KAS Archive-No. 9305.

In the meantime, the PDS can reach out beyond its core voters to a considerable number of frustrated voters with no ideological ties to the communist system. The PDS, with its left-populist image, has succeeded in stoking antiwestern resentment. By playing on east-west divisions, it was able to win over more of east Germany's protest voters in the 1994 election. The PDS was remarkably successful with this strategy, particularly among young voters who have been severely affected by unemployment. In addition, since child care centers have been eliminated, young women lack the flexibility needed in the job market.

The loss of their former social security—employment guarantees, child care, subsidized rent—has been particularly painful. They would like to see the state take on many of the personal risks that reunification has caused, and they are trying to find someone who will represent their interests. The PDS, made up almost exclusively of former SED members, has presented itself as the defender of the "little people." This makes the PDS the party with the Janus face: it continues to be primarily a leftist-radical party for the cadres, but it also functions as a leftist-populist protest party.

According to its own statistics, the PDS lists about 130,000 members—a far higher membership than east German democratic parties (CDU, 98,000; SPD, 27,000; FDP, 5,000; Bündnis 90/The Greens, 2,700). As a result, the PDS can more effectively reach out to disgruntled voters through an extensive network of full-time employees; it can also heavily rely on its active membership. Moreover, it can hook up into the same infrastructure that the SED had used for social control. This goes far beyond the local political level, and extends into neighborhoods and even into homes. The old structures haven't changed, for the present membership continues to use them. Bärbel Bohley, a member of the civil rights movement, states: "There are some PDS members who aren't necessarily black sheep. But the PDS spirit is ancient—it is the old SED spirit—and 97 percent of the PDS are former members."[32] In its sociological makeup, therefore, the PDS represents the aging privileged members of the former state. It is undoubtedly a leftist-radical cadre party that now tries to present itself in public as a revitalized party of purified Socialism.

Gregor Gysi is the party's most prominent functionary, and in his shadow stands a troika of neocommunists: party head, Lothar Bisky; treasurer, Dietmar Bartsch; and head propagandist, André Brie. They rule the party with centralized, almost dictatorial authority. The party's inner core continues to have undiminished absolute power, reminiscent of the former SED's top echelons. Bisky, Brie and Bartsch were all SED cadres. The principle of "democratic centralism"—power increases as one goes up the party structure—has been officially rejected; but now it is returning again through the "back door."

Dietmar Bartsch, the party's treasurer, was ideologically trained in Moscow. Considered a central figure, he is a man with incredible political and organizational authority. André Brie, who waited until October 1992 to say he had worked for the Ministry for State Security (MfS) for twenty years, now controls the PDS's central election office. He was also the chair of the party's constitutional commission, which worked out the proposal for the party's new constitution in January 1993. Lothar Bisky, another former SED member, is considered the man responsible for the remarkable rebirth of the Communist Platform (KPF) within the PDS.

The party's Janus face is also evident in its international contacts and connections. The PDS increasingly wants to play an international role. Primarily, its contacts are with parties that have a communist and class-conscious worldview. The spectrum of these parties runs from rigidly orthodox to more modern, anticapitalist, and ecologically inspired movements. The PDS also has no qualms about leftist dictatorships. Examples of this are its campaigns in support of Cuban communists (e.g., the "workers' community," "Cuba Si") and its friendly relationship with the Chinese Communist Party. The international communist movement—many thought it dead after the collapse of the Soviet Communist Party—is now beginning to reorganize. The PDS should be seen as one of the motivating forces behind its rebirth. Many candidates on the party's European party ticket are members of orthodox communist parties in other countries.[33]

Moreover, in Germany itself, the PDS has numerous personal contacts with organizations with an extreme leftist character: for example, its ties to members of the former SED's sister party in West Germany, the German Communist Party (DKP); Maoists; and Trotskyists. The left-extremist strategy of the PDS is often camouflaged by left-populist tactics. By strategically playing on populist and civic topics, the PDS has managed to increase its acceptance among east German voters since 1992.

To achieve this, the PDS has relied on classic communist modes of infiltration. For example, the party started several interrelated political campaigns, including its "Antifa struggle" and its infiltration of unions. The PDS supports conflicts in the world of workers and is very determined to break into the SPD's traditional voter reservoir. The PDS's activities also extend into environmental, feminist and extraparliamentary groups. In all this, the PDS does not care much about the actual political beliefs of the various target groups (i.e., the views of the unemployed, union members, environmentalists, "antifascists," "progressive" Christians, the youth); these groups merely help to spread political acceptance of the PDS throughout the population, that is, they serve primarily an instrumental function.

The PDS's dictatorial past continues to taint the party. Though the PDS emphasizes its break with the SED state, it endorses continuity with the SED itself. Immediately after the collapse of East Germany, membership in the State Security Service of the regime was considered condemnable; in the meantime, the party considers the past history of its members more or less "unimportant." The PDS represents itself as a modernized communist cadre party. Its internal affairs are characterized by a "pseudopluralism"; it grants internal party movements only limited freedom. The "young comrades" association, for example, declared: "We believe there can be no openness if there are no means of discussion within executive committees; if coalition questions and job placements are decided on behind closed doors; if positions and opinions cannot be openly discussed for electoral reasons; if candidates' nominations are organized like at a marshaling yard—a blatant abuse and violation of the rights of members."[34]

The Communist Platform (KPF), which party chief Bisky states is "incredibly important for the PDS," is considered very influential within the party; several thousand party members belong to it. According to its statute, the KPF supports a "broad left alliance"; it strives to "cooperate with all forces whose goal is to present an alternative to the existing capitalist system and who get involved in the political, social and other debates of the present."[35]

In February 1993, two spokespersons for the KPF articulated their long-term political expectations in *Theses for a Political Statement by the Communists in the PDS*: "The transition to a new level of civilization, the revolutionary transformation of the old classed-based society into a new classless one—this transition will be a long historical process, marked by bitter class conflict, and it will encompass many complicated and arduous phases. . . . How socialist society will develop in this dialectical process and how this transformation into a classless communist society will be achieved, no one at this stage can say."[36] The Communist Platform's primary function is to integrate communist hardliners into the PDS and to make it seem that the party is tolerant of diversity. Therefore, it makes sense for Gysi to declare, "The PDS can become anything—except an anticommunist party."[37]

In order to understand the PDS's ideological identity, it is necessary to evaluate its political strategy in conjunction with its political platform. Since the PDS has adopted many of the demands of the Greens and the SPD, the PDS's political platform does not contain many truly divisive elements; rather, it is characterized by a colorful hodgepodge of communist, Green, Social Democratic and feminist features. In that sense, the PDS's platform projects a leftist-populist image, but it cleverly avoids discussing how these political and economic activities should be realized and how practical the demands are. The platform lists demands such as the immediate creation of jobs, the renovation of apartment buildings, the freezing of rents, the preservation of all kindergartens and sports facilities, the establishment of youth centers and immediate improvements in the infrastructure. Since financially strapped towns and communities are not in the position to support such projects, the PDS can cleverly make itself seem the defender of the socially underprivileged. It tries to suggest that socialism (as the PDS conceives it) will be able to eliminate the root causes of political and social problems.

According to the PDS, socialism can only be achieved by a broad and heterogeneous movement. Its political and strategic goal is to integrate the left on its own terms. To realize this goal, it wishes to thoroughly transform society. The new 1993 constitutional program states: "There is room in the PDS for both those who wish to resist capitalist society and to reject the given conditions as well as those who combine resistance with a desire to reform the given conditions and gradually overcome them." For the party, socialism represents both means and the end. In its 1990 program, the PDS made its commitment to historical communist traditions even more explicit. The PDS, it stated, drew "mostly from the dialectical and material ideas of Karl Marx and Friedrich Engels, Wilhelm Liebknecht and August Bebel, Eduard Bernstein and Karl Kautsky, Rosa Luxemburg and Karl Liebknecht, V. I. Lenin and Antonio Gramsci." By referring to Lenin, the PDS clearly pitted itself against parliamentary democracy—though it continues to profit from its institutions. The PDS isn't very interested in political reform; this is just one small step on a political march that will ultimately lead to more far-reaching, even revolutionary social transformations.

According to polls, however, the PDS continues to be held in high esteem by the east German population, because they see the party representing their interests: 52 percent of east Germans believe that the PDS isn't comparable to the former SED,[38] and only 5 percent consider it "an undemocratic communist party." On the other hand, not many people really understand the true goals of the PDS—a party which, at best, has an ambivalent position toward the Constitution and toward the use of violence as a means of political confrontation. The PDS, after all, does not reject the use of violence, militant forms of protest or illegal actions as a means of political confrontation. For example, the PDS wants to build up broad-based social "resistance" to existing "capitalist" conditions. In its Constitutional Program of January 1993, its goal was to "overcome the rule of capital." In a paper in preparation for the "Resistance Conference of the PDS," drawn up by the "Young Comrades (Belzig)" association, one can find the following statement: "Depending on the form of rule capital establishes, it can lead either to a political strike or perhaps to the use of armed force."[39]

The party uses open electoral lists just to create the illusion of party openness. The truth is, however, that its candidates, even the handful of writers, are merely semiofficial PDS party members. The "Committee for Justice," which was inaugurated in 1992, is a classic case of how the PDS attempts to solidify and organize the spirit of resentment. Moreover, the placement of functionaries and activists from the German Communist Party (DKP) on lists for the Bundestag is a further example of the PDS's close cooperation with the German Communist Party, the successor party of the once banned Communist Party of Germany (KPD). Overall, the PDS represents the most powerful force on the left-radical, extremist spectrum due to the sheer size of its political apparatus.

In sum, it is important to reassert that the PDS is a party with a Janus face. On the whole, it is still a party of the old cadres and the profiteers of the SED regime. The latter refuse to recognize that the PDS must assume its share of blame for the SED's systematic human rights violations, for the

GDR's ruinous policies on the economy and the environment, and for the system's gigantic machinery of surveillance and suppression. What is characteristic of this party is its inner affinity, its continued nostalgia, for the old SED system. The objective of all democratic parties must be to win back the disgruntled voters whose fears and anxieties the PDS is trying to exploit.

It is difficult to say how many votes for the PDS in the recent election were protest votes. Estimates range anywhere from a third to a half. This means that one will have to differentiate between the PDS and its function-aries on the one hand, and its voters on the other. Not every PDS voter wants to return to the old GDR system—even though the majority of those who voted PDS were privileged by the communist system. The writer Günter de Bruyn sees the votes for the PDS primarily as "a reaction against the social conditions, the shock of the market economy, the factory closures, the unemployment, the idea of less money for the same amount of work." He adds, "The feelings of humiliation, to which intellectuals particularly like to refer, are only of secondary importance."[40]

The PDS's efforts to build a broad front with the Social Democrats, the Greens, the Left Socialists, unemployment associations, and so on, reflect an old Leninist principle that one should adapt to the majority status if one does not yet have power. The objective is to conceal communist-inspired ideology. Anyone who attempts to enter into a partnership with the PDS—either directly or indirectly—must be prepared to face the charge that he is helping this party gain acceptance. After all, this party is just an extension of the SED which was responsible for a criminal and inhuman regime. Partnerships with the PDS, moreover, weaken the common front of demo-crats that was successful in keeping the right-wing, radical Republikaner at bay. Enemies of democracy can be found on both the extreme right and the extreme left. Whoever allows the PDS to gain acceptance helps it become a powerful opinion leader in the opposition.

This will have the most negative effect on the SPD. Except for the right-wing, radical Republikaner, who suffered major losses in the recent elections and who weren't able to fulfill the 5 percent requirement at any level, there are currently no significant parties to the CDU/CSU's right. As I have already mentioned, the Greens and the PDS, the two leftist parties competing with the SPD, have a more defined image than the larger national party to their right. The latter must cater to the needs of a rather broad spectrum of voters—from "conservative" unionized workers in the Ruhr to ecologically inspired intellectuals. Often, the SPD doesn't project a strong enough image—particularly among young people—and this is now made worse by the existence of two parties further to its left.

There is another reason why the issue of the PDS is important. Until the emergence of the student rebellion in the late 1960s, an antitotalitarian consensus existed among the West German people. Both forms of extremism on right and left were rejected by the majority of political scientists and philosophers, because they saw the claims of National Socialism and "real-existing socialism" ("institutionalized Marxism," according to Topitsch) as attempts to institute an absolute, totalitarian truth.[41]

Karl Dietrich Bracher often pointed out that—despite certain ideological surface differences—National Socialism and communism have much in common. That is why many "leftist" arguments could find their way into National Socialist ideology—such as the critique of capitalism and democracy, anti-individualism, antiparliamentarianism and antipluralism: "Their methods, criteria and goals were different; but their idea of a transformation through power and through dictatorial rule led to very similar activities and ways of thinking. The most important difference between the two was who should become the ideological subject and carrier of their worldwide transformation: race or class."[42]

With the student revolt, some people began to relativize the antitotalitarian position. Though many intellectuals may not have wanted to realize communism, or even rejected it, they considered it for the most part less ideologically objectionable than National Socialism. The fact that the communists were successful in the first all-German elections—though some like to refer to the PDS as "postcommunist"—signifies a degree of "normalization": communists now represent a political force as in other Western European countries such as France, Italy and Spain. On the other hand, until now open toleration of communists was considered taboo in west Germany, that is, until the taboo was recently broken in one of the east German states. Will this now serve as a precedent for the rest of Germany?

4

The Germans and Their Nation

How do Germans relate to their nation? This remains an open question, and it will remain open as long as Germans continue to search for an identity. How should Germans be able to achieve inner unity if they remain unsure whether division has left them with two separate histories, or if in fact the East German past is really part of the West German past and vice versa? How should Germans be able to perceive themselves as a nation if for many years West Germany reacted as though any stirring of national sentiment was being scrutinized from abroad, forcing it to look for other forms of identity? How should East and West Germany be able to become one nation if "Germanness" is only seen as a means of freeing East Germans from years of state-imposed "antifascism?" How should Germans share responsibility in the world if foreign nations have always called for restraint, fearful of the consequences of Germany's increased power? How should Germans be able to identify with Europe if they still haven't come to terms with themselves?

Only a nation that knows itself, and knows why it acts the way it does, can assume responsibility. The Germans are struggling with the unification of their nation, and Germany's position in the world remains an open question.

THE JOY OF UNIFICATION: THE EUPHORIA OF HARMONY RATHER THAN NATIONAL EUPHORIA

It was the Frenchman Jacques Delors, of all people—former President of the European Commission in Brussels—who demanded self-reflection from the Germans. In a speech delivered on October 3, 1993, the anniversary of German unification, Delors asked: "Is it too much to ask of Germans to embrace unification in their hearts? Is the price for this unification too high? Is there an unwillingness to accept this new world?"

Then Delors went on to exhort the Germans: "Your neighbors in Europe can only be surprised at this timidity. But I am certain that Germany is not the complaining nation presented to us by the media.

"Hasn't your nation created an economic and political miracle over the last decades and contributed with vigor to the reconstruction of Europe, becoming an example of democracy, participatory citizenship and the rule of law? Isn't the social market economy a model for other countries?

"Is it a coincidence that America's president is using the German health care system as a model for his own country?

"I am sure that the joy you people felt on October 3, 1990—the day you celebrated in the streets of Berlin—will become part of your national heritage. I had the privilege of taking part in the festivities on that day, and I can say for myself that I will never forget the image of peaceful and happy people—a people who gave such worthy expression to their deepest joy!"

Those who, like Delors, participated in the celebrations around the Berlin Reichstag will always remember the boisterous mood of that day. The symbols and flags of Europe waved alongside the black-red-gold colors of the German national flag. The end of German division suddenly seemed to mean the end of international uncertainties and tension. Seventeen million people had regained their long-denied freedom. It seemed their indisputable right to express their joy on this historic day of unification. Feelings of joy, relief—even awe—overshadowed euphoria.

The mood expressed in 1989 was *not* one of national euphoria.[1] That year was characterized by a "euphoria of harmony," as many Germans deceived themselves into believing that the collapse of the East Bloc would resolve many of the outstanding world conflicts and that peace would emerge in major international trouble spots.

Considering that all international questions appeared linked to the East-West conflict, this reaction is not surprising. When there is a release of tension, a feeling of tenseness can soon take its place, and the demand for harmony can indicate a lack of self-confidence or timidity, as Delors pointed out.

Perhaps this is all very understandable in a nation that for decades has been both active and passive participant in major international conflicts. That this unpolitical, yet legitimate longing for harmony would be destroyed by the Persian Gulf War should not come as a surprise. The Germans—at the time preoccupied with themselves—had hoped that the horror of war would pass them by. They had suppressed the notion that the end of the Cold War might possibly lead to new areas of conflict.

Civil war in Yugoslavia and other parts of Eastern and Central Europe also revealed that national and ethnic conflicts would soon emerge from the shadows of the East-West conflict and from the truncheons of Marxist-Leninism. No matter where new or merely suppressed conflicts began to appear in the world, the questions were raised: Where does Germany stand on the matter? How will Germany react? What does the German nation actually represent?

For many Eastern Europeans, as for the east Germans themselves, the national ideal represents a means of achieving free institutions, democracy and freedom from foreign oppression. Today, there are more nation-states than ever before—in Europe and throughout the world.

It is certainly not a coincidence that the end of the bipolar world has brought with it a surge of new nation-states such as at no time since World War I. There was an awakening of national consciousness that quite literally fought its way into existence. The people of Poland, Hungary, Latvia, and Lithuania beat back the Soviet empire by laying claim to their own national identities.

On the other hand, *trans*national cooperation had become the norm for countries in Western Europe. It may have been influenced by the circumstances of the East-West conflict, but it was voluntary, and not imposed by another nation's hegemonic force.

Still, after reunification, many Germans began to ask themselves: If countries in East Central Europe had experienced national awakenings— that at times had even resulted in horrible ethnic and nationalistic conflicts—then why shouldn't a reunified Germany and other nations in Western Europe experience a similar renationalization of politics?

But in the end, a euphoria of harmony, resulting from a need for security, cannot serve as the basis for a national identity. National identity is tied to history. Though the joy Germans legitimately felt at reunification is now somewhat more muted, it will still help them in their efforts to take charge of their own history, and this in turn will become a part of their national identity.

Taking charge of their own history: this will be the central goal of the Germans as they try to find their position in the world. It is a goal that German reunification has once again brought into focus.

A COMMON HISTORY: OUTWARD UNITY RATHER THAN INNER UNITY

Naturally, the difficulties of Germany's historical tradition have multiplied. After decades of division, what is needed is to look back into the past for common historical ground, as well as to draw up future plans of cooperation.

"The German Fatherland—what is it?" This has never been easy to answer. Questions related to the national identity of the Germans have always been difficult for the very reason that definitions of the term "nation" have been diverging ever since the last century.[2]

The *regionalization* typical of Germany has been the result of various factors: the religious schism in the sixteenth century, the spread of absolutist state administrations throughout the territories, and the uneven level of economic and political progress within various states.[3] Despite the feeling Germans had of belonging to one "German nation," they had actually always felt a stronger sense of local, rural and regional communality. This, combined with a sense of loyalty toward a regional monarch, formed the basis of local patriotism.

It was not until well into the mid-eighteenth century that something similar to a "national culture" took hold among the educated population. The decision to form a "small German" and thus "incomplete" nation-state in 1871 led to the unification of Germany "from above": the outcome was an authoritarian state structure. As a result, a tragic connection arose, linking the term "German nation" to the idea of the authoritarian state. Compared to other European powers, Germany—the "delayed nation," as Plessner called her—became a late member of the concert of nations.

It was the religious schism within Germany and "the revolution from above" (i.e., unification through decree) combined with the contrast Germans made between a "culture state" and a nation-state that contributed most to Germany's unique development in national affairs. But the goal at the time was *outward* unity, and not a feeling of national consciousness as a result of freedom and self-determination *within* Germany.[4]

This "extroverted" unity prevented an "introverted" unity, which meant that a strong internal unity could not develop into the basis for a solid national identity, and national consciousness could not be linked to democratic principles.

In fact, just the opposite occurred. The concept of nationality in Germany started to develop more and more in isolation from democratic principles. The Weimar Republic may have later realized German unity on the basis of a free and representative parliamentary democracy, but the state remained internally divided. Above all, the political leadership could not find a consensual common ground, and showed little interest in defining its relationship to democracy and to the role of the political parties.

Then, in 1945—after twelve years of National Socialist dictatorship, a world war unleashed by Germans and the horrors of the Holocaust—there could no longer be an intact sense of national consciousness among Germans. Beyond that, the iron curtain fell on Europe. Barbed wire and a wall separated Germany into two separate states, each belonging to a different system and each denying the other political legitimacy and the right to exist. As long as the unnatural division of Germany continued, there could be little hope for the prospect of a (common) national consciousness.

A DIVIDED HISTORY: DICTATED IDENTITY RATHER THAN LIVED IDENTITY

In both parts of Germany, a generation has come of age that has never lived in an undivided nation. It was primarily the older generation that still identified with an undivided Germany. But the younger generation increasingly identified with the West German state itself, particularly through its link to the West.

The strained efforts of the former East German regime to dictate some sort of East German national identity could not conceal the unnatural fact of division. The model it established of a unique "socialist German nation" was only an unconvincing and bloodless ideological construction. Its self-definition as the legitimate cultural heir to the Germany of Goethe and Schiller was another hollow claim. And the celebrations surrounding the five hundredth anniversary of Martin Luther's birth in 1983, as well as the canonization of Carl von Clausewitz and Frederick the Great, were just further examples of these efforts.

But these attempts to form a separate identity were destined to fail; they were just a means of avoiding the competitive pressure from a free and economically prosperous, politically stable community in West Germany. Nevertheless, the leadership of the GDR tried everything it could to associate its state with "progressive" German traditions, while branding the Federal Republic as representative of "reactionary" traditions in German history.

Germany's common history (i.e., commonly experienced history) was now divided in both senses of the word, and the best parts of history were laid claim to and exploited. But most people in East Germany ended up by developing their own identity through inner or outer forms of political opposition, and through the common experience of suffering under a Soviet puppet regime. Their sense of "self-identity" would ultimately find expression in the history-making call: "*We* are the people!"

But Poland without communist leadership still remained Poland. A transformed Hungary without communist power still remained Hungary. It was understandable, then, that within the SED the question was raised what legitimacy a "socialist GDR" would have alongside a "capitalist Federal Republic?"

Despite a doctrine that accorded the party full powers, the East German leadership could not force the population of the GDR to adopt a unique national identity.[5] For years, no one was allowed to sing the East German "national anthem," because the text by Johannes R. Becher, which included the verse "Germany, Unified Fatherland," was treated like classified information.

In 1990, a radio commentary broadcast on the then still active GDR station Radio Berlin International stated: "One of the most fatal political decisions made by the former Honecker regime was to deny outright the existence of the German nation and to declare outright that the German question did not exist. As the events of 1989 proved, it was this policy that proved destabilizing for the GDR, for socialism, and, furthermore, for peace in Europe."[6]

The state structure of the West German Federal Republic, however, was provisional in nature—as expressed in Article 147 of the West German Constitution: "This Constitution loses its legal force the day a constitution is enacted that has been freely decided on by the German people." The Federal Republic did not see itself as provisional in its emphatic commitment to democracy—there was a clear commitment to "freedom *before* unity"—but it was provisional in the nature of its state structure.

A large majority of West Germans stood behind the preamble of the Constitution. Among other things, this preamble challenged the entire German people "to realize the unity and freedom of Germany in free self-determination." Though a broad segment of the West German population supported the Constitution's declaration of reunification, few Germans believed that the political unification of all Germans would occur in the foreseeable future.

West German politics was committed to the decision made by the West German Supreme Court on July 31, 1973. In its examination of the Basic Treaty, the Court stated: "No constitutional branch of West German Government can give up the political goal of restoring state unity. All branches of government are legally obliged to work toward this goal through their policies. This includes the obligation to keep alive the demand for reunification internally and to project it with perseverance externally, as well as to avoid anything that would prevent reunification."[7]

Nevertheless, a growing chorus was calling for a retreat from reunification and for an "acceptance of political realities." Prevented by the Supreme Court decision from "recognizing" East Germany as a foreign country, these people demanded that the GDR be "respected."[8]

Karl Jaspers had demanded renouncing reunification as early as 1966.[9] And in 1983, the former undersecretary in the Federal Chancellery, Günter Gaus, who had also been head of the Permanent Mission of the Federal Republic in East Berlin, spoke up against a "reunification of the Germans,"[10] and suggested removing any statist connotations from the term "German nation."

"We will have to denationalize our idea of the German nation," Gaus said, "which means separating it from the idea that a German Nation is linked to a unified state. Only then will reality be served—the reality of two separate German states with their separate supremacies, their neighbors and their memories."[11]

Here, Gaus was influenced by a typical German way of thinking, that is, separating the idea of the state from that of the culture. He was so supportive of the idea of the cultural nation that he actually believed the Federal Republic's integration into the European Community would make the division of the European continent even more difficult to overcome: "Above all, it is the CDU/CSU and the FDP who continue to lead us down the European road. Along this road, the German Miracle is expected to blossom. But at the same time, they're just solidifying the division of the continent in their attempts to expand the (West) European Economic Community."

Gaus also claimed to see "a policy in Brussels to divide Europe," literally stating, "In the West, the European Economic Community itself is the platform on which the division of Europe is built."[12] Yet this deliberately ignores the fact that it was precisely Western European integration that proved so attractive, helping to destabilize the former COMECON nations after the collapse of the Soviet empire.

Not only were there now more people in West Germany who were beginning to question the goal of German unity, but there were also those who were more generally beginning to question West Germany's integration into the European Community.[13] Even at the parliamentary level, the idea of German reunification was being considered less relevant, even undesirable.[14]

But the Supreme Court decision previously mentioned placed clear legal constraints on West German politicians demanding international recognition of the GDR. Most significant in connection with this was Article 116 of the Constitution, which, in defining the term "German," stipulated one common German citizenship. The legal precedent of a common German citizenship was the most important institutional element linking Germans, because it constitutionally guaranteed the East German citizen the right to be treated as a citizen of the Federal Republic.

It also eventually led to the undermining of East Germany. A massive wave of 300,000 East Germans arrived in the West in 1989; and 3,000 people a day moved from East to West in 1990. (In fact, one of the reasons Chancellor Kohl had to respond so quickly was to prevent a complete hemorrhaging of the former GDR and to secure the functioning of the welfare system, whose services former East Germans now had the right to demand.)

The preamble of the Constitution challenged the German people "to protect their national and political unity and to serve peace in the world as a full and equal member of a unified Europe." With this, the Constitution had firmly established two poles of one basic principle.

Gradually, West Germany regained most of her sovereignty—most decisively through the German Treaties of 1955. This did not mean, however, that she had regained her identity, as repeatedly pointed out by Werner Weidenfeld.[15] Particularly in the formative years of the Federal Republic, it was clear that West Germany was dependent on international policies and on decisions made by the former Allied powers—most of all in matters concerning the after-effects of the war and efforts at reconstruction in a bipolar world. At this time, the Federal Republic needed Western integration to protect itself from the growing threat of communism.

Even though this did not lead to a national identity, it was an identity that arose from a particular historical constellation. It offered protection, security and guaranteed freedom; another more immediate form of identity was not possible under the given circumstances. The frightening lessons of history also recommended caution.

But this poses an interesting paradox: maybe the very fact that it was impossible for West Germany and her postwar generation to establish a German identity in the end actually created a form of identity: namely, a typically *West* German identity—linked to the "Bonn Republic," restrained in its actions, aware of past burdens as well as the future promise of the European Community.

If this is the case, then the historically determined set of conditions has now become reality. It resulted out of the awareness that finding one's own identity is often more a matter of chance than effort. Having understood herself in this way, West Germany became a reliable partner of her Western allies.

But reunification has brought with it an entirely new set of challenges. After all, the "Bonn Republic" has now become a part of history.

In his ten-point program to end the division of Germany, announced on November 28, 1989, Chancellor Kohl proposed a system of "federal structures between the two German states" with the goal of "creating a federation, that is, a federal structure within Germany."[16] The proposal was an attempt to stem the massive flow of East Germans into West Germany, and to ensure an organized integration of both German states.

Even the first openly held elections in East Germany could do little but prop up the crumbling state structure. By insisting on keeping open the German question, Chancellor Kohl rendered legal integration of Germany possible. Kohl's lasting historical achievement was that he acted decisively to exploit the given international historical constellation in order to resolve the German question—despite the fact that many voices in the press and in the political opposition were vehemently opposing reunification.

In January 1989, for example, the copublisher of *Die Zeit*, Marion Gräfin Dönhoff, wrote: "After forty years we must realize that Adenauer's promise to end division through a policy of strength has only stood in the way of the goal of reunification. We must change our way of thinking. It is not a question of having a perfect state structure, but of ensuring that citizens of the other German state lead a normal life."[17]

In 1988, even Willy Brandt called reunification the "self-deception of the Federal Republic."[18] Then, in the fall of 1989, Brandt gained political points against SPD chancellor candidate Oskar Lafontaine by actually supporting German unity.

But the clearest rejection of reunification came from Egon Bahr. He believed that there was an inherent contradiction between the call for unity and the idea of European integration, that one should take a productive stance toward this contradiction and accept the division of Germany: "*That* is our freedom—to say to the two German states: I want [division], because I have to [accept it]. There are possibilities for Germany that arise from division. But there is no possibility to reunify the two German states."[19]

Identities that are dictated can only be temporary; but identities that are commonly experienced need time to develop. Contrary to Bahr's misreading of the situation, this moment of reunification offers the Germans the chance to find a common identity: namely, through a common experience of the present—a time that is demanding new ways of thinking from us all.

THE LIQUIDATION OF HISTORY: AGAINST THE SUPPRESSION OF MEMORY

If one wants to rethink one's views, one must first be able to look uncomfortable truths in the face. Germany's divided past ended in 1989—though it only began in 1945, and became evident to everyone with the construction of the Berlin Wall in 1961. The National Socialist years are part of a *common* past. Historical responsibility for Germany, however, is not divisible, and it is this fact which west Germans must also learn to confront. National consciousness is inextricably linked to historical consciousness—that is, "knowing about the past, and knowing about it as past," (Manfred Hättich).[20] One could add "and understanding it as being in common."

After years of a divided and dictated history, this process will be a painful experience for east Germans. The formerly unfree east Germans will be challenged to come to terms with two forms of suppressed memory—the memory of the Nazi dictatorship and of the repressive SED dictatorship.[21] A nation can only feel a sense of belonging to a community if it knows its own history and, at the same time, stands by it. There hasn't been democracy in the eastern territories since 1933. An east German with experience of the democratic Weimar Republic would now be in his seventies or eighties.

In the next several years, new information will surely surface that will confront Germans (also west Germans) with atrocities committed in the GDR and with the involvement of people in the activities of the SED regime—particularly in the State Security Service. Even if some of these injustices might have occurred a while back, in the early years of postwar history, the consequences of these actions will directly affect Germans now. Those Germans who had to experience almost sixty years of totalitarian dictatorship have been affected at the very core of their existence. The victims have the right to the truth; and the culprits and their followers must face this truth. Many east Germans are upset with the attempts to "shovel up" the past—which some people suggest should be done—or with the suppression of memory by many former pillars of the old regime, who are not willing to deal with their own past in this period of transition.

Politics is therefore faced with two different levels of expectation. Some people are calling for the reintegration of the perpetrators—as long as they have not committed any serious crimes and now support democracy. On the other hand, the former victims are demanding that scores be settled with the perpetrators—and even with their followers. The conflict between the two sides has made the process of integration even more difficult. Many people have the feeling that legal justice is not serving the interests of the victims, and they are disappointed and embittered.

It should be mentioned that east Germans' relationship to the institutions of democracy is not based on broad experience at this point, but rather on hope. And this hope in turn is based on the need to feel that the life one led wasn't all for nothing.[22] People want their individual biographies to be taken seriously—and they have that right. But the people in the east have their doubts. They do not feel their concerns are being acknowledged, and they see that the perpetrators are often protected. This impedes their integration into the present structures after their former, artificially sustained sense of communal feeling in the GDR has been undermined.

It must be difficult for people to accept the fact that many of the most obvious culprits can wash their hands clean and can even legalize their spoils. The people cannot understand that many of the executive functionaries, the compliant judges, the prosecutors and the collaborators will not have to answer for their crimes. This robs the community of the chance to achieve penance through reconciliation, which could then serve as a new common basis. For the second time in their history, many east Germans feel deceived. What is called for is a deep, general catharsis. Only that will be able to purge self-doubts and self-abnegation, and will set free new creative forces. Without this renewal, the people who were damaged by forty years of the SED regime won't be able to develop a new self-image; without a historical memory, there can be no self-confidence; and there can be no justice without memory.

Therefore, the issue here is uncovering the truth—uncovering historical injustices in a consistent and objective manner, and then bringing them to the law's attention; this also means understanding that this injustice is part of a subjective experience. It will further require the Germans to draw lessons and morals from this (often painful) knowledge for the sake of the future. For both the east Germans who were directly affected, but also for those in the west who are now forced more into an observer role, it is important to get to know in detail the various repressive and manipulative mechanisms that the SED functionaries employed—particularly the ways in which the all-encompassing repression of the SED and the state security system influenced the public culture and got involved in all aspects of people's everyday lives.

However, the question must be asked how this unjust system was able to solidify its rule and develop it to such perfection. Aside from finding out about this regime's unofficial and official helpers at all different levels, one shouldn't forget that the actual Moloch was the unjust apparatus of the former state party, the SED: in its very nature and function, it was the cancer eating at society. A look at the SED can tell us how the apparatus—through oral directives and written authorizations—was set into motion and how it kept on functioning.

To come to terms with the past one must also begin to mention antitotalitarianism once again in the same breath as antifascism. As Karl-Dietrich Bracher says:

It should no longer require explanation that National Socialism and communism are comparable—in the sense both of their inhuman objectives and their means. That is why a study of fascism and National Socialism can give us access to the power structure of the SED—in reverse, of course. The SED regime saw itself as the instrument through which fascism would finally be destroyed. In this struggle, it employed all kinds of fascist and totalitarian elements. The conception of totalitarianism, which was long scorned, claims that right- and left-extremist regimes are comparable, and this idea is now making a comeback after the decline of the GDR state.[23]

Joachim Gauck, federal commissioner in charge of Stasi (state security service) files, sees it similarly and makes the following complaint: "All the people who made an issue of the inhuman and illiberal side of socialism have been sidelined to a degree, particularly in west Germany." This is different from France, where the new philosophers and others have seen the need "to criticize at some time or other the eastern brand of socialism."[24] Gauck sees himself on the side of an "anticommunism that has the same emancipatory roots as antifascism." "Antifascism understood in the right way sees anticommunism as something like a brother or sister."[25]

Indeed, fascism and totalitarianism go hand in hand: the citizens of former East Germany experienced a repressive state-run education that linked up smoothly with the period after 1933:

Everywhere, punctuality, cleanliness and politeness were drilled into you. The ruling principle was to subordinate yourself under a collective and under collective norms, which was meant to destroy all individual character traits, opportunities and potential. It was among the highest virtues and duties of every child to sit still, to practice self-control, to exert one's energies and to achieve something, to accept the leadership role of parents without complaint and thankfully and to show obedience. The goal of state education can be summarized as: to hinder individuality and to break the will! This principle was ruthlessly pursued at all levels of the state educational system.[26]

The east German psychotherapist Maaz also refers to "the repressions in the family": "The style of raising children in the GDR was usually authoritarian. Most parents themselves were victims of a repressive education, and they were required to live in a society which rewarded them for conformity and subjugation."[27]

This doesn't mean that the Germans of the old Federal Republic are absolved from responsibility. They too must be interested in clearing up the injustices in the former GDR. They are called on to come to terms with the past on an individual basis, which certainly does not mean passing blanket judgments or making off-the-cuff condemnations. Joachim Gauck repeatedly makes reference to how many west Germans were also caught in the Stasi's web, which will "eventually become very unpleasant for some people": "Some west Germans will find out that they themselves—either consciously or unwittingly—were traitors or spies, or were duped or manipulated into becoming 'conversational partners.' It is a fallacy to believe that the communist regime's power to influence was limited to the east German state security system."[28]

For example, the East German communists managed "to gain considerable influence in the peace movement."[29] West Germans should be cautious about judging the former GDR and be aware that they were lucky not to be in the same position. Considering the responsibilities that all Germans have with reunification, there can be no "outsiders"—neither on the Rhine, the Spree or the Oder. The former GDR's structured world—its closed society, where all people had their specific place, whether they wanted to or not—has fallen apart. An open and dynamic process has taken the place of the rigid conditions, and every person must fight for his or her position.

Former lifestyles must also be adjusted in the west, for everything has changed since the fall of the Wall. This new reality calls on us to shape the future together: it is an opportunity for Germans to establish a new, common identity: "The unification process is suffering from the fact that each side nurses its own disillusionment, but fails to understand the sense of disillusionment that it inflicts on the other side."[30]

THE ROLE OF INTELLECTUALS: AGAINST A FEELING OF LETHARGY?

Where do intellectuals stand on the national question?

The classical battlefield of ideas—the features section of German newspapers, or *Feuilleton*, in which German intellectuals debate over issues—

never really dealt with the national question, and remained relatively free from the pros and cons of German intellectuals. After brief debate on the German term *Heimat*, the idea of "nation" once again became a taboo subject, particularly if it called for a so-called conservative position.

Some intellectuals avoided the subject altogether; or, it offered them the opportunity to let off "a barrage of petulant verses that say more about the mood of German intellectuals in the fifth year of unification than many other texts" (Ulrich Schacht).[31] Cora Stephan, a journalist, found that Germans suffered from a "cult of empathy," a daily mood of "engagement," a moralistic, at times almost sentimental relationship to the world that had replaced a true national identity.[32] More bluntly, she even refers to a "typical German self-hatred."[33]

German intellectuals weren't unanimous in their evaluation of division. In his 1959 book, *Mutmassungen über Jakob* (Assumptions about Jacob), Uwe Johnson described the injustices of the SED regime in excrutiating detail. Johnson lived in the GDR until 1959, and his book in the meantime has become a classic, but it has still not been discovered by a broad readership.[34] Quite a few intellectuals, either silently or vocally, appealed for an acceptance of division, though it was the GDR's intellectuals in particular who urged people to defend their country—more so than intellectuals in other East Bloc states. As Günter de Bruyn pointed out, critical intellectuals were more rooted in Marxism than many of their colleagues in other East Central European countries.

On November 4, 1989, for example, Christa Wolf, Stefan Heym (who ran as an independent candidate on the PDS list, and was elected to the German Bundestag in October, 1994) and Friedrich Schorlemmer stood on Berlin's Alexanderplatz and called for a renewal of the old GDR. However, this appeal—"for our country"—went against the wishes of the east German population; but people like Martin Walser, who went against the majority opinion of intellectuals in the question of German reunification, had to reckon with painful confrontations.[35] The enthusiasm with which the east Germans embraced reunification showed that they had little in common with the intellectual opponents of reunification: socialism had fallen apart, eliminated by its own population.

When intellectuals argued over the term "nation" after 1989, it most often revealed where they stood on the issue of reunification. Günter Grass and Martin Walser were prime examples of "two opposite sides of the 'national conscience.'"[36] Beyond that, there were supporters of the "cultural nation" (Günter de Bruyn), representatives of a utopian "other nation" (Heiner

Müller), and writers for whom democracy and not "nation" represented the consensual common ground.

In a book published in 1980, Günter Grass spoke of "two states, one nation," and of a literature that would act as a unifying common bond: "Literature is the only thing that the two German states have in common; it disregards the border even though the border has tried to restrict it."[37] During the unification process, Grass called for a "confederation of the two German states, including a declaration that would reject a unified state." This would accommodate European unification.[38]

In an interview with *Spiegel* magazine,[39] Grass stated: "For reasons of security in Central Europe [*Mitteleuropa*], the status of two German states should remain." Responding to the question "What can the GDR contribute in a partnership of two German states, whatever form that might take?" Grass almost waxed nostalgic over the GDR: "Anyone who has often visited the GDR might have noticed something there that we here are missing: a slower way of living, meaning more time for discussions. A subculture of social niches . . . has formed there—something like the Biedermeier culture during the Metternich era."

In opposition to Grass stood Martin Walser, a writer who strongly endorsed German unification: "I refuse to participate in the liquidation of history. In my heart, another Germany still has a chance." And further: "We must keep open the wound that is Germany." Words such as these were rare for intellectuals before 1989, and met with open hostility.[40]

Walser admitted to having a "feeling for history," and spoke up against a "rationalization of division."[41] He saw Germany's integration into Europe as a counterbalance to Germany's position of hegemony in Central Europe. Again and again, he expressed optimism toward German unification—for example, in the statement "Unification will not fail."[42]

According to Walser, love for one's country did not in any way mean becoming uncritical to events that occurred in Germany. Speaking up "against the lethargy in the media," Walser wrote: "Apparently, there are people who are always in a bad mood, who can't put up with their own personal lethargy. Thus, everybody should share this lethargy. In every season, the masters of lethargy come up with a new emblem of crisis."

The German media, Walser believed, were the most teary-eyed in the world. Walser's own diagnosis of the problems of German unification, on the other hand, was very concrete: "We're suffering from one true problem: unemployment. That is the really serious illness of this society."[43]

Then, there was Günter de Bruyn, a writer from east Germany who supported the idea of a cultural nation instead of a nation-state. He had reservations against a unified state, because it would jeopardize "European stability," would ignore the divisions between rich and poor, and would eventually destroy regional cultural diversity.[44] Turning to Herder and Jean Paul as models, de Bruyn referred to the role of tradition in his arguments.

The playwright Heiner Müller supported the idea of an "other nation," seeing Stalingrad as "the end of the German nation."[45] Because of the failure of a socialist utopia, Müller's concentration on German history was now to prepare for an "other" European cultural nation.

Finally, there was Hans Magnus Enzensberger, who saw German unification as a means of achieving the political responsibility of all German citizens and as a commitment to democracy in practice: "The Germans are not concerned with the spiritual side of the nation . . . but with work, apartments, social security and wages."[46] He recognized that the European utopias had failed in their major promises: the end of the state and the failure of internationalism. The call for freedom had yielded to the call for equality. All citizens, not just intellectuals, were responsible for the creation of a national identity ("*We* are the people!").[47]

In a similar vein, but even more pessimistic, was Günter Kunert's view. For Kunert, there was no national identity, only the "nation as a drug"[48] and "the myth of Germany."[49]

The spectrum of opinions briefly introduced here clearly shows how many intellectuals had lost touch with the concept of "nation." "When someone attempted to understand the nation in its original unified sense, he was accused of nationalism and, against his will, placed in association with radical right-wing demagogues. How agitated people became in 1988 when Walser insisted that his country should continue to exist as a cultural whole! Opinions of this kind caused disturbance; they broke the inner peace of the two German states."[50]

The feeling of alienation that often exists when Germans from east and west meet, their mutual sense of uneasiness, also stems from a "self-willed alienation": if we do not have some sort of conception of "nation," then we're missing the unifying "third party" through which both sides can communicate.[51]

The problem that many intellectuals have with the German nation perhaps also results from the fact that although some of them may have been against the "real existing socialism" in the GDR, and particularly against the human rights violations there, deep in their hearts they are more positively inclined toward east Germany's tradition of antifascism and basic economic structures than they're willing to admit in public. Thomas Rietzschel, literature critic from Dresden in east Germany, thought this was why many West German intellectuals held up East Germany as "an example of a socialist utopia" despite the discrepancy between the reality and the ideal. "And if the leftists in the West now refuse to get involved in the critical appraisal of the east German past," Rietzschel wrote, "then this is less a reflection of noble restraint than of fear of revealing their own emotional involvement. Through their engagement, after all, they had improved the external conditions that favored dictatorship and that helped conceal totalitarianism.

"But even despite all this, they . . . had always encouraged their colleagues in the East to hold on to socialism, defending it as an alternative—but from within a liberal democracy. That is, from a position of freedom, divorced from any sense of moral responsibility. For how else could one support the promises of communism after June 17, after the revelations of Stalinist terror, after the construction of the Wall, after the violence of the Prague Spring?"[52] The author Peter Schneider, one of the leaders of the 1968 student movement, hits the nail on the head with his laconic statement: "Obviously, the left has a hard time accepting the fact that their ideological mentors had a quasi monopoly on the title 'intellectual' for forty years."[53]

NATION AND DEMOCRACY: A PROCESS, NOT A CONDITION

What does the identity of the Germans mean today?

What is meant by identity, in the first instance, is the sum of all orientative experience that makes up the whole of individual existence.[54] Factors that influence one's own personal identity are experiences and reflections from the past, influences from the present, social and political allegiances, the image of oneself and the contemplation of future action.

In a certain way, collective identity—whether understood as a simple feeling of togetherness or as national consciousness—also represents a level of orientation that encompasses the categories past, present and future. The Germans are presently confronted with four differing varieties of communal experience:

1. A sense of heritage, cultural tradition and (until 1945) a commonly shared history
2. The experience of the Federal Republic
3. The experience of the former GDR
4. The need and desire to develop a new communal German identity out of the above (only temporary) partial identities

Today, Germans are confronted with the historic challenge of establishing a common identity, without which unification cannot be realized. The goal is nothing less than to combine the concepts "nation" and "democracy" in the hearts and minds of the people. The powerful link between the concept of nation and democracy will prevent the danger of an exclusively ethnic interpretation. At the same time, the idea of the nation will be associated with the European ideal, which will protect it against any anti-European interpretation solely favoring the nation-state.

But a collective identity requires both rational and emotional components of a national consciousness: the identification with a free constitution, human solidarity and a common history rich in tradition—both the highs and the shameful lows. A collective identity lends security, and it can give strength in times of turmoil; it can help give the Germans a vision by falling back on proven concepts, by recognizing obsolete models and by understanding the necessity of innovation.

Identity conveys the sense of security (particularly at the psychological level) that allows the Germans to be open to new goals and to help them understand that national isolation has long become a thing of the past. The worldwide trend of migration, the suffering of the poor in the Southern Hemisphere, worldwide environmental problems, organized crime at the international level: these are problems that we can no longer avoid or be isolated from.

Borders no longer divide Germany, and they no longer divide Europe; but they can also no longer protect us. In this situation, people almost instinctively fall back on the national community—even now, in the era of the European Domestic Market and the Treaty of Maastricht. For many, having roots in a nation, in a region and in Europe has become important— even if the once divided Germany has only been a nation-state since 1990.

What are the consequences for Germany? Today, the "nation" again must become part of an active agenda, rather than just an object of analysis. The "nation" is not a condition, but a process; it is not static, but dynamic; a "nation" needs to be lived and experienced; it at times has to be questioned and needs to prove its worth. Above all, this calls for the active participation especially of young people. They must recognize and live up to their responsibility for democracy—this, of course, presupposing they feel a part of it, and feel that their dreams and goals are being accepted and taken seriously.

But responsibility for democracy means more than this. It is a matter of inner unification; but it is also a question of taking on Germany's international responsibility—in common with other democratic European nations—as well as responsibility for issues such as the maintenance of peace and environmental protection. Politics increasingly has to convince citizens that the international arena has assumed greater importance for the individual. Here, at this international level, he must both take on responsibility and feel at ease—reassured in the knowledge that his need for security is taken seriously by the state.

What are Germans proud of? Polls reveal that west Germans are most proud of their successful economy. German symbols and a common language and culture are mentioned less often. For the younger generation too, the pride of being German is primarily associated with economic criteria. Thirty-one percent of those surveyed, when asked, "What does the word 'nation' mean to you?", responded "Absolutely nothing." All the same, 52 percent were proud of being German. This discrepancy is easily explained. When asked "What can Germans be proud of?" 47 percent clearly answered "German products" and 41 percent "The performance of the German economy."[55]

People in the former GDR continue to be proud of their athletic achievements. Keeping this in mind, German politics, particularly political education, must be responsible for pointing out the positive features of German history and culture—even despite the tragic aberration of the Holocaust: events such as the Movements of Liberation, the Hambacher Fest, the democratic tradition of the old Federal Republic, as well as the peaceful revolution within the former GDR and, not to forget, the workers' revolt in East Germany of June 17, 1953.

Of course, it is not possible just to dictate a new feeling of communality within a new nation-state. In order to resolve the momentary difficulties and tensions resulting from the unification process, we must also be willing to express mutual trust and to overcome egotistical behavior at both the individual and group levels. In public debate, there is presently talk of a mood of crisis within Germany. But maybe this will offer us the chance for a new beginning.

Perhaps people must feel the interests of the nation are at stake before they can once again concentrate their energies on those interests. "The nation should never become the highest value in itself; nor should it be treated as substitute religion. Instead, the idea of nation must be firmly linked to the idea of freedom and to the self-determination of nations."[56]

5

The Economic Challenges of a Reunified Germany

In the economic sphere—as in the political, social and cultural spheres—reunified Germany is faced with a twofold challenge: the need to transform the east as well as to modernize the west. It will be years before the two German economies will have reached the same standard. As the minister president of Thuringia, Bernhard Vogel, says: "It's like building a house: you need one-third of the time for the frame and two thirds for the overall construction. In building the foundation, we have set our future objectives. And for that foundation we needed to become a free country and a functioning democracy."[1]

THE DIVIDED ECONOMY

At the end of World War II, the three Allied occupied zones of Germany received a total of $1.3 billion from the Marshall Plan (approximately DM 10 billion in today's terms). Just in the two years between 1991 and 1993, the net transfer from the former states of West Germany, from the European Community and from the social security system into the new east German states was as high as DM 360 billion. This can be considered the greatest financial transfer in world history. Whereas the $1.3 billion from the Marshall Plan acted as a considerable financial stimulus, having a multiplying effect on the entire economy (though one that certainly did not occur from one day to the next), the solutions to the economic problems of German reunification are much more difficult than was initially assumed.

Despite the avowedly "socialist" principles of the National Socialist regime, the economic order that emerged in West Germany from the war was primarily a "capitalist" one. Forty years of communist dictatorship in the east, however, led to a thoroughly socialized economic order which was diametrically opposed to the West German economic system. Private ownership of the means of production was all but eliminated; some artisans' professions and small private enterprises survived—but only barely, and against the odds.

This process was particularly detrimental to the agrarian sector. The spirit of initiative—one of the central principles of a market economy—was stifled in those forty years of socialism. Major aspects of the legal system developed in totally different ways as a result of the regime's attempts to sever all ties to West Germany. Moreover, there were no independent insurance or banking systems. The state—through its party, the Socialist Unity Party of Germany (SED)—took full responsibility for the care and welfare of its citizens. This led to a system of privilege within the "Workers' and Farmers' State" itself—though the leadership continued to claim it was upholding egalitarian principles.

In analyzing the economic integration of the two Germanies, one should not forget these basic economic conditions. In fact, the economic situation in the former GDR was far worse than many specialists—including prominent economists and intelligence services—had ever thought. The West, after all, had accepted the falsified East German statistics: "Only the positive aspects of the developments were recorded. The negative figures— for example, the high level of indebtedness—were treated as 'confidential' information so that it was impossible to form a clear picture of the actual economic situation."[2]

Figures for East Germany's foreign debt ranged between a gross debt of $20 billion (GDR Minister President Modrow's estimate of November 1989) to a net debt of $10 billion (according to Western estimates). On the qualifying date December 31, 1989, the East German state bank announced to the West that its total net debt amounted to $18.5 billion. But in fact, the total debt of the GDR with foreign countries (primarily the West) amounted to $55.6 billion in 1989–90, partially offset by foreign claims amounting to $36.3 billion (primarily from socialist countries and developing nations, i.e., from countries with limited financial resources).

Aside from the indebtedness of the East German state, there was the further dramatic level of debt that had been run up by East German businesses (DM 115.8 billion).[3] What these (before unknown) figures reveal is that the GDR had skirted the edges of insolvency in the last years of its existence. In principle, it was only the billions in West German loans that had helped keep the East German system afloat.

East Germany's level of production was also overestimated: the chemical industry's rate of production was estimated to be 56 percent that of West Germany's; in reality, it was only 31.5 percent. In the field of electrical engineering, the rate of production was considered to be 65 percent of West Germany's, and in the textile industry, 57 percent; but in truth, they were 40.2 percent and 33.7 percent, respectively. We also know today that worker productivity in many of East Germany's industries was only a third of that of West Germany's. Moreover, the poor quality of East German products made them uncompetitive in the West. Overall, the extent to which East Germany needed hard capital had been underestimated. Even in 1990, the assumption was that DM 350 billion from state funds would be enough to revive the East German economy by the year 2000.[4]

Another huge problem in the former GDR is the poor condition of housing. The SED regime left a legacy of dreary, shoddily built buildings and satellite towns. Approximately 40 percent of family housing complexes reveal serious structural deficiencies; 11 percent are even considered uninhabitable by west German standards. The transport system is also in shambles. In 1993, every second German mark from the investment expenditures of the transport budget had to be used for the immediate improvement of the east German transport infrastructure. Other objectives that will require full attention during the reconstruction of the east German economy are the expansion of the postal and telecommunications systems, the cleanup of the environment, the creation of a competitive agricultural sector and the formation of successful research facilities. In addition, the health care system—once the pride of the former GDR—has to be completely rebuilt.

One major challenge is unemployment. In the GDR (where most women worked), unemployment was (officially) nonexistent. But even in the highly centralized economy of the GDR, just as in any bureaucracy, hidden unemployment existed. Personnel was not reduced during periods of limited demand and production cutbacks; the level of personnel remained static—though the same level of production could have been sustained even with a dramatic reduction in the workforce. In January 1994, there were more than 4 million unemployed people in all of Germany—the rate was 8.8 percent in west Germany but 17 percent were in the east. If one includes those now involved in work creation programs, the figure would rise to 6 million for all of Germany.

These statistics indicate that it will take years before the German economy is reunited. In west Germany, the concern is that the massive financial transfers were like an enormous black hole, whereas people in the east feel things aren't going fast enough. But most people there aren't familiar with the workings of a social market economy. East Germany's economic system needs a complete overhaul, since the entire East Central European market has collapsed and most standard import nations have discontinued purchasing goods and services from east Germany. And although most of the 13,000 formerly state-run businesses have been privatized since September 1990, thousands of ownership questions still remain unresolved.

A recent trend in the east, exemplified particularly by the PDS, has been to glorify the past achievements of the old system. They point to the state welfare system, to the cheap rents, the kindergartens at work, and they praise the supposed equality of life that existed there. For many people in the east, unemployment represents a new phenomenon, and they feel that they have lost out through reunification. As a result, socialist ideals are undergoing a momentary renaissance, whereas the issue of human rights violations is downplayed. The emergence of a new west German–style bureaucracy in place of the old one has also not helped foster an all-German identity, since many in the east do not consider the new market economy to be simpler, but rather more complicated. It requires them to adapt to a thoroughly restructured legal system and to the complex administrative and judicial procedures of a democratic state.

Richard Schröder, SPD party whip in the first and last freely elected People's Chamber in the GDR, declared:

People say we are drifting apart. Nonsense! After the euphoria, we will again settle into our daily routines, and only then will we experience the discomforts. They will have to be worked out. True, some people in the east may have reason to complain. But there is also much to be thankful for. Hundreds of billions are flowing from west to east. Some of that will go to waste. Some of it could be put to better use. But without that help, we wouldn't be better off."[5]

Indeed, some of these figures are impressive:

- In 1990, the year of reunification, the average social security payment in the east totaled DM 672 per month. Three years later the average is DM 1,188.
- Incomes in both parts of Germany are also beginning to reach the same level. In 1990, the gross monthly income of an employee in the east was about 39 percent of the average western income; in the first half of 1993, however, that figure had risen to 68 percent (the standard of living and the rents in the east are generally cheaper than those in west Germany—though that difference is gradually diminishing). Since 1994, the average income in the east can be as high as 80 percent of western income.

- The number of independent businesses grew from 258,000 in 1990 to 425,000 in 1993.

- The number of people employed in trades grew from 426,000 in 1989 to 850,000 in 1992.

- In road construction, the overall volume rose from DM 15 billion in 1991 to DM 25 billion in 1993.

Chances are good that the new states will eventually develop into a modern economic region, particularly since people have a high level of technical training. However, the general worldwide trend toward deindustrialization will aggravate the reconstruction process. But by adopting the western German social system and by putting the massive financial transfers to good use, east Germany should be able to solve its problems faster than other countries of the former East Bloc. On the other hand, the worldwide recession hit Germany hard—right in the middle of its reunification process. It only affected Germany later because the numerous investments in the eastern economy had created an artificial boom that helped stimulate demand.

GERMANY'S ECONOMIC SITUATION

I have looked at several economic indicators in connection with German reunification. But what about Germany's overall economic situation? Germany's economic viability has been the focus of political discussions for quite some time. The political high tide for these discussions came in the years 1975–76, 1981–82 and 1987–88, periods when the West German economy was going through a recession.[6] The present debate concerning Germany's international competitiveness and its economic future is heavily ideological—just as the last three ones were. The purpose of the debate often seems to be to reintroduce old (often protectionist) measures that are held up as the cure-all for society's problems. Some of these arguments seem to be improvised: for example, whereas certain individuals see the need for an improvement in regional factors—such as a high level of education or a well-maintained infrastructure—they complain about spending too much money and carp about excessive state interference. But these are simply two sides of the same coin.

THE STARTING POINT

In the 1980s, the Germans were spoiled by an economic boom, so that the negative economic figures of the last two years—such as increasing unemployment (in 1994, the level of unemployment exceeded 4 million for the first time in the Federal Republic's history), a relatively high inflation rate (4 percent in 1993) and negative growth rates—came as a big surprise. Moreover, since reunification, there has been a deficit in the balance of payments; this means that all the economic projections laid down by the economic stability law of Germany will not be realized.[7]

Besides these macroeconomic statistics, the growing problems of the German economic region are revealed in the cumulative balance of accounts in direct investments, considered an important indicator of a region's economic health. In 1990–92, there was a deficit of DM 70 billion—and rising.[8] This means that companies are not investing as much in Germany. In trying to analyze the root problems of this crisis—which affects not only Germany, but all her major trading partners—it is important to separate two causes, which, however, lead to the same result.

For one, there is the structural crisis. Certain economic sectors are confronted with a decline in demand that may either be short-term or even long-term. The agricultural sector is an example of this, but so are the coal and steel industries, and even traditional German businesses, such as the auto and machinery industries. These examples point to a decline in German industry's competitive edge, at least in those cases where there was no sudden drop in demand (such as in the 1970s when the demand for black-and-white televisions suddenly plummeted). A structural crisis can turn into a general economic crisis when all sectors of an economy are similarly affected by a long-term decline in demand. This does not seem to be the case in west Germany today, despite negative economic indicators.

East Germany, however, has been plagued by this kind of economic crisis ever since the inception of the single German currency union. By becoming part of the west German currency market, the east had to start calculating its production costs in west German currency terms, suddenly putting itself at the mercy of West German economic forces. What this process revealed was that many east German products were not competitive enough on western markets because of their high production costs.[9] The policy of equalizing salaries in east and west allowed those costs to rise faster than overall productivity, and this surely sealed the fate of many east German businesses. These problems were further exacerbated by the fact that the former country's original foreign markets in the East Bloc fell away after the German economic union: foreign trade payments that had been made in "transfer rubles" now had to be made in a foreign currency that East Bloc banks couldn't access.

Second, the Federal Republic was in a cyclical economic downturn that occurs in all market economies when demand for products—and therefore labor—declines. Debates over a nation's economic viability arise when these crises occur: in a recession the growth rate declines, markets contract and so do business profits. Whereas boom periods create better markets and thus help to "cover up" economic problems, these problems clearly emerge in times of shrinking markets, and they become the focus of intense public debate.

Business cycles, of course, are of serious concern to economists and political decision makers, but they do not say much about the overall international competitiveness of the economy. They are generally short-lived, on average lasting a period of two to three years; and all of Germany's trading partners go through similar cycles. A recession cannot make Germany less competitive than other foreign countries.

If one considers the laws governing foreign trade, even a long-term restructuring of supply-demand relationships that occurs in downward business cycles is not overly serious. The international labor market and a country's economic structures are such that they adjust to the comparative costs of production in various parts of the world, that is, where goods can be produced most efficiently. Adjustment costs are usually figured into the cost of transferring production to another location, and so an ideal division of labor results, because all goods can be produced efficiently with a minimum amount of resources.

But serious economic problems can arise if German businesses transfer production outside the country because the country no longer offers a positive production environment—and this excludes the normal barriers to international competitiveness, such as tariffs, subsidies and other trade obstacles. Unemployment will usually arise due to the immobility of production factors as well as the time needed to adjust costs. Political action only becomes necessary if unemployment gets serious and lasts over the long term, and people begin to fear that jobs are scarce or that the country cannot produce enough jobs for those willing to work.

What is new about the current debate is that it concerns Germany's international competitiveness. This is best reflected in an image which shows the German economy caught between two grinding millstones.[10] Under the upper millstone, one sees the "higher" end of industrial production—that is, the high-tech products that require a high level of capital intensity and a well-skilled labor force. This sector of the German economy has been falling behind Japan and America for the last several years. Above the lower millstone, one sees the goods that can be produced by a less qualified labor force. In this area, the German economy must now face competition from both the low-wage countries of the Far East and the countries behind the former iron curtain that can produce at a tenth of Germany's present labor costs.

Keeping these factors in mind, I will look more closely at those features that continue to make Germany an attractive economic location. What will become apparent is that (1) a large majority of Germany's economic problems are not the inevitable consequence of free international markets but are "homegrown," that is, they result from politicians who have—partially in response to domestic pressures—increasingly intervened in the workings of the economy; and (2) the economy also has clear strengths aside from its weaknesses, particularly the "soft" data aspects of competitiveness, and these strengths should alleviate many of the fears concerning the German economy's future. However, a comparison of international economic conditions will show that Germany's economic competitiveness can certainly be improved. I will then analyze certain measures based on economic theory that might help in this regard.

AN ASSESSMENT OF GERMANY'S ECONOMIC SITUATION

It is difficult to find a single indicator that might tell us something about a national economy's international competitiveness.[11] Though the balance of payments account is often mentioned in this connection, it is insufficient for the following reason: a positive account (i.e., a trade surplus) might tell us that a country's products are selling well on international markets, but it also indicates that a deficit will probably arise in capital accounts over the long term (i.e., a deficit in the net export of capital). This would lead to a decline in economic viability, because investment projects would be channeled from the domestic economy to nations abroad.

As already indicated, what also tells us little about an economy's competitiveness is the balance of payments. For one, this might be achieved through devaluing the currency, which in turn would lead to a decline in real national income. But a rise in a country's international competitiveness is usually associated with a rise in the standard of living.

The direct investments account is also not an adequate single indicator of a nation's economic viability. According to a report by the Institute of the German Economy from 1990, roughly two thirds of the foreign invest-ments made by German businesses go into foreign markets.[12] Direct invest-ments today are a major part of a company's global strategy, and they need not be seen as a rejection of the production standard in the home country.[13] For example, no one would say that Japan's economy is uncompetitive just because it has the highest international deficit account in direct investments (in 1990, DM 70 billion).

Usually the best way to determine a national economy's competitiveness is by analyzing microeconomic standards.[14] But this process is also far from perfect, since it is often very difficult to measure and compare the various factors. Moreover, the same factors can be very different or not equally important, depending on the economic sector, which means that economic decisions should ultimately be based on an analysis of factors in each of the various economic sectors and industrial branches. Nevertheless, I will only attempt a macroeconomic analysis of the various factors, because this can give us a general view of the fundamental strengths and weaknesses of the German economy.

WEAKNESSES OF THE GERMAN ECONOMY

Comparing Germany to her major international competitors reveals the following weaknesses:

(1) *Production Costs*: The production cost of capital has risen due to the high interest rates that stem from the reunification process, and this has led to a general rise in Germany's production costs in comparison to foreign countries. Even more serious is the question of labor. The Federal Republic has the shortest work week and machine operating times combined with one of the highest wage rates. The DM 42 an hour average wage (1992) is one of the highest in the world. Compared to other countries, Germany lies in the middle of the spectrum in workers' take-home pay (DM 22.50). Significant are the additional costs of wages: for industrial workers, it is DM 19.50 an hour, which puts Germany way at the top of the international list.[15] And these high wage costs are not offset by a higher productivity rate. For the past fifteen years, for example, Japan and the United States have been much more successful in raising their productivity rate. As a result, German unit prices are the highest in the world; and the competitiveness of German industry has declined in many key sectors because of the inflexi-bility of the pay-scale system and the difficulty in correlating wages with productivity.

(2) *Low Innovation*: Contrary to public perceptions, Germany's rate of investment is about average in international comparison (in 1992, 21.5 percent). Japan's level is significantly higher (with 31.1 percent).[16] This low level of investment becomes more apparent if one looks at other periods in German history. During the years of Germany's "economic miracle," for example, the rate of investment was 5 percent higher. Both in process modernization and product innovation, German industry has failed for the last several years to rationalize and innovate—partially because reunification has allowed it to make up in mass sales what it has lost through the general slowdown in economic activity. The production of mass goods did not become so efficient that it could make up or compensate for the increase in costs in comparison to foreign countries. In many key product areas and economic sectors (particularly in new and important technologies), Germany has failed to catch up to Japan and the United States. This development is the most worrisome of all because a nation's economy cannot expect to maintain its position among the group of nations with the highest standard of living if it does not specialize in areas that require a high intensity of human capital. High wages in the long run can only be secured through a high worker productivity rate. If Germany cannot catch up to its competitors in the fields of information technology or in the production of new materials, then she will eventually drop from the group of nations with the highest per capita income.

(3) *The Bureaucracy Barrier*: State regulations in many industries have become another serious investment problem for Germany. An overextensive bureaucracy means licensing procedures take much longer in Germany than in other nations. For example, BMW needed more than five years to be allowed to build a new office complex in Munich, whereas a similar building in an earthquake-prone region near Tokyo got its license in just six weeks. But most of all, in the pharmaceutical industry, there are many examples of German companies that had to transfer production and sales abroad because excessive bureaucratic security and control regulations (though well intentioned) had made investment in Germany a risky proposition. The reason for this high regulation level in Germany (it primarily affects "key industries") derives in part from prejudices in the population (e.g., in the field of gene technology—though a 1994 change in the gene technology law should now make things easier) as well as the higher level of environmental consciousness that exists in Germany compared to other countries (resulting in high industry costs for environmental protection).

(4) *Tax Burdens*: With a 43.7 percent tax rate, Germany—according to a Bundesbank figure from early 1993—was in the front rank of countries

with the highest tax rate (along with France and Sweden).[17] By the beginning of 1994, the rate had even increased to 44.1 percent. That not only places Germany far ahead of Japan (29.3 percent) and the United States (30.7 percent) but also makes the present rate even higher than it was before the three-phase income tax reforms of 1986–90. Though a law was passed in 1993 to improve Germany's economic viability, lowering the corporate tax and improving corporate write-offs, the high tax rate remains one of the major obstacles to Germany's international competitiveness. (But the nature of this argument is ambivalent: many of the strengths I will mention can only be financed by a relatively high tax rate.)

Except for the bureaucracy barrier, all of the above-mentioned factors threatening Germany's economic viability are so-called "hard" data aspects of competitiveness: they are represented by figures and can be brought into economic balance fairly easily.

STRENGTHS OF THE GERMAN ECONOMY

Aside from these negative factors—which have been discussed intensely in connection with Germany's international competitiveness and which have prevented the nation's economic report card from being as good as it could be—there is also a series of positive factors worthy of mention. But because the latter are associated with what are primarily considered "soft" advantages (i.e., those that cannot be recorded statistically) they do not have the same level of force or persuasiveness in discussions. These strengths include:

(1) *Key Market Position*: Germany is the largest single market in the European Union (EU) and in the European Economic Area (EEA). The Federal Republic lies at the geographic and economic crossroads of Europe. The economies of scale that this large "domestic" market has created is no longer that significant, nor is the decline in transport costs that result from this central position. But what is decisive is that Germany, as largest economic power in a "trade bloc," can more easily influence the "rules of the game," that is, the conditions that determine international trade.[18] She can use her field of maneuver to influence the rules to her advantage—for example, in monetary policy—and can therefore improve her economic competitiveness.

(2) *A Balanced Economic Structure*: Germany, it is agreed, produces a broad spectrum of goods, and she has an economically and technically experienced management as well as a flexible and creative middle class. These factors all point to a high level of economic resilience. Unemploy-

ment and structural crises can more easily be tackled in such an economic environment than in more uniformly structured state-run economies.

(3) *Material Infrastructure*: Another one of the key advantages of the German economy is its transport and communication systems. An economy's infrastructure is an extremely important factor in a business's decision to invest in a certain production site, but something like this must of course be financed (the opposite side of the same coin). However, the positive nature of this factor is somewhat cancelled out by the fact that the state does not run its infrastructural services in efficient, cost-effective terms, making these services needlessly expensive (e.g., the German railroads).

(4) *The Educational System*: Despite weaknesses in some high-tech areas, research and development meet international standards. The educational system serves as a model. At an international level, German employees are highly trained. This qualification is a precondition for high labor productivity and for quickly adapting to innovations introduced into the production process. As in the case of material infrastructure, the educational system also suffers from a lack of state efficiency.

(5) *The Political, Economic and Social Stability of Germany*: Germany is considered socially, politically and economically stable and can offer a high sense of security. Germany's democracy is in many ways exemplary; and its system of social security and right to free collective bargaining, though essentially improvable, have made Germany into one of the countries with the least amount of strike-related production delays. The atmosphere of social stability therefore relativizes somewhat the effects of the shorter workweek. In this sense, the nation's economic policy deserves credit. Though the high level of state involvement in business and the debt that results from that must be criticized, German economic policy still grants German businesses a relatively high degree of autonomy in comparison to other countries. The national economic policy is geared toward creating essential overall stability in the economy. Potential investors are not, for example, scared off by recurring waves of nationalization and privatization, as is often the case in other countries. And recent figures point to generally low levels of inflation (estimates for 1994 lie below 3 percent); the stability of the German mark is another factor that helps to make the economy attractive.

Weighing these various weaknesses and strengths, one can say that there are few grounds for pessimism:

- Germany is also in good condition if one compares her unemployment, growth and inflation rates with those of other countries. Though some of her statistics could be improved, Germany continues to be one of the world's most stable countries.

• In international studies, Germany continues to have one of the world's most competitive economies: she assumes anywhere from second to fifth place, depending on the measurement criterion. However—and this is grounds for concern—the gap between Germany and other nations has grown smaller.

• According to a 1992 study in the *Wirtschaftswoche*, a German economic weekly, Germany received three fourths of a total of 1.600 points for its level of economic competitiveness (though the method used to achieve this score was somewhat questionable).[19] Even if one should be skeptical about these kinds of studies, it does indicate that Germany's level of economic competitiveness can be improved.

One of the main reasons for these strengths is Germany's Social Market Economy—the social economic system introduced after World War II that has contributed substantially to securing Germany's social stability, primarily through the principle of social balance. Economic and political policy help create a stable relationship between the state and the economy, which makes people trust the economy as a whole. Since many of the present weaknesses of the economy seem to arise from the country's departure from these principles, it will be necessary to look more closely at the functioning principles of this system before I turn to a discussion of the measures needed to improve Germany's economic viability.

THE SOCIAL MARKET ECONOMY AS AN ECONOMIC FACTOR

The theoretical framework for the Social Market Economy came from studies carried out by the Freiburg School—a group of independent social scientists and legal scholars, including Franz Böhm, Constantin von Dietze, Walter Eucken, Wilhelm Röpke and Alexander Rüstow. The central idea behind this conception arose as early as the 1930s. The people involved were preoccupied with the question of what kind of economic, social and political model—or "irenic" conception,[20] as Alfred Müller-Arnack referred to it—would be best for postwar Germany. The system was eventually introduced into West German society through the political efforts of Ludwig Erhard and Alfred Müller-Arnack.

The market economy offers the highest degree of personal freedom combined with the highest overall economic efficiency. But aside from that—and Eucken recognized this level of interdependence—it is also the necessary cornerstone of any stable, functioning democratic order.[21] Though a rejection of market economic principles might have led to an economically powerful state, history has shown that a state will end up abusing this economic power by also trying to take over the reigns of political power. Democracy is not conceivable over an extended period of time without a democratic economic order (i.e., a market economy).

This idea of linking market principles to a system of social balance arose from the lessons of experience, that is, by recognizing that market economies are not by nature "social." What was required instead was a system of social security and a mechanism that would counterbalance the forces of total economic supremacy, which Marx and Engels envisioned as the end of all capitalist societies. This theory's guiding principle is that the market economy can only serve social goals if a democratic and pluralistic constitution—as well as workers' rights and other social guarantees—are made part of the political system. The Social Market Economy's most important principles are[22]

- The guarantee of private property, for private ownership is a productivity incentive; it guarantees the principle of decentralization and secures individual freedom.

- The guarantee of individual decision making—particularly the freedom to make contracts—for that is the only way consumers can make contracts with suppliers who best suit their individual needs. It is also the guarantee for the greatest level of efficiency.

- The guarantee of a competitive pricing mechanism, which helps to channel resources into the most productive sectors and ensures that the demand fulfills the needs of the consumer.

But a system of competition like the one described can still result in injustices, which works against the ideal "irenic" consensus. As a result, (regulatory) interventions by the state are necessary

- To secure the stability of the monetary standard, a precondition for an effective pricing mechanism.

- To prevent monopoly influence when competitive forces fail to function properly.

- To take appropriate action when the market fails to do the job. Many people believe this is the case in the environmental sector.

- To cover people who cannot compete in the workforce. The market economy doesn't distribute rewards according to moral criteria, that is, it rewards people for their productive input, not according to their individual needs. The elderly, the sick, the disabled, the unemployed must be compensated through a secondary income distribution system based on the principles of social security and social justice.

The social market economy produces a highly competitive economic environment, and its success has made it into a model for many foreign countries. State involvement in economic activities must conform to the system, that is, it must take place within the social and political framework, and it cannot disturb the functioning principles of the market economy.

But this principle has not always been respected, which means that the social market economy is not able to function to its full capacity. For example, the state in some instances has gotten in the way of business freedom and has worked against the market's inherent pricing mechanism. According to some pessimistic figures, only a third of all prices are truly determined by free market forces; all other prices have been influenced to some degree by state intervention.[23] Subsidies distort the pricing mechanism, and this prevents or delays business from making the appropriate production adjustments. Measures must be taken to bridge the gap between the theory of the social market economy and the reality of the German market so as to improve the economy's overall efficiency and its international competitiveness.

MEASURES TO IMPROVE ECONOMIC COMPETITIVENESS

International competitiveness is a relative term. If foreign countries improve their competitiveness, then the home economy's competitiveness will decline if nothing is done to improve domestic economic structures. That is why it is important to observe the measures taken in other countries so as to be able to draw lessons from their successes. However, at the same time, one must keep in mind the differences in the systems and adhere to the fundamental principles of one's own system. The Federal Republic needs to rediscover the strengths of its own Social Market Economy and to take steps to improve its functioning. One of the ways in which the system can regain its energy and viability is by deregulating and privatizing sectors of the economy. In theory, the same economic policies essentially apply to both east and west, though the individual measures might vary in practice:

(1) Competition and private property must act as the key incentives, for only they can force businesses to achieve maximum efficiency and to

implement the newest technological advances. In east and west, privatizations must continue; regulations inhibiting competition must be eliminated; and national and international markets must remain free and open. Here, the Uruguay round of the GATT (General Agreement on Tariffs and Trade) conference represents an important victory. After all, history does not know of any examples where a country's protectionist policy could yield greater productivity and secure "infant industries"[24] from the pressures of the world market.

(2) Subsidies that bolster uncompetitive industries are a burden to the state, and they lead to fossilized economic structures. They prevent structural adjustments and distort prices by inefficiently allocating resources, damaging the country's competitiveness. Subsidies are only acceptable within the system if free markets aren't doing the job, for example, in the production of environmental products.

Unless they are phased out over time, subsidies that protect jobs prevent competition and remove pressures to adapt to technological advances. Germany's economic situation will worsen if subsidies are continued to be paid over a longer period of time. Whenever possible, subsidies should be eliminated in tandem with other foreign countries. If some key industries (such as agriculture, which must be preserved for environmental reasons; the coal industry, one of Germany's most important domestic sources of energy; and the shipping industry) require continued subsidization, then those subsidies must allow for productivity-enhancing incentives.

(3) Bureaucratic regulations and licensing procedures are only sensible to a certain degree. If they become too complex, lengthy or inscrutable, they can actually prevent investment. The situation needs improvement, particularly in the east (though some advances have been made), so that living standards can be adjusted, which will lead to concomitant increases in productivity. Two laws have been passed that are very welcome: one has made investments easier; the other applies to construction projects. Among other things, these laws have simplified and speeded up housing construction procedures and urban renewal projects; have made it easier to grant licenses in cases involving environmental emissions; have strengthened the contractual basis in urban construction projects; have decreased waiting times in development projects; and have curtailed (at least for the time being) the use of legal intervention in administrative proceedings, which in certain cases has speeded up the investment process by up to two years.

(4) Job market regulations only make sense if they help protect the rights of the employee. They do not serve a purpose, however, if they produce

employee disincentives or if they hamper business's flexibility in the creation of new jobs. Deregulation should also apply to the job market.

But it is here where the principles of the system have been abused the most—and with catastrophic consequences. Protectionist measures—including the minimum wage, unemployment compensation and maternity regulations—were introduced to protect the interests of disadvantaged groups. But what has happened instead is that "protected" groups will often have a more difficult time finding jobs in a downward business cycle because they incur higher costs than other workers. An insider/outsider problem emerges, further contributing to unemployment. Though these measures may be worthy, one should actually reassess their usefulness in terms of the system, because there might be better, more economically effective means of protecting workers and ensuring that they are reintegrated into the market as efficiently as possible.

Private employers, for example, could split the cost of maternity leave with their female employees—a practive already observed in many small businesses—and this would improve the employment opportunities for young women. We also must learn to think more positively about flexible work hours. Extending or shortening the workweek may not be a cure-all for the problems of unemployment. But on the whole, the preferences of individual workers should be taken into consideration, since many people would prefer better work conditions and more free time to greater material benefits. Rigid work times and wage agreements have become an anachronism in a modern society.

(5) The German social security system has grown so large that it threatens the underpinnings of the Social Market Economy. The ideal behind Erhard's and Eucken's original proposal was to help finance social security through economic growth;[25] but what we now have is a struggle over allocations, and a system that tends toward social leveling. The costs needed to run this system have begun to affect both wage costs and the rate of taxation. Economic and social policy must try to reduce these costs by eliminating abuses to the system, by increasing efficiency and by transferring certain services over to private suppliers. Self-sufficiency must once again become the objective of social policy.

(6) Another measure that would help improve Germany's economic viability is a reform of corporate taxation. This measure has often been announced and only recently has it been initiated in a bill to parliament. Germany has a high profit tax compared to other countries, which decreases investment incentives in the domestic economy and leads to the export of capital. Instead of a tax based on profits, there could be a tax unrelated to

the profit margin that would have less impact on overall productivity. The goal must also be to tax work and reinvested capital less; instead, there should be a coordinated European policy to tax energy consumption and environmental violations. This would reward environmental protection rather than punish hard work.

Of course, it is not possible here to present a thorough analysis on how Germany's economic competitiveness can be improved. This list, I realize, is incomplete and somewhat eclectic. But it was only meant to refer to general ways in which policy can improve the nation's economic situation. In order to enhance Germany's economic viability, it will most of all be necessary to enhance the market conditions for business. This cannot be achieved through stimulating demand, but only by gradually improving the economic conditions of the system as a whole. Such a strategy, focusing on the supply side, would strengthen market forces and would improve the system's efficiency. This is also the approach favored by the Council of Economic Experts (whose views have gone largely unnoticed since 1976).[26] The government's economic policy should play more the referee in the economic marketplace.

However, an active German or European-wide industrial policy is not needed at the moment. This kind of policy was recently made possible by Article 130 of the Treaty of Maastricht, which revised the original EC Treaty on this point, and many Germans are seriously considering this very issue. But in a social market economy, the state cannot begin targeting certain products, hoping in this way to enhance its own domestic market. It is industry's job to act on these opportunities; and it can do this job much more effectively because of its proximity to market forces and economic trends. The profit motive is the incentive for businesses, whereas state agencies are immune from such incentives. Even Japan's megaministry MITI, the model for many industrial policy proposals worldwide, has not always been successful in finding and nurturing "key industries." In the early 1970s, for example, it recommended that Japanese producers abandon the computer market because of poor market opportunities and declining competitiveness.

It is not the role of governmental economic policy to point to the direction the economy should take. This job can only be done on a decentralized basis, that is, through free price-setting mechanisms. Industrial policy only makes sense if it works within the market economy. Supporting research projects can also be problematic—as Germany's experience with the high-speed railroad project (Transrapid) illustrates. However, governmental support of business can be effective if it involves "pure research." There are two reasons why the market will not respond to this need:[27]

- There does not often seem to be a direct correlation between expenditures for research and the eventual development of a competitive product. As a result, many meaningful investments are not made because businesses do not expect high returns.

- The goal of "pure research" is not necessarily the direct profit resulting from the exclusive use of a product, because the technological advances that help spur on the general economy only occur after patent expiration.

A policy supporting this kind of research has already been initiated by the Federal Ministry for Education and Science, Research and Technology; it can also be encouraged within the current framework of industrial decision making. A "new industrial policy" as such is not required.

As a nation dependent on exports, Germany has important links to the world economy. It therefore must be one of the major goals of her foreign policy to secure export opportunities (which will be discussed in Chapter 6).

ECONOMIC CHALLENGES OF GERMAN REUNIFICATION

How can the economic challenges of a reunified Germany best be tackled? Here are some brief suggestions.

(1) Up until now, financial transfers have not brought about long-term investments. The primary goal of these transfers has been to standardize east and west German living conditions, which has only led to a higher level of consumption. What is now necessary is to make east Germany more attractive as an investment site and in this way secure long-term investment in the region. The role of the state, however, should not be unnecessarily expanded; rather, it should only help establish the framework (e.g., through taxation) to stimulate long-term investment and job creation. Barriers to investment must be eliminated through a variety of measures—for example, relaxing the licensing procedures in construction projects, changes in urban construction laws, a simplification of the law involving environmental emissions, shorter waiting times for developmental projects, a standardization of construction and environmental protection laws, faster licensing of waste disposal complexes and more efficient administrative procedures. Some of these proposals have already been implemented.

(2) For many businesses, it has become too expensive to locate production in Germany (and even in east Germany). Countries like Hungary and the Czech Republic now offer production conditions similar to those in Taiwan and Korea. In the end, only higher worker productivity can enhance

Germany's competitiveness. It is questionable, however, whether proposals such as those introduced by Volkswagen and Opel (four-day workweeks) are a solution to these problems. But the demand for greater part-time solutions—and here Germany has fallen way behind the example of the Netherlands—could create up to 2 million additional jobs, according to the Federal Labor Office.

Moreover, it is necessary—though admittedly risky—to grant favorable loans to innovative business ideas, because new jobs must be created in innovative economic sectors: they are the ones that offer new products and services. Since Germans are more interested in keeping their jobs than having higher incomes, there is the need for greater flexibility in the workplace. The last two decades have shown that after every recession Germany has emerged with higher levels of unemployment. There must be new proposals to combat unemployment because jobs are continuously becoming more scarce. Of course, one cannot compare the situation now with that of the Weimar Republic, because fewer people were working back then and the unemployment rate was over 30 percent. Today's social safety net is much better developed than it was back in the 1930s. Still, it is not possible to be dismissive about the present level of unemployment in east and west, for it is a serious challenge. One only need think about the ranks of young graduates with excellent academic qualifications who have not been able to find adequate positions because of hiring freezes in the economy. Though the safety net has helped to soften the blow of unemployment, the potential explosiveness of mass unemployment has not been defused.

(3) Germany on average has needed less time than other nations to climb out of recessions. But Germany is now confronted with two objectives—the need to modernize its western economy and to transform its eastern economy into a functioning capitalist system. Both these endeavors will require great effort. Though government should help improve the conditions for those involved in the economic process—for example, by establishing a positive economic environment—it should not get too involved in the workings of the economy. At the moment, the state's intervention level is too high: in 1994, 54 pfennigs of every mark spent in Germany came from the state (either through the federal government, the states or the local government)—a result of the indebtedness brought about by reunification. Yet, the more government spends and intervenes in the marketplace, the more difficult it will be for the economy to recover on its own terms. Raising taxes will not help economic recovery in Germany.

6

Germany's International Role

Germany's foreign policy could not remain immune from the dramatic series of events of the early 1990s. German reunification and the other changes transforming the face of the continent led to feelings of insecurity in Europe. The Germans must now find their own identity and project that new role in their partnership with other countries. The "German question" that had stood at the center of the Cold War was resolved on an international basis; not nationally, however. The resolution of the "old" German question through reunification has produced a "new" German question: that is, Germany must confront the concerns and skepticism of its partners and friends toward a nation that has regained its unity and sovereignty, and has assumed a powerful role in a new international constellation.

FOREIGN AND SECURITY POLICY

The Basis for German Foreign and Security Policy:
The Sovereignty of a Larger Germany

The Germans are now faced with a new situation because the day of reunification officially restored Germany's international sovereignty. Neither the Federal Republic nor the former GDR were ever truly sovereign, because the postwar order still reigned supreme in Europe: the four victorious powers (the United States, Great Britain, France and the former Soviet Union) continued to decide on Germany's future on the basis of their rights derived from victory over Germany—though West Germans hardly seemed to notice.

This situation was clearly reflected in the status of Berlin. Having been divided into four sectors in 1945, the occupied city of Berlin became the center of East-West conflict and the focal point of German division during the iciest moments of the Cold War.[1] The West was willing to confront the hegemonic East over the issue of this city. Berlin was also the reason why West Germany opted to side with the West. Though the Soviet Union claimed the GDR had regained her full sovereignty, it too ultimately retained its control and rights over the country "through valid bilateral and multilateral agreements" (e.g., in the "Treaty of Friendship, Cooperation and Mutual Assistance" between the Soviet Union and the GDR on October 7, 1975),[2] an indication that the Soviet Union understood its commitment to the three Western powers.[3] But also the Paris Treaty on Germany (May 26, 1952) in its revised version of October 23, 1954, referred to the reserved rights of the victorious powers.

Even though the lack of full sovereignty that existed until October 3, 1990, no longer mattered much to citizens of West Germany, diplomacy in both Germanies remained dependent on the four victors of World War II. In the United Nations, for example, the German question was a recurrent issue. Moreover, a "Bonn Group of Four" meeting was usually held once a week between the three Western allies and the West German government (including the Senate of Berlin).[4] Since almost all negotiations between West Germany and Warsaw Pact nations ended up touching on the status question of Berlin, the three Western allies remained well-informed about steps the Federal Republic was taking in its *Ostpolitik*. Indirectly, therefore, they had a participatory role.

In (West) Berlin, the Western allies clearly made use of their occupation rights. West German laws, for example, first had to pass through the Berlin legislature before they could be enacted in the city of Berlin—a result of Berlin's special legal status. During periods of East-West conflict, West Germany had to seek protection from her Western allies, but its diplomacy also had to consider the interests of the three Allied powers—the United States, France and Great Britain. And though the United States strongly supported German reunification, diplomatic circles in France and Great Britain were far from enthusiastic about the prospect of having diminished influence on Germany's foreign policy, particularly her *Ostpolitik*.[5]

The most important outcome of the "Two-Plus-Four Negotiations"—it was mostly the French and the British who liked to refer to it as "Four-Plus-Two Negotiations"—was that Germany as a whole would unconditionally become a member of the Western alliance. This meant membership in the European Community[6] as well (though East Germany was already, indirectly, a member of the Community through its special trade ties to West Germany). In the end, reunified Germany did not become an East-West hybrid or a bridge between East and West. West Germany's ties to the West were just extended to the east after the east had merged with the Federal Republic, that is, when the treaty between the two Germanies was signed. Another important result of Germany's new sovereignty was that Germany's borders with Poland and former Czechoslovakia (today's Czech Republic) were cemented so that Germany could not again make territorial demands in the East. (Though relevant legal questions remained, such as the issue of reparations, which was not adequately resolved.)

But Germany only regained its full sovereignty after Russia had pulled its last troops out of east Germany in August 1994. As Germany was reunifying, there were still 350,000 Red Army troops on the territory of the former GDR, equipped with the latest in military equipment and tactical nuclear warheads. The "Two-Plus-Four Negotiations," signed September 1990, and the German-Soviet "Treaty on Good Neighborliness, Partnership and Cooperation," were not ratified by the Supreme Soviet until March 4, 1991; and the German-Soviet treaty that settled the "arrangement for the scheduled withdrawal of Soviet troops from the territory of the Federal Republic" was not ratified until April 2, 1991. The withdrawal of Soviet troops from Germany signified an historic turning point in the relations between these two countries.

It is amazing that the withdrawal even occurred—and without major incidents. But this new chapter in the German-Russian relationship did not begin with the Russian withdrawal; it was already under way by July 1990, when Kohl and Gorbachev met in Moscow and at the foot of the Caucusus.[7] By fulfilling all contractual obligations, Moscow has taken a major step in overcoming old suspicions—and this is partially due to Kohl and Yeltsin's solid partnership of trust. The Soviet Union (later Russia) gradually withdrew all its troops. By June 19, 1991, it had withdrawn from Czechoslovakia; by June 30, 1991, from Hungary; by the fall of 1992, from Mongolia; by August 31, 1992, from Lithuania; by September 17, 1993, from Poland. Parallel to the withdrawal from Germany, Russia also removed its troops from Latvia and Estonia.[8]

The Guiding Principles of German Foreign Policy: Politics as the Geography of a Smaller World

As long as Germany remained divided, Europe remained divided. In that sense, the German question was truly international, rooted in the postwar situation. So the question should not be—what will change for Germany as a result of reunification, but rather what will the consequence be for the rest of Europe. What will be the guiding principles of reunified Germany's foreign policy? What will be Germany's security problems and her specific responsibilities?

(1) Germany has more neighbors than any other country in Europe. The saying "politics is geography" applies to no other country as well as it does to Germany. One is reminded of Bismarck's dictum: geography is the only constant factor of foreign policy. For the first time in many decades, Germany is surrounded by friendly nations. The nation once divided by the iron curtain has now moved to center stage of a "reunified Europe." Gregor Schölgen ranks Germany as a "great power" alongside France and Great Britain;[9] Christian Hacke refers to an "unwilling world power";[10] Hans-Peter Schwarz states that Germany has now "clearly assumed the leadership role within the Community";[11] in "the medium term," one can even expect "Germany to be in a higher rank—both quantitatively and qualitatively—than France and Great Britain."[12] With its "return to the world stage," Germany has become the "central power in Europe."[13] David Marsh refers to a "hesitant giant."[14]

But one should be aware that—in the short term at least—reunification will weaken Germany, because all political, financial and economic energies will first and foremost be devoted to its eastern half. Yet, in the future, an economically and politically consolidated Germany will be a source of stability within the framework of the European Union and in the rest of the continent. For example, the stabilizing influence of the German Bundesbank presently extends well beyond the borders of Germany. In London and Paris, people are starting to realize that Germany will master the challenges of reunification.

(2) The East-West conflict in its past form is over. This is an important fact that cannot be overestimated (particularly in its psychological dimension), since the conflict produced negative stereotypes on both sides and made Germany the focal point of confrontation. These stereotypes helped to integrate the Germans. It was clear against whom Western policy was directed—that is, against the inhuman, antidemocratic and expansionist policy of the communists. But at the end of the Cold War, many politicians and others were suddenly faced with a philosophical vacuum—even though new philosophical constructs did emerge to try to take the place of the old.[15]

Often, it is easier and more persuasive to present voters with negative images than come up with one's own positive perspectives. The collapse of the East Bloc has therefore left an enormous vacuum (e.g., the conflict in former Yugoslavia or the civil wars in the former Soviet republics). At the moment, there are no viable security structures to protect East Central Europe or even Europe as a whole. But aside from the purely military dimension, there is a further foreign policy consequence: with communism's demise, Eastern Europe's cultural and intellectual isolation from the modern world has come to an end.

(3) Parallel to these events, we are witnessing the "decline of the American century" (Hans-Peter Schwarz).[16] We can assume that America in the future will be less interested in the affairs of Europe since it will be preoccupied with its own domestic affairs. Moreover, America will also be less willing to play the "world's policeman." The United States will continue to be the most powerful member of NATO, "but its days as an hegemonic power and as the sole protector of Western Europe are numbered."[17]

(4) The rise of Islamic fundamentalism will also mean a greater likelihood of conflict facing liberal Western democracies. Turkey is more threatened by this development than many observers are willing to admit. The crisis within the country has led to a strongly resurgent Islamic fundamentalism, intensified by the rise of poverty in parts of the population, and all this can eventually lead to a rejection of the West. The earlier East-West conflict may now be replaced by the conflict between Islamic fundamentalism and European-American values, between poor, overpopulated nations and prosperous nations, between nuclear and nonnuclear nations, and so on.

The American political scientist Samuel Huntington was right in his assessment that fundamental international conflicts will no longer arise between individual nations but between opposing cultures. This clash of civilizations will determine future international policy, and new fronts will emerge between nations with different cultural traditions.[18] Economic stratifications will exacerbate the cultural oppositions. These future conflicts might arise as a result of a renewed oil crisis, because the dependency of the North Atlantic states on Middle and Far Eastern oil is substantial: in 1989, 43 percent of crude oil was imported from those regions.[19] It is not the threat of a complete turnoff of oil supplies that causes the greatest concern: EU law require nations to stockpile at least a ninety-day supply, and many countries have even larger reserves. The real danger would be from the dramatic rise in oil prices that would result from an international crisis. This could seriously affect Western welfare systems.

(5) We are presently living in a more complicated but smaller world; and we are increasingly growing more interdependent. Issues such as

environmental protection, peacekeeping, gene technology and the protection of energy reserves can no longer be treated on an isolated basis or an individual national basis. How sovereign can a nation really be in matters such as currency speculation and immigration? What control does Germany have if a nuclear power plant somewhere in Europe spins out of control or thousands of refugees knock on the doors of a prosperous Europe? This breaks down the classical division between foreign and domestic policy. In many areas, foreign policy has already become an extension of domestic policy, which means many more international actors must now be brought into the decision-making process—also within the framework of the European Union.

(6) Another crucial role is played by the so-called CNN factor. From all corners of the world, the individual is swamped with images received on his living room TV set. Many people may be more informed now that they can see live broadcasts of coup attempts (e.g., in Moscow) or can be immersed in events directly as they occur; but it can also lead to oversaturation. The mass of images and information can no longer be digested, and people begin to lose their sense of orientation.

Many of these factors have existed for a while—but it is the interplay of these various factors that will now play a role as Germany defines her new foreign and security policy. What are some of the important strategic questions that will define future German policy? Germany is not the only country going through these changes; the entire international order is facing radical transformations and a major restructuring process. Within this context, what will be Germany's future interests?[20] Germany's vital interests can generally be defined as follows:

- To maintain its territorial integrity and to establish democracy firmly in Germany as a whole
- To protect Germany from external pressures that pose a threat to her security
- To secure free international trade, since Germany's prosperity is highly dependent on exports

The Goal of German Foreign Policy: Willingness to Assume Responsibility

Because Germany is located at the heart of Europe, it always stood at the center of European conflicts. That is one of the reasons why Konrad Adenauer, West Germany's first chancellor, was such a vocal supporter of German integration into Western Europe and into the Atlantic alliance in the early years of the Republic. He wanted to achieve security for Germany and wanted Germany's partners to feel secure with Germany.[21] The Montan Union of 1952, establishing the European Coal and Steel Community (including the three Benelux countries, France, Italy and Germany); the Treaties of Rome of 1957, creating the European Economic Community (EEC) with the same countries; and the European Atomic Energy Community (EURATOM) were the first successful stages toward Western European political and economic integration.

Even after reunification, the integration of Germany into the West is still as relevant an issue as ever. Germany is now asked to fulfill many (sometimes contradictory) expectations. Foreign Minister Kinkel expressed this situation with a very figurative image: "As a nation of 80 million and as the country with the strongest economy, situated in the center of Europe, we are sometimes like a St. Bernard in the living room: when it starts to wag its tail, it threatens to knock over the coffee cups."[22] Though she must continue to come to a consensus with her other partners, Germany must also clearly define her own national interests within the framework of the European Union (EU) so that she can have an influence on the European integration process. This is also what is expected of Germany. The times when Germany could play the passive bystander at international events are now over.

After the reunification of Germany, several European nations liked to point out that there were certain old geopolitical models that could still pose a threat. They show how vulnerable Germany has become as a result of her new central position; this is why her foreign and security policy will be strongly challenged. Ralf Dahrendorf posed the question in the following way: "Does a reunified Germany belong to the West or not?" He answered the question himself: "When we say the West, we mean certain value systems, to which the old Federal Republic unconditionally adhered. This is why Helmut Kohl is such an important figure. In England and France, he is considered by many to be one of the last of the Western-oriented German politicians."[23]

Since security itself has become a much more encompassing term, security policy must be defined more broadly. It has now become more important than ever to have an early warning system for conflict situations so that we're not suddenly faced by a "problem overload." In this sense, stability in Eastern Europe is crucial, and it means recognizing the interdependence of economics and security policy. European security is no longer just an issue for NATO strategists or ministries of defense; one must appeal to investors and bankers, to diplomats and the European Commission, to contribute their share as well. Security policy should serve to forestall military conflict situations.

A German Europe or a European Germany: Three Questions

Three questions are particularly relevant:

1. How can Europe effectively coordinate a foreign and security policy that integrates East Central Europe?
2. How will Europe react to outside security threats?
3. What is Germany's relation to power—most of all, military power? Or do Germans want to remain just an economic power?

Each of these questions will be addressed in a section below: "Historic Changes and Open Questions" (question 1), "International Institutions and Free Trade" (question 2), and "Worldwide Challenges and the Fear of Power" (question 3).

These questions show that the precondition for any political discussion is Germany's common identity with Western Europe. The fact that EU members could not settle on a common policy in the Balkan conflict disillusioned many people. The solidarity of interests that was supposed to exist among European nations—that is, in those issues which demand decisive action, governing and intervention—actually needs time to materialize. What is necessary is a common foreign and security policy, like the one envisioned by the European Union and NATO, though the latter (because of American and Canadian membership) would introduce a non-European, Atlantic dimension. But what is Germany's position?

Germany has irreversible links to the West. The Federal Republic's membership in the European Union and in NATO are basic principles of German policy. Even before reunification, Germany often repeated that she had common interests with Europe—though some continued to have doubts.24 That is why many ask: will there eventually be a German Europe or a European Germany? Germany's too weak to act unilaterally in international matters, yet too strong to play a secondary role on the world's stage.

Historic Changes and Open Questions

The transformations in East Central Europe—and particularly in Russia—reveal a complex picture. More than a dozen different nations have emerged, not including regions that are looking for independence, such as Kosovo. The situation in this region is precarious, much like the period between 1917 and the early 1920s. But after years of communist oppression, many of these East Central European nations are more open to Western influence than they were in the 1920s or 1930s, even though they have fallen dramatically behind the West in economic terms.

In fact, the economic situation in all the nations once under Soviet rule, including the nations of the Warsaw Pact, is miserable, and it will take them a long time to catch up to the West. Mass unemployment and even incidents of hunger have shown how difficult it is to make the transition from a communist command economy to an economy based on the market. But Germany's eastern neighbors—particularly the Czech Republic, Poland and Hungary—and some of the Baltic states are slowly reviving their economies.[25] However, it will take decades before these nations fully recover.

A look at the GDP figures of the Central European group—Slovakia, Slovenia, the Czech Republic and Hungary—show early signs of a recovery. In Poland, the trend started as early as 1992; in Slovakia, it started in the first quarter of 1994; and in the other countries, the first signs of recovery appeared in 1993. At the same time, inflation went down—though it will not fall into single digits anywhere by 1995.[26] What is encouraging about the recovery is that it is not only being spurred on by private consumption but also by a growth in investments.

But the situation is more discouraging in the southeastern European nations—Bulgaria, Romania, and stricken Croatia. Russia, the Ukraine and the other former Soviet republics lie at the very bottom of the list. A survey by the reputable Viennese Institute for International Economic Comparisons has made a more optimistic economic prognosis for the region, even though its prognoses for 1994 and 1995 are generally more pessimistic than the official statistics given by the countries themselves (Table 6.1).

In some elections, people voted in communists to share governmental responsibility. This will not make it easier to bring these nations into the European Union, or, more specifically, into NATO. On the whole, however, the projections for a speedy economic recovery in these nations were too optimistic. The transformation processes will take time and patience.

At the moment, all eyes are turned to Russia. Once again (as often in Russian history) there seem to be two principal forces at work. On the one side are the supporters of a national-imperialist agenda, who reject Western values and who'd like to isolate Russia from Western influences. Though somewhat idealistic, their thinking is reactionary and dangerous. On the

Table 6.1
Selected Economic Indicators and Prognoses for Central and Eastern Europe

| | GDP[1] | | | Balance of payments | | | Inflation | | | Unemployed Rate | | |
	(Change from year before in %)			(Balance in Mio. $)			(in %)[2]			(Yearend, %)		
	1993	1994	1995	1993	1994	1995	1993	1994	1995	1993	1994	1995
Bulgaria	-4	-2	-1	-900	-250	-400	74	80	60	16	18	19
Croatia	-6	-3		293	400	n.a	1 518	115	n.a	17	18	n.a
Poland	4	4	4	-2 329	-1 900	-2 500	35	30	25	16	17	20
Rumania	1	-2	0	-1 345	-1 000	-1 000	256	180	100	10	12	14
Slovakia	-4	0	1	-599	-500	-300	23	16	10	14	16	16
Slovenia	1	3	4	196	500	500	32	20	14	15	15	n.a
Czech Rep	0	2	3	580[3]	0	-500	21	10	10	4	4	5
Hungary	-2	2	1	-3 455	-3 000	-2 500	23	22	20	12	12	12
Russia	-12	-10	-5	6 231	6 000	5 000	866	300	300	1	3	4
Ukraine	-18	-20	-5	-390	n.a	n.a	3 141	700	500	0	2	n.a

[1] Croatia: Gross Material Product. [2] Change in consumer resp. retail trade prices from previous year. [3] without Slovakia. n.a = not available

1. Croatia: Gross Material Product.
2. Change in consumer and retail trade prices respectively from previous year.
3. Without Slovakia.

Source: Vienna Institute for International Economic Comparison, in Neue Zürcher Zeitung, July 9, 1994; see also Peter Havlik et al., Transition Countries: The Economic Situation in Early 1994 and Outlook until 1995. Research Reports, No. 207, Vienna, July 1994, p. 25.

other side are the reformers, who'd like to lead Russia out of her isolation and open up the country to the West. This would also mean opening the country to the values of European civilization and the Enlightenment. The reform forces would like to see a modern Russia, one that is a respected member of the community of free and democratic states.

The question whether Russia wants to retreat into the Eurasian wilderness or to bind itself politically, economically and spiritually to Europe is one that has been discussed for centuries, and the country always seems to come up with different answers. This time, Russia might opt for a future in a modern Europe. But serious internal conflicts—including the coup attempt of October 1993 and the subsequent "tolerance" that the Russian judiciary displayed toward it—show that the confrontation between modernizers and supporters of Europe and those who wish to return to the past has not been settled, and will continue to destabilize Russian society. The conflict in Chechnya, in particular at the end of 1994, illustrates how unstable Russia is.

The results of the elections to the national Duma on December 12, 1993, came as a shock to Europe. The left-extremist and left-oriented parties (including the Russian Communist Party and the Agrarian Party) and the right-extremist parties (such as the Liberal Democratic Party of Russia) together received a total of 270 out of 450 seats, while the reform-oriented groups (such as Choice Russia, the Javlinsky-Boldyrev-Lukin group, and the Party of Russian Unity and Harmony) only received a total of 160 seats. The danger is that the political center will be torn apart by the two extremes.[27]

The elections to the national Duma have not solved the crisis of political power in Russia. On the contrary, most prognoses are dire—even for the economy. One American analyst says that the problem of Russian politics "is not if democracy, but if the state itself survives."[28] He concludes that it is unlikely Russia will develop into a stable, liberal-democratic order anytime soon, and he sees several possibilities—from "fascism, to a constitutional government, right on up to the dissolution of the state itself." In his analysis, a form of "Peronism" would be the best of all possible scenarios.

The general goal of Western policy must continue to be—despite such negative prognoses—to support reform forces in Russia. Yet, only the Russians themselves can fight against revived nationalism. The expansionist positions espoused by the right-extremist Vladimir Zhirinovsky show us that extreme Russian nationalist ideas exist and can find resonance among the population as a whole. Even the reform-oriented forces have not remained free from their influence. The collapse of the Soviet Union, the loss of its great power status, and the decline of Russia's supremacy in East Central Europe are considered humiliating by many Russians—even though Russia was victorious in World War II. When Russians see their soldiers returning from the West, some see a defeated army. It strikes a chord with many Russians when Zhirinovsky promises to restore the Russian Empire, the country's previous greatness and her former superpower status.

Many members of the Russian military in particular have open ears for such promises. But the forces of xenophobia, anti-Western bias, anti-Semitism and racism are not new to Russia, and they did not just emerge for the first time in the Soviet Union. After the elections to the national Duma, it is uncertain whether the military would once again side with Yeltsin if another coup attempt occurred. But on the whole, it is becoming clear that Russian foreign policy is pursuing greater Russian and imperial ambitions along the same lines as the former Soviet Union. In that sense Russia is standing at the crossroads: she has not yet decided between empire and democracy.

It is now in Russia's national interest—and it has become one of the strongest components of her foreign and security policy—to try to extend her sphere of influence into the nations in former Soviet territory. It is from this perspective that one must evaluate the Russian military doctrine enacted on November 2, 1993, whereby Russian troops can be deployed within the territory of the Commonwealth of Independent States (CIS). This doctrine is interesting in that it identifies these nations as "neighboring foreign countries." Since there are ostensibly 25 million "Russians living abroad," Russia reserves the right to intervene in nations with a substantial Russian minority when it claims human rights abuses are taking place.

Yeltsin publicly asked whether Estonia had forgotten "certain geopolitical and demographic realities." If this were the case, Yeltsin continued, then Russia would have the means to remind her of this reality.[29] Even if this undisguised threat was intended for a domestic audience, it still shows how loaded the term "neighboring foreign countries" is within the framework of Russia's military policy. On the one hand, Russia dismantled the common supreme command of the Commonwealth of Independent States in June 1993—a rebuke to communists and nationalists who dreamt of restoring the Soviet Union. Many of Russia's troops stationed in its "neighboring foreign countries" are scheduled to return by 1995. On the other hand, Russia is trying to establish approximately thirty military bases in some of her other former republics.[30]

Moreover, Russia seems to be stirring up, rather than containing, civil war–like conditions in areas of Abkhazia, the northern Caucusus, Moldova and Tajikistan. In the case of Georgia, for example, there can be little doubt that the Russian military intervened on behalf of the Abkhazian rebels. How else could the rebels have resisted the numerical superiority of the Georgian forces? It was not until President Shevardnadze and his troops were cornered that Georgia agreed to become a member of CIS and to strengthen its ties to Russia (including permission to station permanent military bases on Georgian territory); and only then did it receive support from the Russian military. Economic sanctions (oil and natural gas) and the offer of generous support (the ruble zone) have also become instruments of Russia's great power politics.

Vyacheslav Kostikov, President Yeltsin's press spokesman, said: "The era of political-democratic romanticism is over. It is only a matter of time before the political union with the former Soviet republics will be restored. The roads leading from the capitals of the republics to Moscow have not yet been closed."[31] One wonders if the conflict in Ukraine will follow the same pattern. Russia "turns automatically into an empire if it subjugates the Ukraine" (Brzezinski).[32] Using the Crimea as a lever, Moscow has a means of destabilizing Ukraine. Many Russians, particularly members of the political elite, are still not able to grasp the fact that Ukraine has become an independent, sovereign state. Many politicians are concentrating their attention on Belarus and Ukraine. Even democratic reform politicians have not come to terms with the loss of these territories.

But it has become as difficult to decipher the political situation in these two states as in Russia. There have been changes in government in both states, since the people were not satisfied with the way things were going. Yet, it is still uncertain whether this means the two states will now be reintegrated into a Russian empire. The Ukrainian minister president Leonid Kuchma, who defeated the former head of state Kravchuk, officially assumed leadership on July 19, 1994. Though he said he'd be cautious, he has promised to vigorously press for reforms, and has spoken up for Ukrainian sovereignty while also pushing for closer economic ties to Moscow.

The vote for Ukrainian independence in December 1991 came primarily from ethnic Russians, who make up a fourth of the total population of 52 million. They hoped that they would eventually have better living conditions than in Russia. But these expectations were not fulfilled. It has been estimated that the economy in 1993 only achieved 60 percent of the mid-1980s level of production. The rate of inflation was probably as high as 2,000 percent in 1992 and 1993. Practically 60 percent of public expenditures are in the form of price subsidies and go into the state industrial and agricultural sectors.[33] And except for the western Ukraine, Ukrainian national identity is not very strong. Though the western Ukrainians are also primarily of Slavic origin, their cultural background is quite diverse: in 1939, Stalin annexed this former Polish region.

Belarus also elected a new president in June 1994—Alexander Lukashenko. He has plans to set up a currency union with Russia, though not in violation of the nation's sovereignty or of the Belarussian constitution. However, this will hardly be possible, since the constitution stipulates that monetary policy must remain solely in the hands of the Belarussian National Bank.[34] During the elections, Lukashenko said that cooperation with Russia might be possible, but in the meantime he says he intends to defend the country's sovereignty. How long he can maintain this autonomy in the present miserable economic climate is questionable. It is extremely important for the still vulnerable countries of Poland, Slovakia, Hungary and Romania to have a strong Ukraine as a neighbor. It is certainly preferable to having a Russia next door that might once again want to expand into the countries of Central Europe.

Because of the oppressive economic situation in many former Soviet republics, it is not only Russia that might want to create a network of interdependent economic spheres: there is also the danger that the countries themselves might want to reimperialize. One important German weekly newspaper tried to dispel those fears: "The fact that troops were withdrawn from Germany and the Baltic states on time and on schedule dispels many suspicions. It is clear that Russia is retreating geographically to the East in order to arrive politically in the West."[35] Russia is trying to create a common economic area where goods, capital and labor can be traded without obstruction. By mid-1998, there are plans for a CIS currency union. What is significant, however, is that these plans[36] for an economic area are supposed to be implemented along with a military sphere—a cooperative project to develop arms and defend mutual borders. An "Intranational Economic Committee" is also planned, with its seat in Moscow, and it is expected to have full executive authority.

Moreover, Russia has been sending many confusing foreign policy signals. On the one hand, Russia's President Yeltsin declared on state visits to Prague and Budapest in August 1993 that he would have no objections to the Czech Republic or Hungary joining NATO. But several weeks later, in memos sent to Western European governments, he relativized and then revoked this position. Russia, it seems, is trying to revive its imperial past and to fill the vacuum suddenly left with the collapse of the Soviet empire. In this sense, Central Europe's attempts to join NATO would be seen as harmful to Russian interests.

In September 1993, Yeltsin sent a letter to government heads in the United States, Great Britain, France and Germany, which the countries of East Central Europe treated with great skepticism. The letter seemed to suggest that a "partnership" should be established that could serve as a "common security guarantee" for both NATO and the Russian Federation. The geopolitical balance, however, should not be altered to Russia's disfavor.[37] Russia clearly wants to be able to veto future attempts by former Warsaw Pact countries to join NATO. Moreover, Russia's new military doctrine states that "any expansion of military blocs and alliances harms the security interests of the Russian Federation," and must be considered one of the "primary sources of military threats."

Russia's proposal that NATO should become a subdivision of the United Nations—a reference made by the Russian defense minister, Pavel Grachev, at the May 1994 meeting of NATO defense ministers in Brussels[38]—is simply unacceptable. Equally unacceptable were Grachev's demands that Russia receive consultation rights in all political and military matters that affect European security.[39] For the West, NATO must remain at the center of all thinking on security, for this is the only way to bring America into the political decision-making process in European affairs. The proposal to include Russia as a member of NATO would only lead in the end to the dissolution of NATO itself. (Later in this section I will have more to say on the issue of including Russia in NATO's "Partnership for Peace" program.)

Shortly before his death, ex-President Richard Nixon said that the West would be wrong to give Moscow the impression that it considered Russia's interests to be equal to its own interests. Instead, Nixon said the West should clearly state their differences, but should then formulate the conditions whereby a limited partnership was possible.[40] However, it is important to integrate Russia as much as possible into the world's economic mechanisms, because then Moscow would have to pay a high price if she tried again to do it alone. At the same time, Germany's policy on Russia is to make sure Russia does not get the impression that the Western industrial powers are trying to treat her as an undesirable economic competitor and isolate her from the world's markets. For that reason, one should seriously consider allowing Russia to join institutions such as the International Monetary Fund (IMF); the GATT, that is, the World Trade Organization (WTO); and down the line, even the OECD (Organization for Economic Cooperation and Development).

But one should not condone Russia's demands for its own sphere of influence in the regions of the former Soviet Union. Essentially, the West's caution and concessions have helped more to further the extreme nationalists and communists than they have helped President Yeltsin. The West's hesitation proves that extremist positions and the threat of a national resurgence have been effective to some degree. If these threats prove effective, then they can always be used over and over again in foreign and security policy questions. The West (particularly America) very much tailors its foreign policy around Yeltsin, whose position we are trying to secure within Russia. Western policy, it seems, is based less on a worst-case scenario than on best-case hopes. This foreign policy approach has its detractors in the West, but it is difficult at the moment to come up with alternatives.

Russia is at a dramatic crossroads in its history, namely, whether it should opt for democratic or imperial structures. Through a combination of determination and a spirit of conciliation, the West must help Russia find a predictable role for the future and must prevent her from making authoritarian decisions in its internal and foreign affairs.

In light of this, what should Germany's foreign policy be?

Before answering this question, one should look at the complex membership structure of European-Atlantic security institutions. Figure 6.1 shows how many countries are presently integrated into the various cooperative structures.

(1) Individual nation-states can no longer establish durable security structures on a bilateral basis. This also applies to the Federal Republic, which is at the moment not in a position—because of her current economic problems—to take a large foreign policy role. Moreover, the Federal Republic must try to prevent any attempts to revive a Rapallo-like scenario. At Rapallo, on April 16, 1922, the German Republic and Russia surprised the West by settling on several of their mutual concerns (e.g., the question of reparations and prewar debts). France and Great Britain are once again concerned that Germany might use her special relationship with Russia to come to new Rapallo-like agreements. On the other hand, Germany should make use of her close ties to Russia (when possible, in consultation with her Western partners) and to the other states of the former Soviet Union. But one thing is clear: Germany would be well-advised to avoid going her own way.

But what is not clear at the moment is how these durable security structures should be set up. One should not overestimate the security role of the United Nations in Europe—as the conflict in former Yugoslavia and

Figure 6.1
Membership in the Institutions of the European-American Security System

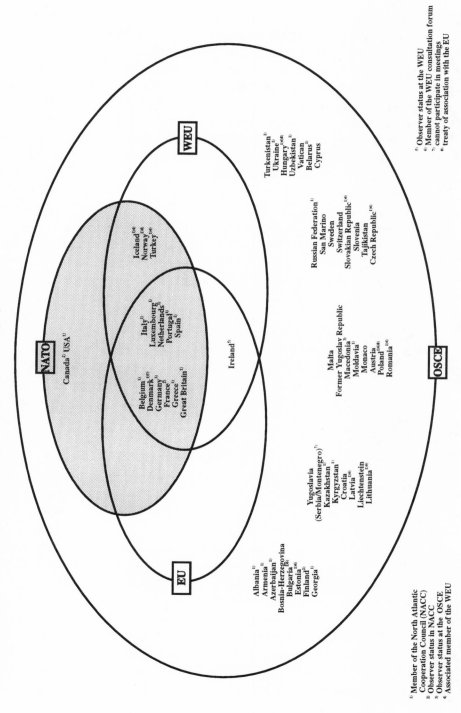

1) Member of the North Atlantic
   Cooperation Council (NACC)
2) Observer status in NACC
3) Observer status at the OSCE
4) Associated member of the WEU

5) Observer status at the WEU
6) Member of the WEU consultation forum
7) cannot participate in meetings
8) treaty of association with the EU

the defensive position of the United Nations on this issue proves. Though it was founded as a bulwark against Soviet imperialism, NATO should not be allowed to become a relic of the Cold War. But what should be its fundamental security responsibilities in the present climate?

The New Strategic Concept that NATO decided on in its Rome meeting of 1991 firmly declares that the Alliance will "deter and defend against any threat of aggression against the territory of any NATO member state;[41] and second, it emphasizes that the Alliance provides "one of the indispensable foundations for a stable security environment in Europe, based on the growth of democratic institutions and commitment to the peaceful resolution of disputes." Third, the Alliance, according to Article 4 of the North Atlantic Treaty, serves as a "transatlantic forum for allies to discuss questions that concern their vital interests as well as developments that might pose risks for the security of its members; and as a forum to properly coordinate efforts in areas of mutual concern." Fourth, and last of all, the Alliance wants to maintain "the strategic balance of power in Europe." We will need to fulfill these obligations (both political *and* military) if we wish to prevent the erosion of NATO—especially since the United States and Canada, as two non-European powers, are firmly integrated into a security system whose main objective is European security.

The NATO summit meeting on January 10–11, 1994, was important in this regard. Three points were the focus of this conference: namely, the security and defense identity of the Alliance; the continued development of Alliance structures, such as taking over some responsibilities from the United Nations; and the extension of security to the countries of East Central Europe (such as through the "Partnership for Peace").[42] Can the Conference on Security and Cooperation in Europe (CSCE)—since January 1, 1995, Organization for Security and Cooperation in Europe, or OSCE—develop durable security structures? Can NATO be subordinated to the structures of the UN or the OSCE, as the Russians would like? These proposals cannot be in the Western interest. Further building blocks for European security structures (aside from NATO and OSCE) are the European Union (EU) and the Western European Union (WEU). Up until now, the CSCE has not had effective mechanisms at its disposal.

With the end of the Cold War, the United Nations has not proved very effective—especially since its involvement in many regions of the world (including Africa and the Middle East) prevent it from being more seriously engaged in Europe. Only NATO has the proven military structures that can serve as effective deterrence. The multiplicity of political institutions—one could add the Council of Europe in Strasbourg—also carries with it the danger of clashing competencies.

(2) An extension of the European Union to the East must be possible in theory; the same holds true for NATO. However, immediate admission of East Central European states into the European Union is quixotic. To this day, the European Union suffers from its southern expansion—the incorporation of Spain, Portugal and Greece, but also Ireland. In essence, three important preconditions exist for admission to the European Union:

(a) Countries interested in joining must be democratic, politically stable and respect human rights.

(b) A country's economic conditions must be compatible with EU requirements. In many countries of East Central Europe, there is no well-functioning banking system and no laws governing economic competition, which makes it all the more difficult for foreign countries to invest. Moreover, the judicial system and legal protection for foreign investors have not been developed sufficiently. Of course, the situation varies from country to country. For that reason, the membership of the so-called Visegrad countries—Poland, the Czech Republic, Slovakia and Hungary—should be evaluated on a case-by-case basis.

(c) The third condition is the willingness of potential members to work on the democratization process in the European Union (more on this later). The original European Community (today, the European Union) was not formed as an exclusive club. In theory, it is open to all countries that can fulfill the requirements discussed here. What we must begin to consider are transitional stages toward full membership in the EU—for example, through an "affiliated membership status." In that way, some states could already begin to participate and cooperate in a common foreign and security policy or could work with the common domestic and legal policies established at Maastricht or could perhaps have an official say in areas of economic policy.

On the one hand, these countries want to be integrated into a Western community of nations for foreign political and security reasons; and on the other hand, their economic interests are important as well. Flexibility in the European Union's structure would thus give East Central European countries the opportunity to feel a part of Western Europe, and it would signalize—not only symbolically—that they belong to the "family" of Europe. At the same time, potential member states from East Central Europe could send observers to the European Parliament, in the same way that east German observers were once involved in the European Parliament after reunification: they were accorded a special participatory status before the

European elections of June 1994. Several East Central European countries have signed European agreements with the European Union, and are now one step closer to membership.[43]

(3) Unfortunately, the European Union does not take advantage of the Common Foreign and Security Policy (CFSP) apparatus established by the Maastricht Treaty as a means of deepening the European Union. As opposed to the EC's European Political Cooperation, institutionalized in 1970, this new apparatus grants the European Commission formal participatory rights; up until now, however, the now fifteen member states of the Union have only made reluctant use of it.

The failure of the European Union in the Balkan conflict, however, should signalize that a common foreign and security policy is now more necessary than ever, since from now on the United States will only be involved in European security and foreign policy affairs when her own security interests are directly at stake. These security interests are—aside from international trade matters—ones that involve nuclear weapons and the relationship between the United States and Russia. As the Balkan crisis has shown, the United States will be more disinclined to intervene in political and military conflicts, at least ones that are primarily of regional, European significance.

Within the framework of the CFSP, the Western European Union, founded in Paris in 1954, should develop into one of the European pillars of a common foreign and security policy. The member states of the WEU include Belgium, Germany, France, Great Britain, Italy, Luxembourg, the Netherlands, Portugal, Spain and Greece. In the past, the WEU lived silently in the shadows of NATO, but it could develop into an effective apparatus, enabling (EU member) Austria as well as the new members Sweden and Finland—for whom neutrality has always been state policy—to participate in a Western-oriented security policy, especially since support is more unconditional than with NATO. And if Norway, as a NATO member, one day decides to join the European Union, then there might eventually be a sense of common identity between European NATO members and members of the European Union. (Exceptions are Turkey as a member of NATO; Ireland as non-NATO member; and France, where there now seems to be a renewed interest in participating in the military infrastructure of NATO.)

To organize the CFSP, it is practical to use already existing institutions such as the WEU, because forming a completely new treaty-backed military structure would not be very popular. Turning the WEU into a security pillar of the European Union is somewhat controversial—even within member states—since some members fear that, by having an independent, clearly

defined security and defense identity, the Western Europeans might relativize NATO's significance and United States influence in Europe. It is
presently in Germany's interest to avoid any conflict between European
security structures and the Atlantic alliance.

But with the continued presence of approximately 100,000 American
soldiers in Europe, which represents a considerable security guarantee for
NATO member states, the fear of a separate European military identity can
be countered. East Central European states such as Hungary and Poland
clearly state that NATO membership is more important than being a part of
the EU or the WEU, and that the American presence in Europe is also crucial
to their interests.

But the key question is how to turn the WEU into one of the pillars of
European security, and how to keep NATO and the WEU two separate
entities. It is in Germany's interests to broaden the role of the WEU—but
alongside NATO, *not separate* from it. There should be no parallel structures at the leadership level. Instead, the WEU should be able to tap
collective NATO resources (e.g., its communication network, transport
capacities, command structures, headquarters, etc.). This would prevent a
conflict between the two institutions, for the WEU would then merely be a
complement to NATO. These issues will probably play a significant role in
the forthcoming governmental conference of EU member states in 1996,
which will discuss ways of broadening the Community's political and
democratic structures.

In Luxembourg, on May 9, 1994, the WEU (which includes all EU
members except Denmark and Ireland, which have observer status) admitted nine new states as associated partners: Poland, Hungary, Romania,
Bulgaria, the Czech Republic, Estonia, Latvia and Lithuania.[44] Though
association is not the same as full membership, it does allow for regular
consultations and cooperation in crisis management. Up until now, only the
NATO states Turkey, Norway and Iceland have had association status. Their
level of association has now been upgraded. This will allow them to send
officers to the WEU's military planning center, just as the other member
nations. Unlike the North Atlantic Cooperation Council (NACC) and the
"Partnership for Peace" program, only those states interested in becoming
members of the European Union can be considered for association with the
WEU.

(4) With Finland's entry into the European Union, the EU will, for the
first time, share a border with Russia. But Russia does not welcome NATO's
general expansion to the East, and it is therefore controversial even within
the Western alliance itself, as it would mean a change in the alliance's

character. Yet, this discussion is highly hypothetical in nature, since it presently only involves Europeans, and every expansion of NATO would require an extension of America's security guarantee. The question is, then, how far should NATO expand? Should it admit just the Visegrad countries of Poland, the Czech Republic, Slovakia and Hungary—or should it also incorporate the Baltic states? Can the latter expansion truly be in NATO's interest? Wouldn't that bring NATO even closer to Russia's borders? And wouldn't this kind of expansion just play into the hands of imperial, antireform forces in Russia, who would have an easier time finding support for an anti-Western policy?

In the end, it was consideration for Yeltsin's position in Russia that convinced government heads to withhold immediate membership from several East Central European countries.[45] At their summit meeting in Brussels on January 11, 1994, the government heads of NATO member states in turn proposed a "Partnership for Peace." The North Atlantic Cooperation Council—to which NATO's former enemies would belong—was not considered an adequate framework. The proposal for a "Partnership of Peace," accepted by the East Central European states, will bring new partners into Western security structures without having them become full members of NATO. The possibility of common military exercises was discussed; partners were invited to send permanent liaison officers to NATO headquarters; in addition, "NATO will consult with any active participant if that partner perceives a direct threat to its territorial integrity, political independence, or security."[46]

Perhaps Western states will one day see that their decision not to grant immediate NATO membership to East Central European states was a historic miscalculation. Or, perhaps the "Partnership for Peace" will be seen as having been the more viable option, because it keeps all doors open while events in Russia continue to develop. It is not feasible to allow Russia to join the European Union or NATO: her sheer size and her Eurasian connections stand in the way. At the same time, Russia should not be isolated, because what is needed is a system of reliable security partnerships. How this structure will eventually look will depend on Russia's future inner development.

It is necessary that we continue to broaden our security dialogue with Russia, particularly with her military establishment, which still tends to view NATO as an anti-Russian alliance. Russia should not be given the impression that it has been excluded from Europe or that a new iron curtain has separated her from the rest of the continent. It cannot be in NATO's interest to create a security system without Moscow's cooperation or one that is directed against Russia.

On the other hand, NATO cannot condone a "Yalta II"—that is, an agreement with the Russian leadership that would negotiate spheres of influence in Europe. For that reason, it is particularly important for Germany that Russia and NATO agree on an institutional framework that will prevent confrontation—one that would meet on a regular basis to resolve international problems and that would help establish close and open forms of cooperation. NATO's "Partnership for Peace" offers Russia such an opportunity, and it takes into account Russia's special status as a nuclear superpower.

(5) Military conflicts that could jeopardize Germany's existence have become more unlikely; but many countries in the world are still trying to obtain weapons of mass destruction and the necessary launching systems. More than twenty countries possess short- and middle-range missile systems. And now, aside from Russia, Ukraine, Belarus and Kazahkstan, other countries have the know-how to develop nuclear weapons, or even have them already. By the end of the decade, according to German military experts, thirty countries will have the potential to make chemical weapons, and ten will be able to engage in biological warfare.

On former Soviet territory, there are approximately 10,300 warheads on mobile strategic missiles, and about 15,000 primarily land-based tactical nuclear weapons (short-range missiles, artillery grenades and mines) and their launching systems. Since mid-1992, all tactical weapons are located on Russian territory. According to information supplied by the German government in 1994, the strategic nuclear weapons can be divided up as follows:

- Russia: A total of 7,000 warheads (over 4,000 of these can be found on 900 land-based strategic intercontinental missiles, about 2,700 warheads on about 800 sea-based intercontinental missiles and about 300 warheads on 25 heavy bombers).
- Ukraine: A total of about 1,640 strategically deployable warheads on 42 bombers, 130 SS-19s and 46 SS-24s.
- Kazakhstan: A total of about 1,400 warheads on 40 bombers and 98 SS-18s.
- Belarus: A total of 81 SS-25s, each with one warhead.

All strategic nuclear weapons were put under a unified command as laid down by the Minsk Agreement of December 30, 1991; its commander in chief until June 1993 was Marshal Shaposhnikov. According to this agreement, the president of Russia—in consultation with the government heads of Belarus, Kazakhstan and Ukraine—makes the final decision on use "until that moment when all nuclear weapons have been scrapped."

The disarmament process is very important. On January 3, 1993, U.S. President George Bush and Russian President Boris Yeltsin signed the START II Treaty, which builds on the START I Treaty of July 31, 1991, and which continues its technical regulations (including verification procedures)—as long as they were not modified by the new treaty. START II once again sets lower limits for nuclear weapons, and would eventually reduce the stockpile of warheads to a third their present level.[47] In a supplementary protocol, the "Lisbon Protocol" of May 23, 1992, Kazakhstan, Belarus and Ukraine committed themselves to the elimination of all strategic nuclear weapons from their territories within a seven-year period.

In principle, there are strict personnel and technical security measures to prevent an accidental or unauthorized use of nuclear weapons. But the greater mobility of tactical nuclear weapons, which are relatively small and light, makes the risk of potential misuse inordinately higher than with strategic nuclear weapons.[48] One of the major problems is that—due to the dissolution of the previous power structures—there is an increased risk in nuclear proliferation, mostly in connection with fissile material used in weapon production, but also with nuclear technology and atomic know-how.

Ever since the fall of 1992, there have been signs of atomic smuggling, and CIS states (including Russia herself) have been named as the countries of origin. Caches of plutonium that were discovered in Germany between May and August of 1994 clearly point to a growth in the export of radioactive material. As a result of the collapse of the Soviet Union, there are presently many (badly paid) specialists willing to deal with interested buyers, and this would explain why construction blueprints for weapons systems as well as difficult-to-obtain materials for missile propellants have been uncovered.

The Federal Intelligence Agency of the Federal Republic expects that future threats will come from states that have access to missile launchers with nuclear, biological or chemical warheads.[49] With these launchers, missiles with a range of approximately 1,000 kilometers might be possible within the next several years. Although one cannot expect quick and thorough solutions to this problem of nuclear proliferation and leaking military expertise from countries of the former Soviet Union, a series of measures has already been implemented with the Federal Republic's participation.

For example, the German government has earmarked a part of the budget for an area entitled "disarmament aid," which will help finance projects to eliminate the material used in weapons of mass destruction in CIS states. Moreover, Germany has made contributions to a technology center in Moscow that is expected to put a stop to the "brain drain," that is, to prevent former Soviet nuclear scientists and weapons designers from being lured away by prosperous newly industrializing countries. Germany also actively participates in nonproliferation agreements—namely, the Nonproliferation Treaty (NPT) and Missile Technology Control Regime (MTCR).[50]

Furthermore, the security of Germans and other Europeans is seriously jeopardized by the nuclear power plants of East Central Europe. It is imperative that the disastrous Chernobyl reactor be closed down soon. A study sponsored by the World Bank has concluded that the West should come up with about $10 billion between 1995 and 2000 to improve the nuclear and the conventional energy supply systems in East Central European countries. Two reactors, according to the study, had to be shut down because it would have been prohibitively expensive to modernize them.[51] The poor security standards of Soviet-built nuclear power plants (fifty-six remain in operation and still more are being constructed) are exacerbated by the bad economic climate.

(6) It will be difficult to influence inner developments in Russia. Financial transfers are needed more than anything. But one should not underestimate the role that institutions such as German political foundations can play in transferring knowledge to Russia and other countries of Central Asia and East Central Europe. They relay information on how democracy functions, how a country is governed by the rule of law, why an independent judiciary is important and why a legal framework creating a friendly environment for investment is a prerequisite for economic growth.

Because of Germany's traditional relations with the Soviet Union, she is more likely to pursue an active Russia policy than other Western European states—even though she should avoid going her own way. One should mention, for example, that Germany is paying the lion's share of aid to Russia. According to an estimate by the EC Commission, German support for Russia and the other former Soviet republics amounted to DM 80 billion by the spring of 1993—more than half the Western total.[52] In the same period, the United States gave DM 13.5 billion, Japan DM 4.1 billion, France DM 4 billion and Great Britain DM 1 billion. The European Community has contributed DM 6.1 billion.

(7) Since security today must be understood in broader terms and must deal with the inner stability of potential conflict nations, economic ques-

tions have become extremely important. In particular, Western markets must begin to accept products from East Central Europe—even if it might cause economic problems for Western Europe. By encouraging these countries to help themselves, we can help them achieve a sustainable economic growth, for this is the only way democratic and political stability will arise. Up until now, Western Europe has been shamefully protectionist, despite the fact that the EU allowed for a system of "asymmetrical" trade that was supposed to work out to the advantage of these nations.[53]

The European Community's trade balance surplus has grown considerably. The OECD concluded that the EC achieved a $3 billion surplus in 1992, and that Western European exports to countries in the East Central European region rose 25.3 percent in 1992, whereas imports from those countries only increased by 19.7 percent.[54] In 1991, according to OECD estimates, East Central Europe's share of agricultural imports in the Western European market was 2.4 percent; for textile products, it was 2.8 percent; and for chemical products, it was 1.7 percent. Their share of the EC market in iron and steel—which was affected by an antidumping tax of 1993—was less than 3 percent.

On the other hand, one should mention that East Central European countries primarily supply the kind of goods produced in crisis-stricken Western industries (agriculture, iron, steel, coal, shipping, etc.). Yet, one should not underestimate the importance of the European Union for these reformed countries. About 50 percent of total foreign trade from these countries is picked up by—up until recently—the twelve (now fifteen) member states of the European Union. Just several years ago, it was only 25 percent. East Central Europe's democratic future will ultimately depend on the health of its economy.

At the moment there is no clear answer to the question of how Europe can effectively coordinate a foreign and security policy that integrates East Central Europe. New security structures are just beginning to emerge with the decline of the bipolar world. A lot will depend on developments in Russia and on the future form of Russia's own foreign and security policy. Germany's security depends on NATO, as well as on the countries of East Central Europe, particularly Russia and the Ukraine. But Germany also needs to cooperate with the Scandinavian states to promote stability in the Baltic. And Turkey's new role must also be considered. On the whole, Europeans must assume greater responsibility for the security of Europe; but at the same time, Europe must continue to actively incorporate the United States in her affairs.

International Institutions and Free Trade

Several points should be repeated:

(1) Even after the Cold War, regional conflicts both inside and outside Europe could have consequences for Europe's security and her economy (conflicts in the Middle East, developments in South Africa, etc.). Massive waves of migration from unstable regions in the world could spill into the industrial nations of the West. The danger is that civil wars could be imported into Germany—that Kurds, Serbs or Algerian Muslims, for example, could act out their conflicts on German soil.

(2) Moreover, the energy supply will become a major problem. According to the International Energy Agency, oil consumption will grow 30 percent by the year 2010. Western Europe is interested in maintaining the stability of the regions which supply her with oil and natural gas. If energy sources got into the hands of anti-Western fundamentalists, it could create an economic crisis in the West.

(3) More foreign countries are developing atomic weapons. Biological, chemical and nuclear capabilities could one day fall into the wrong hands. There is a potential for nuclear terrorism.

Developments in North Africa, but most of all in the Middle East, significantly affect German and European interests. Almost all Arab states are, to a certain degree, politically, socially and economically unstable. Although problems will surely continue even after the Israeli-PLO agreements, the Middle East peace process is a hopeful sign in the future development of that region.[55] Other areas of possible future conflict in the region are a potential increase in nuclear proliferation, a decline in water supplies and a resurgence of religious fundamentalism (both Islamic and Jewish).

Despite continued terrorist attacks and other problems, including the status of Jerusalem, it no longer seems unrealistic to expect a peaceful resolution sometime in the near future. Unlike the earlier attempts to promote negotiations, both sides now seem generally interested in peace (ever since the Israeli-Palestinian declaration of principles in September 1993). Germany and the European Union are interested in this neighboring region—the most important aside from Eastern Europe—because of its general political significance and because of the many economic and historic ties they share. But the EU's Common Foreign and Security Policy must make great advances if it wants to have an impact on Middle Eastern policy. Crucial in this respect would be a concerted EU policy that would incorporate the entire Mediterranean region, for all Arab states south of this region are (potential) conflict zones.

To address Europe's foreign security challenges one should consider three very significant factors:

Germany and the United Nations

Ever since the Cold War ended, the system of international relations has become increasingly complex, since earlier divisions of the globe into categories such as First, Second, Third or Fourth World have lost their relevance. From World War II's end to the beginning of 1988, there were thirteen UN peacekeeping missions; since then, there have been fifteen more.

In 1992 alone, the number of troops involved in such activities has increased fourfold. In 1993, more than 80,000 UN troops ("blue helmets") from seventy different countries were deployed in 13 different peacekeeping missions. With the end of the East-West conflict, the UN has been confronted with new challenges. There have never been as many UN peacekeeping forces deployed in crisis regions throughout the world than at the present time.

In Germany, the possible deployment of German soldiers in UN peace missions was a hot political topic, and it became a legal debate for many years. Before the Supreme Court decided on the issue on July 12, 1994, Chancellor Kohl had worked toward gradually ending German diplomacy's self-imposed isolation. A controversial legal point was the relationship of Article 87a of the Constitution to Article 24, Paragraph 2. According to the supporters of German deployment in areas outside of NATO territory, so-called "out-of-area" missions, these constitutional articles need not be changed. After all, the Federal Republic had joined the United Nations in 1973 without reservations, meaning that it had agreed to all obligations set down by the UN Charter in principle. The SPD opposition wanted the deployment of German soldiers limited to "blue helmet" missions (i.e., to peacekeeping missions), and did not want to extend it to peace-making measures.

On July 12, 1994, the Supreme Court decided that in the future the German Armed Forces, or Bundeswehr, could also be deployed in regions outside of NATO territory if a simple majority in the German Bundestag supported the measure. With this decision, the Supreme Court put an end to the constitutional debate surrounding out-of-area deployments and established that the Constitution does not block deployments either within a UN framework or in other potential collective partnerships (e.g., with NATO).

Yet, as the Court went on to say, the government had not requested Bundestag approval—as it should have—in its deployments in the Adriatic, in its use of AWAC missions, or in its involvement in Somalia. Having lived in the shadows of the Cold War and acted according to a restrictive interpretation of the Constitution, (West) Germany until recently practiced a "culture of restraint" in international military matters.

Germany was not directly involved in the Gulf War (though military bases in Germany were used for allied deployments). Instead, Germany contributed logistically and financed a considerable share of the mission's costs.[56] Though at first restraint seemed to be reasonable politically, it soon seemed that legal arguments precluding involvement no longer made sense. Chancellor Kohl's initial reactions after the Supreme Court had handed down its decision, however, show that Germany is in no way falling into the other extreme; instead, it is looking for ways in which military deployments can be used cautiously. Since 1991, the Bundeswehr has been involved in a series of UN missions and humanitarian aid projects. Therefore, a gradual shift in German policy has already taken place. Germans no longer consider international deployments out of the ordinary. Several examples prove this:

- From April 6, 1991, to June 15, 1991, Kurdish refugees in Turkey and Iran received 1,900 tons of air supplies from Germany to relieve them from the casualties of war. Through German assistance, for example, a field hospital was built.

- At the end of Operation "Desert Storm," the Bundeswehr helped to remove mines in the Arabian Gulf. The operation was coordinated by the WEU.

- A German medical corps was involved in Cambodia in 1991. At first, it participated in UN excursionary missions. The last group of Germans returned on November 12, 1993. One German soldier was killed.

- Since August 1991, Germany has been assisting the Special Commission of the United Nations to disarm Iraq by supplying German air force transport planes and army transport helicopters.

- Since July 4, 1992, the German air force has been involved in a Balkan airlift, including a fleet of AWACs to control and enforce the flight ban over Bosnia-Herzegovina. Moreover, since July 18, 1992, the German navy has been involved with NATO and the WEU to enforce an embargo against the remnants of former Yugoslavia.

- Since 1992, Germany has contributed considerably to hunger relief in civil war–torn Somalia through the humanitarian aid program of the United Nations. One thousand seven hundred soldiers were stationed at the operational base of

Belet-Uen in central Somalia. On February 28, 1994, the last German soldier
left Belet-Uen.

For constitutional reasons, the German government was obligated to
refer to these UN operations as peacekeeping and humanitarian projects,
not as peace-making measures. But at this point, the Bundeswehr is not
prepared for international crisis situations—neither in its equipment, nor in
its organization. In the "White Book 1994," published on April 5, 1994, the
government reported on the efforts made to readjust the present Bundeswehr structures so that they will be able to meet these new responsibilities.

In the meantime, the German government is actively pursuing membership in the Permanent Committee of the United Nations Security Council.
Japan is highly interested in membership. Some people argue that the
preeminent position of the victorious powers in the Security Council is just
a vestige of World War II, and it no longer reflects the true power balance.
The highly populous countries of India, Brazil, Nigeria, Egypt and Indonesia are all pressuring to become permanent members of the Security
Council—especially since it is dominated by the industrial nations.

There are demands for a more just and democratic distribution of power.
But of course any change in United Nations structures requires both a
two-thirds majority and the ultimate approval from the five veto-wielding
powers. For that reason alone the reforms will probably take years. There does
not seem to be a broad consensus on this issue. France and Great Britain are
not very supportive of the proposal to let the European Union as an institution
represent the Western European member countries through rotation. But for
the supporters of European integration, this proposal makes sense.

However, the more that Germany tries to force the issue of Security
Council membership, the higher the admittance price she will have to pay
in New York. Today, the Federal Republic contributes approximately 9
percent of the United Nations budget; but as a late member of the organization, its share of the personnel is rather low. But the issue of Germany's
permanent membership on the Security Council is not only a question of
how fast the United Nations can reform its structures. Germany should not
force itself on the United Nations. When it is in the interest of this
organization to grant Germany greater participation in the United Nations,
then the question of Germany's UN membership will resolve itself.

The Role of the United States

Germany must be interested in strengthening and broadening its strategic
partnership with the United States. But at the moment, America's foreign

policy seems to be lacking a "grand design." America has its own problems coming up with a coherent foreign policy strategy, because we are all presently living in a historic age of transition. Despite the dangers and confusions of this age, the decisive advantage is that superpower rivalries no longer directly threaten world peace.

At the present time, America is undoubtedly affected by a mood of isolationism, particularly since the North American continent is no longer directly threatened by communist Cuba. The Europeans (and especially the Germans) must begin to realize that the superpower America will increasingly be dominated by its domestic agenda[57]—most of all by the reduction of its national debt. That is why at the moment American foreign policy— and as sole surviving superpower, the United States cannot avoid playing a role—seems more to be *re*acting to events than acting on them, which has been demonstrated by the Balkan crisis.

In the first year of his presidency, Clinton seemed to take little interest in foreign policy. It took him more than a year to visit Europe for the first time (January 1994). Then, Europe began to take on greater significance in Clinton's second year, as was demonstrated by two further visits to Europe in June and July 1994. Clinton's interest in German politics was demonstrated by two of his major reform proposals—health care reform and vocational education. Clinton has looked to German models.

Comments made by Secretary of State Warren Christopher in November 1993 led to overall irritation in Europe: he stated that Western Europe was no longer the central region of world conflicts and that American policy should begin to overcome its traditional Eurocentrism. Then, at the following Asian-Pacific summit meeting in Seattle (November 1993), American diplomacy attempted to downplay Christopher's remarks. In foreign policy, the emphasis has shifted from security issues to foreign trade policy, and here the Pacific Rim has become America's central focus: it is the most important trade area for the United States and is presently recording the world's highest growth rates. It is not necessarily true that American foreign policy has downgraded Europe; rather, it has upgraded Asia.

America has made investigations into these matters, and they now seem to inform its economic policy. The Economic Strategy Institute, a Washington think tank, revealed that trade with China and Japan has led to a 70 percent trade deficit, whereas America's trade with Europe records a 70 percent surplus. America exported raw materials to Far Eastern countries, and received high-tech products in return; with Europe, however, the relationship runs in reverse.[58] In 1992, 24 percent ($107.5 billion) of America's exports went to the European Economic Area (EEA) (the EU states and the seven EFTA [European Free Trade Association] member states). Nineteen percent of American imports ($105.3 billion) came from EEA countries. But in its trade with East Asia, the United States has consistently recorded high deficits ($89 billion in 1992!), so that despite an overall higher trade volume (29 percent of American exports, 40 percent of American imports) there remains a considerable trade gap.[59]

Moreover, transatlantic economic relations are primarily based on direct investments and the trade that is carried out within companies, which now make up about half the trade volume over the Atlantic. In 1992, about $239 billion of America's direct investments went into Europe, and $249 billion of the Community's went into America; these amounts made up more than half the total volume. About 12 million jobs (or more than 11 percent of total employment) are linked to American exports to Europe, and to European investments in the United States; more than 4,000 European firms operate in America.[60] Though the United States often appears somewhat ambivalent toward the European integration process and to the idea of "Brussels," America is in general agreement with Europe on the future of the world economic order. Besides, "Asian values" are not what attract the United States to the region: though the United States might seek economic cooperation with Asian countries, the human rights policies of China, Korea and Singapore, for example, and the protectionist measures in Japan, have also created a good deal of reservations.

Washington is aware of the important political changes that are occurring in Europe after forty years of Cold War. It would be foolish if she did not want to influence these events. At the same time, America is clearly concerned with the resurgence of ex-communists in the former East Bloc. President Clinton's visit to Riga in June 1994, was a clear sign of how seriously America takes Russia's policy toward its "neighboring foreign countries." With his visit to Poland, Clinton must also have seen that America's leadership role in NATO and Europe continues to be important.

Moreover, Washington understands the nature of the radical changes presently confronting its Western European allies. England and France have undoubtedly lost some of their former power. Spain is faced with political problems, and in 1994 Italy's head of government took office in a pact with neofascists. These are some of the reasons why America will not too publicly play its "Asian card" in front of Europe, and why it continues to see Europe not only from an economic, but also from a political perspective. It is very much in Europe's interest to keep the present level of American troops in Europe (not below the agreed upon level of 100,000). After all, this continued presence serves American interests: by withdrawing from

Europe, America would allow Germany, with its effective military forces and the most prosperous economy in Europe, to become the leading power on continental Europe.

But the Germans and the Europeans are just as unsure of America's future foreign policy goals as America is in regard to theirs.[61] However, since America under Bill Clinton gave absolute priority to domestic concerns, it was inevitable that the administration would create uncertainties at the outset concerning American foreign and security policy. This administration has not yet discussed its point of view on Europe with its European partners. As a result, many Europeans now feel a bit helpless, since they have long grown accustomed to America taking on a leadership role.

On the other hand, the Clinton administration generally has a more positive attitude toward a larger, more stable and prosperous European Union than the previous administration had. The United States and (Western) Europe will continue to have to rely on each other. Neither of the two partners will be able to solve its serious external problems on its own. What is important, however, is that neither of the two try to turn to a third party for more effective support. This holds true for GATT's evolution into the World Trade Organization (WTO), as well as for questions involving international conflict management—not to mention the necessary reform of NATO. I have already referred to their shared values in the area of human rights policy.

Free Trade

Within the realm of foreign and security policy, world trade policy has assumed a central importance (particularly for America). Many people in Europe have yet to realize this. We are presently witnessing a trend toward worldwide economic regionalization, toward the formation of larger trade blocs. Further regional organizations have been founded in response to the increasing economic and political integration of the—up until recently—twelve EU member states as well as the creation of a European Economic Area (EEA), that is, the European Union and the current seven member states of the European Free Trade Area (EFTA) (Austria, Switzerland, Liechtenstein, Finland, Sweden, Norway and Iceland).

These regional organizations include the free trade zone between the United States, Canada and Mexico (NAFTA), Asia-Pacific Economic Cooperation (APEC) and the Asian Free Trade Area (AFTA), which the six ASEAN (Association of Southeast Asian Nations) states are currently trying to organize. Economic regionalization can be effective, but it would mean a step backward if it led to economic isolation. For both the developing nations and the industrial nations, economic isolation through regional economic blocs would prove fatal.

Yet, internationally oriented countries need larger markets (more than their nations on an individual basis can provide) to promote their highly capital-intensive products. In this sense, regional cooperation is often attractive, because nations with their regulatory mechanisms can avoid getting involved in economic particulars: their political and legal structures are not nuanced enough to cope with larger markets. Despite the overall positive outcome of the Uruguay round of GATT on April 15, 1994, protectionist tendencies still remain. However, through GATT, it was possible to avert the long-feared trade war between the United States and Europe.

Many people do not understand GATT's significance for the world economy. The GATT agreement was signed in Geneva by twenty-three countries in 1947. In this multilateral agreement, the participating states laid down the rights and obligations that would govern their international trade relations. In some cases, the treaty replaced existing bilateral trade agreements, and it served to create a more liberal international trade environment.

GATT ultimately gained in prestige through the expansion of worldwide trade and the globalization of the marketplace. After seven and a half years of negotiations, the recent eighth world trade round ended in Marrakesh with the signing of an agreement establishing a World Trade Organization (WTO). The origins of the Uruguay round go back to a meeting of ministers in Geneva in November 1982. In September 1986, after numerous lengthy negotiations, the process was officially ended in Punta del Este, Uruguay. The final agreement commits the 125 participants to broaden multilateral trade conditions through the establishment of the WTO.

Moreover, trade in the service sector and the legal protection of intellectual property are issues that have been incorporated for the first time within the framework of a global treaty.[62] GATT's most important liberalizing principles concern the treatment of goods within a member state: (1) a country cannot treat an imported foreign product as inferior to a domestic product, and (2) the most favorable tariff accorded one trade partner must be accorded to all (the most-favored-nation principle).

The negotiations were particularly successful in the area of trade in industrial goods. As a result of the Uruguay round of GATT, the average import tariff fell from 40 percent to approximately 5 percent. However, in the area of non–tariff-related trade obstacles and in the question of service industries and subsidies (particularly the subsidization of agricultural products), there remains considerable hindrance to trade. For a long time, these obstacles in fact seriously threatened to undermine the last round of negotiations.

But multilateralism (as the GATT treaty foresees) and greater regionalism (i.e., the emergence of free trade and tariff zones) aren't compatible. Regional alliances, as experience shows, often result in a disadvantaged third party. The European agricultural market is a clear example of this. Many of the measures taken by the European Community (today's European Union) to secure the jobs and incomes of farmers end up protecting the European market from world market forces. The European consumer ends up with the costs, for he must pay the inflated food prices as well as the cost to house the surplus.

But the European Union, being the largest trade power in the world, is more dependent on foreign trade than any other country, and thus had the greatest stake in the successful conclusion of the GATT negotiations. In 1988, the European Community had a 20 percent share of world trade, whereas the United States and Japan had shares of 15 and 12 percent, respectively. In 1989, 20 percent of the European Community's gross national product was related to foreign trade. The following trade statistics reveal the extent of Germany's dependence on exports:[63]

- America's export quota per capita is $1,500.
- Japan's is $2,300.
- Germany's is $5,000.
- Fifty-five percent of Germany's exports go to EU member countries. If one were to include the seven EFTA nations (i.e., the European Economic Area), that percentage would increase to 72 percent (10 percent to North America, 4 percent to East Asia, of which a fourth goes to Japan).
- One out of every six jobs is directly linked (and one out of three indirectly) to exports to EU member countries.

The export of goods and services as percentage share of gross national product is as follows:[64]

- 10 percent in the United States.
- 11 percent in Japan.
- 32 percent in Germany.
- 23 percent in France.
- 21 percent in Italy.
- 25 percent in Great Britain and Canada.

The Federal Republic is considered the champion of exporters: statistically, every third job depends on the export of her domestic products. A policy of protectionism according to the motto "beggar my neighbor" would probably result in countermeasures from other countries (one only has to recall America's "super 301" legislation),[65] and this would have disastrous consequences for Germany as a prominent exporter. The protection of domestic products, which can only be produced at a comparative disadvantage, is not in Germany's interests. Rather, production should concentrate on those many sectors where German products continue to have an edge—either in their prices, or in their quality. Since, as stated, 72 percent of Germany's exports go to countries in the EEA, the priority of Germany's trade policy has been to liberalize intra-European trade.

Germany's prosperity and the security of her jobs depend to a large extent on export within the EC and the EEA. But the developing market economies of East Asia (also in parts of China) demonstrate that the economic balance is shifting. Considering the competition from the Far East, general prosperity and social security in Europe can only be maintained if Europe's partner nations cooperate effectively and engage in a unified policy—and not only in the economic arena. The developing nations must also be interested in liberal world trade, for that is the only way they can obtain hard currency.[66]

Worldwide Challenges and the Fear of Power

The German word *Angst* has become a standard term in many languages. In a survey carried out simultaneously in Japan, Great Britain, the United States and Germany, the question was asked: "What do you consider the greatest problem in the world today?" Forty-two percent of Germans answered "war"; that same answer was given by 27 percent of the Japanese, 26 percent of the British and 8 percent of the Americans.[67] No other country in Europe developed such a strong pacifist movement as Germany; politically it is represented by the Green movement, and there is a tradition in some parts of the Social Democratic Party as well.

This German pacifism can be seen as a reaction to the fact that Germany started two world wars, and that Germany is responsible for the horror of the Holocaust. Probably no other country has such a well-organized pacifist movement. After World War II, political and civic education classes taught Germans that they should never be allowed again to play a significant role in world affairs. Self-restraint became an official state policy. West Germany placed practically the entire Bundeswehr under the auspices of the NATO Supreme Command, decided not to own, produce or deploy any nuclear weapons and instead was active in trying to push European integration—which, in the final analysis, was also motivated by its dependency on the three Allied powers—while refusing to take its own unique foreign political course (*Sonderweg*). In a sense, Germans liked observing world events from the bleachers. The admittance of both German states into the United Nations on September 18, 1973, for the first time forced West Germany to take a position on many international questions.

At the moment, there are no signs of a renewed German "will to power," such as existed in many periods of Prussian and German foreign policy until 1945. This "will" was dismantled after the war; the Germans were, as Hans-Peter Schwarz puts it, "tamed"; they moved from an obsession with power to a neglect of power.[68] Hardly anyone in Germany disputes that the Bundeswehr should defend the nation: 90 percent in the western states and 92 percent in the east agree that this is the Bundeswehr's responsibility. Eighty-nine percent in the west and 79 percent in the east think that the army serves to promote peace; 64 percent of the population in the west and 41 percent in the east want to continue membership in the Western alliance in the future.

But surveys show that opinions are split on the issue of the Bundeswehr's deployment within the United Nations. Even peacekeeping operations, that is, "blue helmet" missions, are only accepted by 74 percent in the west and 61 percent in the east. Military missions of UN troops—peace-making actions—are rejected by every second German in the west and 61 percent of the eastern population.[69] Germany's hesitance toward the deployment of the Bundeswehr outside NATO territory is revealed by another survey: 42 percent of Germans would accept this unconditionally, 37 percent are totally against the idea ("not at all") and 21 percent are uncommitted.[70] What is interesting is that full support for the idea was considerably higher in west Germany (48 percent) than in the east (22 percent). When asked "Do you think your country should send soldiers to crisis regions throughout the world to enforce peace projects if it is called upon to do so?" 57 percent of the Germans said "yes" (in comparison, 72 percent of the British, 59 percent of the Americans and 36 percent of the Japanese).[71]

Military conscription is also no longer taken for granted. The number of sixteen- to eighteen-year-olds who intend to refuse military service has risen by 30 percent. The number of conscientious objectors is considerably lower in east Germany.[72] In 1993, 130,041 Germans eligible for military service registered as conscientious objectors; in 1992, it was 133,868; in 1991, during the Gulf War, 151,212. Forty percent of west Germans and 12 percent in the east consider the American military presence in Germany "important"; whereas 41 percent in the west and 34 percent in the east consider it to be an insignificant factor. Thirty-nine percent in the west support a complete withdrawal of American troops.

According to a survey made by the United States Information Agency (USIA), two thirds of Germans in east and west believe that the United States will remain their most important security partner in the future. The approval level for NATO is similarly high. In eastern Germany, the approval rating rose from 45 percent in 1993 to 55 percent in 1994. The approval and acceptance levels (70 percent) haven't changed much in west Germany over the last several years.[73] At the same time, opinion is split on the question of the American troop presence: 41 percent are calling for a complete withdrawal; another 30 percent would like to see a further reduction in American forces; less than 20 percent support the maintenance of present troop levels. On the other hand, there have been no significant demands calling for the removal of the troops. In the areas where the Americans have pulled out, major structural and economic problems have resulted.

For many decades, it was rarely talked or written about that Germany might have specific foreign policy interests of her own. Hans-Peter Schwarz points out "that many of our politicians, and some of our foreign policy specialists, have lost sight of the state. They consider the goals and views of mankind to be most important. A realistic appraisal based on one's own interests is considered indelicate."[74] There is a further basic question that is not only relevant for Germany but for all parliamentary democracies with conscriptive military services—namely, whether parliamentary democracies are capable of taking timely preventive measures in their foreign and security policy. One must ask if Germans are prepared—in view of scarcer public funds—to make economic sacrifices that might prevent conflicts in Eastern Europe.

To deploy a conscriptive military service in regions outside the country, the political leadership will need the population's approval. For authoritarian governments, it is always easier to plan foreign and security policy. But the fact that military conflicts lately have not occurred between countries with democratic systems shows how important it is for democracy to succeed in the rest of the world.

But if a German were to believe that his country only needs to make *economic* contributions to world peace, he would not be facing reality. That's not to say Germany should be actively involved in all of the world's crisis regions: it must also be in the national interest to keep problems away from Germany. But Germany's options as an economic power are limited. Germany will need more time to get used to the new international circumstances. But whatever Germany decides to do in future foreign policy matters, there is bound to be a critical echo. If the Germans had been involved in the Gulf War, for example, there would have been talk of a new German militarism. For decades, politicians and the media told Germans that they must stay out of world politics because of the nation's past, and so Germany cannot now be expected to take on a new world role from one day to the next. A new discussion needs to take place in Germany on the responsible use of power. But foreign policy, just as the policy on Europe, demands a social consensus.

What will be Germany's future foreign policy? The majority of Germans do not approve of their country becoming a "world power." Even if the Supreme Court decision now allows Germany to deploy troops outside NATO territory, this kind of move would be unpopular with many Germans. And even if Germans thought that their country should carry greater responsibility in the world, Germany would still neither be willing nor able to fulfill many of the expectations (such as former President Bush's "partnership in leadership" concept). It will take Germans many years to grow into their new role. So for now, Germany will continue to concentrate her energies on furthering European integration and expanding Western integration. Germany's interest will be to maintain NATO's structures and the Western European Union and to develop the WEU into one of the security pillars of the European Union. It is in this sense that Germany will use her international clout.

EUROPEAN POLICY

Europe: Between Gravitational Center and Unknown Greatness

Within the European Community, the Federal Republic, and Helmut Kohl in particular, were the engines behind the European integration process. But now, after German reunification, the European Union is faced with a new series of questions: Is the principle of integration theoretically sound? If the European consensus continues in Germany and elsewhere, how should the European ideal evolve in a changing world? Is the Maastricht process meaningful, and what is Germany's position? Is the expansion of the European Union a good idea—and if yes—under what conditions?[75] What does the new situation in Europe look like? Two apparently contradictory developments can be diagnosed in Europe today: On the one hand, there have been increased efforts by the now fifteen member states since the Treaty of Maastricht to strengthen the European Union and to engage in closer cooperation; at the same time, many new states have applied for membership. On the other hand, never before have there been so many European nations as at the present: about a dozen new states have formed since 1989 in East Central and southeastern Europe.

In the latter region, it was the decline of international communism that led to the creation of these nation-states. They were the symbols of respected human rights and a free national identity. But within the EU, problems have arisen concerning further expansion. In the past, the most important factors for integration were economic, for example, a common policy in the areas of coal and steel, the creation of a unified European internal market and a common environmental policy.

But after the proposals agreed on in Maastricht—including the Common Foreign and Security Policy, cooperation in the areas of domestic and legal policy as well as the creation of a common European currency and, along with that, a European Central Bank—the central question of state sovereignty must be seen in a new light. In all member states, enthusiasm for European integration has declined somewhat. The speed with which the European integration process progressed surprised many people, and probably asked too much of them. This also has to do with the fact that many people are badly informed about Europe. General approval that is based on insufficient information can easily turn into careless rejection. Until Maastricht, Europe was a low-key subject for most of the media. This resulted in Euroskepticism, which drew its strength primarily from misinformation, and then from a sudden overflow of information.

The Treaty of Maastricht was partially a reaction of the eleven other member states to German reunification; it was supposed to make Germany's integration into a supranational alliance irreversible. But the pace was also set by the Germans themselves. The worldwide changes in connection with the end of European division did not cause the majority of the population to question (Western) European integration, but rather led to efforts to speed up the integration process through the Treaty.

But the public debates about the Treaty were much more critical—and not only in Germany—than people expected. The former president of the European Commission, Jacques Delors, offered several reasons for this: "For a long time, Europe was built by secret diplomacy, isolated from public opinion in the member states. This was the method of the founding fathers of the Community—a type of enlightened despotism. Competence and intellectual independence were considered sufficient legitimacy to take action, and it was also considered sufficient to gain the population's approval after the fact."[76]

Another reason for the confusion is the complexity of the Treaty itself: "This Treaty will certainly not make it into the ranks of literature. It is difficult to understand without detailed instructions. It is the result of many compromises, and it is written by lawyers."[77] The complexity of the Treaty is also a reflection of the institutional complexity of the European Community and its successor the European Union, a reflection of the inscrutability of its political decision-making process and its lack of a persuasive informational policy. A further reason for the confusion of the populace is that the Treaty doesn't offer "a clear blueprint for the future Community" (Delors). Rather, an evolutionary process was poured into a legalistic framework, which allows for a variety of political and legal interpretations: the Treaty attempts to combine both supranational elements of a federal state and intergovernmental elements of a confederation.

Opinion surveys reveal that Germans continue to react positively to European unification, though dissatisfaction remains in the sense that many citizens feel the relationship between costs and benefits is unbalanced. Many people still consider Germany to be the "paymaster of Europe." Twenty-five percent of Germans surveyed in December 1993 thought that "Germany is only being used by the European Community."[78] This is one of the reasons why people in Germany are calling for more effective parliamentary control in the European decision-making process through the European Parliament.

The picture I have drawn clearly shows that the majority of Germans are fundamentally pro-European, but that there have been some signs of an increasing skepticism over the years.[79] According to surveys taken shortly before the European elections in 1994, 70 percent of the Germans more or less agreed to the position that Germany's membership in the EU will secure Germany's economic competitiveness over the long term (21 percent disagreed with this opinion, 9 percent had no opinion); 69 percent agreed that Germany had many more chances of exerting influence in the world within the European Union (26 disagreed, 9 percent had no opinion).

On the other hand, 83 percent declared that Germany should be doing more to enforce its interests within the Union (15 percent disagreed, 2 percent had no opinion); and 49 percent believed that, as a result of European integration, "too much of what defined Germany got lost" (44 percent disagreed with this, and 7 percent had no opinion).[80] If one compares this to the results of other institute surveys, then one would find this ambivalence toward Europe reconfirmed. For example, according to a survey carried out by the EU Commission in early 1994, 50 percent of the Germans consider EU membership a "good thing" (52 percent of west

Germans, 45 percent of east Germans).[81] This "divided" opinion toward European integration puts the spotlight on the question of German identity: the Germans are looking for security within Europe, but at the same time are afraid of losing their identity.

What is interesting about the "Eurobarometer" surveys is that they compare Germany with other EU member states (see Table 6.2). Here, Germany is in a middle position (with 50 percent seeing membership in the EU as a "good thing," compared with 54 percent for all EU countries). The countries with the most positive outlook toward Europe are the Netherlands (77 percent), the Irish (72 percent), Luxembourg (71 percent), followed by the Italians (68 percent), the Greeks (64 percent), the Belgians (56 percent), the Portuguese (54 percent) and the Danish (53 percent). The French and the Spanish are at the same level as the Germans (50 percent). The British (with 43 percent) have less enthusiasm toward Europe. On the other hand, only 12 percent of the Germans consider membership a bad thing; the Danes top the list in this category (with 26 percent), followed by the British (with 22 percent).

Compared to the fall 1993 survey, 3 percent fewer Germans are now convinced that membership in the European Union is a "good thing," and a growing skepticism is particularly evident in east Germany (the negative value of 7 percent is surprisingly high).

Germans (compared to the European Union average) also have a relatively low opinion of the advantages they see deriving from membership. This results from the opinion, persistent in Germany, that the Germans are the "paymasters of Europe." If one considers that the Germans contribute approximately 28 percent of the EU's budget, then this might explain why (along with the state's momentary indebtedness) people reacted in this way (see Table 6.3).

If one compares these figures with earlier surveys within the European Community (for example, the spring 1982 survey) one can see that there have been alarming shifts of opinion in all member states of the European Union. It seems that now, because of the debts brought about by German reunification, the Germans are much less willing to finance activities outside the country—even within the EU. Moreover, the Germans know that East Central Europe will further burden them with increased responsibilities, which other EU member states won't pick up in equal measure. This has caused some people to become insecure about Germany's future economic situation. The individual has little patience with this (perceived) unequal share of burdens. This also applies to the public debate on the

Table 6.2
Is Membership in the European Union a Good Thing?

Question: "Generally speaking, do you think your country's membership in the European Community/Union is a good thing, a bad thing, neither bad nor good?"

(EB = Eurobarometer)

Col 1: EB41-Result / Col 2: Change from EB40	Belgium		Denmark		Germany West		Germany East		Greece		Spain		France	
A good thing	56	-3	53	-5	52	-2	45	-7	64	-9	50	-4	50	-5
A bad thing	10	+1	26	+4	13	0	8	-1	9	+5	14	0	13	-1
Neither bad nor good	30	+4	18	+1	31	+3	41	+7	20	+5	31	+5	33	+7
No opinion	4	-1	3	+1	5	0	6	+1	7	-1	6	0	5	0
Total	100		100		101		100		100		101		101	

Col 1: EB41-Result / Col 2: Change from EB40	Ireland		Italy		Luxembourg		The Netherlands		Portugal		Great Britain		EU 12	
A good thing	72	-1	68	0	71	-1	77	-3	54	-5	43	0	54	-3
A bad thing	7	-1	5	-2	9	+3	5	0	13	+1	22	0	13	0
Neither bad nor good	16	+1	20	+2	17	-3	16	+4	32	+6	29	-1	27	+2
No opinion	5	+1	7	+1	3	0	2	-1	3	-1	7	+2	5	0
Total	100		100		100		100		102		101		99	

Source: Eurobarometer No. 41, published by European Commission, Early Release, June 7, 1994.

Table 6.3
The Advantage of Membership in the European Union

Question: "If you consider all Aspects, do you think your country has derived an advantage from European Community/Union membership or not?"

	Belgium		Denmark		Germany				Greece		Spain		France	
					West		East							
Col 1: EB41-Result Col 2: Change from EB40	R	Ch	R	Ch	R	Ch	R	Ch	R	Ch	R	Ch	R	Ch
Advantage	49	+1	64	-1	41	-1	40	+2	69	-10	38	-2	39	-1
No advantage	27	-1	26	0	38	-1	37	-5	18	+9	43	+4	40	+1
No opinion	24	+1	10	0	21	+2	23	+4	14	+2	19	-3	22	+1
Total	100		100		100		100		101		100		101	

	Ireland		Italy		Luxembourg		The Netherlands		Portugal		Great Britain		EU 12	
Col 1: EB41-Result Col 2: Change from EB40	R	Ch	R	Ch	R	Ch	R	Ch	R	Ch	R	Ch	R	Ch
Advantage	81	+1	55	+3	67	-2	71	+3	70	+1	41	+8	47	+1
No advantage	11	-2	23	0	19	-3	13	-4	23	+1	43	-5	34	-1
No opinion	8	+1	22	-3	14	+4	17	+2	8	-1	16	-2	19	-1
Total	100		100		100		101		101		100		100	

Source: Eurobarometer No. 41, published by European Commission, Early Release, June 7, 1994.

"Treaty on the European Union," the Treaty of Maastricht, which will change present structures and will introduce new impulses.

At the same time, the discussion on Maastricht is a sign of greater "normalcy" in Germany: the European integration process has become a controversial political topic just like other important questions. In the past, European policy was practically a taboo subject; it was kept out of political debate; Germany's history and the catastrophic course that National Socialism charted for the country made almost all Germans recognize the importance of Europe. But the referendum in Denmark showed that even good democrats could be opponents to the Treaty of Maastricht. Thus, the future of Europe is no longer a topic for Sunday discussion panels but part of the difficult opinion-making process in German political culture. European policy has become part of the general malaise that people have toward industrial society, it is an extension of the fears and concerns, the demands and expectations that are directed at the political party structure.

The Treaty of Maastricht significantly strengthened the European Parliament's status within the institutional framework of the EU;[82] however, there are historical and legal reasons why the European Parliament (EP) has not enjoyed the full rights of a parliament. With the Treaty of Maastricht,[83] the EP—whose members are elected in the member states according to their own election laws—at least received new rights in the appointment of the European Commission, in the European legislative process and in the budgetary process. The first direct elections to the European Parliament were held in 1979.

In the last European elections, on June 12, 1994, the CDU/CSU parties received a total of 38.8 percent—an improvement over their 1989 election results (when they received 37.7 percent, though without the participation of what was still the GDR). The SPD received 32.2 percent (in 1989, 37.3 percent). The two large national parties thus received a combined total of 71 percent. The Greens received 10.1 percent (in 1989, 8.4 percent), whereas the FDP only received 4.1 percent, not enough to make it into the European Parliament.

What is significant is that the right-wing radical Republikaner—who managed to pick up 7.1 percent in 1989—only received 3.9 percent; and a specifically anti-Maastricht party ("Alliance of Free Citizens") was only able to pick up 1.1 percent. The communist SED successor party, the PDS, received 4.7 percent of the votes. These results show that pro-European parties were elected, and specifically anti-Europeans (such as the Republikaner) and the "Alliance of Free Citizens") were soundly rejected, despite the emergence of Euroskepticism—a clear signal *for* Europe.

In other European countries, the ruling governmental parties encountered setbacks (e.g., in Britain and Spain). In France, parties opposed to Europe— right-wing extremists, communists and the party list of the archconservative Count Villiers—were able to pick up 30 percent of the vote. If one included the Maastricht opponents who voted for the conservative combined party list (RPR/UDF) or for the left-radical dissidents, the proportion of voters who opposed further European integration would be similar to the percentage who voted against the Maastricht Treaty in the referendum of September 1992, when the Treaty passed by a very slim majority.

Germany's Union parties—CDU and CSU—succeeded in capitalizing on their competence in European and economic matters. A headline of the Dutch newspaper *De Volkskrant* (July 14, 1994) read "Kohl Is the Last True European." The article stated: "It's high time that Europe reconsiders its verdict on Germany's head of government. He manages to go against all the populist trends—'the German mark will be eliminated,' 'refugees are robbing us of our homes and jobs'—and succeeds in keeping the European ideal alive in Germany. When he said that German and European integration are two sides of the same coin, he kept his promise."

Expanding the former European Community into a political union and creating a Currency Union are the main goals of the Maastricht Treaty. It is mostly the latter objective that has become a focus of political discussions. What goes largely unmentioned is the fact that Frankfurt will most probably become the seat of the future European Central Bank (ECB). Both the Treaty and its supplements as well as the statute for the ECB meet—on almost every point—the high requirements which the German government and the German Federal Bank had set for the future European Currency system. In some of its regulations (for example, that monetary stability should take precedence), the contract in fact goes beyond the German Federal Bank's own regulations.

A timetable was also set for the Currency Union. But in the meantime, every member state must go through preparatory stages and meet certain economic criteria in the transition to a single currency. This applies to areas such as the inflation rate, the exchange rate, the long-term interest rate, the net lending rate and the deficit levels of the national budget. Considering the high deficit level incurred by German reunification, even the Germany of 1994 would have had difficulties joining the Currency Union. Whether the Currency Union can be realized by 1999, as the Treaty of Maastricht foresees, is highly questionable from today's vantage point.

A single European currency would quickly become the second most important reserve currency. Whereas the German mark's share in the currency reserves is 20 percent compared to the U.S. dollar's 57 percent, a single currency would have a share of more than 35 percent. That would strengthen Europe's financial position, would reduce the risk of currency rate fluctuations and would increase the willingness of non-European firms to invest in EU-Europe. The German economy, with the highest percentage share in intra-Community trade, would probably benefit most of all, for her cost-effectiveness would become even more apparent.

In fact, the Treaty of Maastricht realized the majority of Germany's central interests concerning the Economic and Currency Union. In the Treaty, the following principles were unconditionally accepted:

- The future ECB would be completely independent from government interference or interference from other agencies of the Community.
- Member states would give their central banks full autonomy by the start of the third phase of the Economic and Currency Union.
- The major goal of a unified currency policy would be price stability (which is also Article 3 in the German Federal Bank's regulations).

But the Germans continued to be gripped by a traumatic fear: that the Economic and Currency Union, as formulated in Maastricht, would destroy the German mark and would foist an unstable single currency on them. Over the long term, this "esperanto currency" (so the argument went) would rob Germans of their hard-earned savings and undermine the future of their economy. The Germans went through two currency reforms. One German tabloid stated years ago: "The good German mark has to die." This formulation shows to what extent psychological factors play a role when it comes to eliminating Germany's (apparently) most important national symbol—the German mark.

It now seems that the German currency's importance in shaping national identity was underestimated. Germans felt that their currency was being "sold out" for the dubious advantage of a less stable European currency, a mere "abstraction," and they feared that this simultaneously meant a "sell-out" of their cultural identity—as vague as that was. Here, too, the question of security set the tone of political debate.

With the ratification of the Maastricht Treaty in all European member states, Europe made the qualitative leap from "Community" to "European Union." An intra-governmental conference is planned for 1996. It will bring together European heads of government and state with members of the European Commission to discuss how the Community can be furthered and what kind of political decisions will be needed to realize these goals. It should help to bring about a consensus on the future development of the political union. In connection with this, the German Supreme Court decided on October 12, 1993, that the government should make sure the democratization of the European Union continues at the same pace as the integration process. There are structural problems within the European Union, and this situation is bound to become more complicated when new members join after 1996.

For example, the system of a rotating presidency, whereby a representative from a national government occupies a chair for a half-year period, has already reached its limits. The "troika principle" only barely covers up the fact that the six-month cycle of rotating presidencies is not very efficient, if one considers the volume and the complexity of the problems that need to be solved. New members, and smaller nations in particular, could be inordinately burdened or even overwhelmed. Besides, an increase in membership will make it increasingly difficult to achieve unanimity in policy questions. The present procedure requiring a qualified majority has its drawbacks, which will probably only intensify as the Union expands.

Moreover, the legislative authority of the Parliament has not reached its full potential; the procedures of controlling and engaging the EU's political decision-making process are too confusing; a strengthening of the European Parliament's structures has become essential. One of the most important ways to increase the Union's legitimacy is to develop it further into a bicameral system: the European Parliament would form one chamber, and the other would be a European State Chamber formed from the Union's Council. This would combine both democratic and federal principles. At the same time, the Commission—as guarantor of the European Treaties—must be made even more independent from national governments. But for now, most of the legitimacy will continue to derive from the member states. What the European Union needs is a catalogue that clearly defines competency distribution.[84]

The individual reform proposals will also have to take into account the "subsidiarity principle"[85]—one of the goals written into the Treaty of Maastricht. This holds that Europe should only take on responsibilities if these cannot be realized better and more effectively at a national or regional level. The negative image of a European "superstate," which is often presented in public, but which only distracts from the fact that it is the member states who push off their problems onto Europe, should not become the goal of European policy. But this is unlikely, since nation-states will continue to be the decisive factor in most political questions.

Often, the idea of European integration is more attractive outside the European Union than within the member states themselves. This is clearly revealed by a long list of candidates seeking entry into the Union. Following the accession of Austria, Finland and Sweden, there are several others waiting to get in (Switzerland, Malta, Cyprus and Turkey). Moreover, several East Central European states (such as Hungary, Poland, the Czech Republic) have indicated a desire to join. But, as the experience with a country like Greece has shown, allowing some countries to join too quickly (except for prosperous EFTA countries that as net payers would contribute their share to the EU budget) could endanger the present economic and political stability of the Union.

The essential dilemma is the question to what extent the extension of the Union conflicts with the strengthening of its democratic foundations. This is demonstrated in the following connection: the more members that the European Union has, the more complicated its decision-making procedures will become—if those procedures aren't changed by the intra-governmental conference of 1996. There are some people within the EU who would like to see candidates be admitted quickly because it would make it more difficult to strengthen the democratic political foundations of the EU.[86]

Moreover, the four less prosperous nations of the EU—Spain, Ireland, Portugal and Greece—will probably want to drag their feet when it comes to new EU memberships, because they are not too keen on sharing funds from the regional and structural funds with countries even poorer than they are—unless the Community's coffers can be filled through the admission of richer partners. These will continue to be explosive issues in the European Union.

Moreover, equally significant is that the expansion of the European Union could change its political power constellation. Without question, European integration in the past proceeded only if Germany and France agreed on the course. The Franco-German Friendship Treaty of 1963 established the vision of a common European future. The most effective initiatives for the continuance of the integration process came from both France and Germany. The two countries were an engine that jump-started the integration process after many stalls and crises over the years. But this privileged Franco-German relationship also led many of the smaller member states to think that they were too dominant within the European Union and that they passed over the smaller states when it came to agreements. The fears of a Franco-German supremacy were recently revealed in the difficulty of finding a successor to Jacques Delors as president of the European Commission.

How sensitively other member states react to German proposals on European political issues was demonstrated when the CDU/CSU's party whip, Wolfgang Schäuble, announced the party's "Reflections on European Policy" on September 1, 1994. He proposed five interrelated points, namely, (1) the further institutional development of the Union and the realization of the subsidiarity principle, including the transfer of competencies; (2) the further solidification of the "core"; (3) the intensification of Franco-German relations; (4) the strengthening of the foreign and security policy potential of the Union; and (5) the extension to the East.

These reflections are based on a "flexible method of integration": what is important here is "that the countries who are willing and able to go further in their level of cooperation and in the process of integration shouldn't be obstructed by the vetos of other members." This refers to the idea that Europe proceed at different speeds—a taboo subject in discussions over Europe until then. Though Maastricht had also accepted the principle of varying time frames, no one had thought of taking this very realistic principle and making it into one of the organizational aspects of European policy. The discussion in response to these reflections show how (at times emotionally) people can react to German proposals. It showed that people were already beginning to discuss the future model of the European Union (partially in preparation for the 1996 intra-governmental conference).

On the whole, differences remain between Germany and France as well. The French political elite—as opposed to the large majority of the population—reacted to German unification with restraint. France's main motive for European integration was to incorporate Germany into Western Europe, which German reunification made clear yet again. Moreover, the French react very sensitively to any comment Germany makes about her political future, and they need to be reassured repeatedly that there will be no change in Germany's Western integration.

In that sense, France has a problem with discussions about the expansion of the EU. Whereas in the past France was the *political* leader in the EC and Germany was the *economic* powerhouse, the EU now threatens to expand to the north (becoming more Protestant) and potentially (in the next stage) to the east. Some in France fear that their influence could diminish in a larger Union, and that new political constellations—perhaps even between England and Germany—could emerge. But it is hardly likely that Germans in principle will forsake their privileged relationship to France, particularly since they have built up a solid consultative network—more intensive than with any other nation—that provides for a common political course.

At the same time, many Germans recall France's reluctance over German reunification—whereas many Frenchmen are afraid that their country will become more "German" through the "backdoor of Europe." France's particular sensitivity to German influence was shown in her reaction to the German government's efforts to promote German, along with French and English, as one of the three official procedural languages. (Altogether there are actually eleven official languages since the 1995 expansion.)

The European integration process is a response to centuries of European conflict. The European states' decision to join under the roof of the European Union is less of a reaction to the challenges of the Cold War and to communist expansion than a realization that peaceful cooperation between states has become a necessity. Jean Monnet, considered by many "the Father of Europe," wrote in 1944 (i.e., still in the midst of World War II), "There will be no peace in Europe if states organize solely on the principle of national sovereignty and on the policy of prestige and nationalist protection." He stated further, "Europe must be united, and not only through cooperation, but also by voluntarily transferring some of its own national sovereignty onto a form of central union—a union that would have the authority to lower tariffs, to create a larger European market and to prevent a nationalist resurgence."[87] Thus, the actual motivating factor behind European integration is overcoming a bellicose nationalism; moreover, it is also based on the realization that mankind's most important questions are no longer solvable within the framework of the nation-state.

One look at European policy shows that the European Union remains the magnetic force that attracts the individual states; and as a community, it is also able to offer political and economic stability. At the same time, there is still a lot to do in order to guarantee the system's effectiveness in the face of new challenges and to make the system more transparent to the citizens of Europe. "A Europe of Citizens," as the slogan goes, can only be realized if the citizens see and understand that Europe is there *for* them.

DEVELOPMENT POLICY

Democracy as a Policy for Peace

According to a wise old Indian saying, we have not inherited the world from our fathers but have borrowed it from our children. If the developed nations do not live up to their responsibilities to the Third World, then this will have repercussions for the next generation living on the planet. The realization that we no longer live in separate regions of the world, but in *one* world,[88] may seem like a truism to many. But in order for Germany and other industrial nations to survive, there can no longer be small pockets of prosperity while the rest of mankind suffers from hunger, poverty and unemployment, or experiences economic and financial instability.

It is an outdated idea to think that events in industrial nations and in developing countries can occur in isolation from each other. The world is growing smaller, and television brings us live broadcasts from around the world. But television coverage actually makes the prosperous "West" and "North" appear a lot more attractive to people in developing nations; thus international media coverage precipitates migration. A brain drain from these countries often results, because it is often the most prosperous and educated who decide to sell their belongings and look for refuge, that is, asylum, in Germany and other industrial nations with the help of so-called dragnet organizations.

It has become increasingly clear that the fundamental problems of mankind cannot be solved within the borders of the nation-states. Some people say we are living in a "global village." Moreover, the problems of development policy can no longer be solved using the classical instruments of diplomacy or foreign policy. In many ways we already have a "world domestic policy." In any case, most individuals still focus on the nation-state in which they live. It is difficult to convince them that the processes in developing nations—above all in the medium to long term—will also affect developments in the more prosperous regions of the world.

The following questions show how serious the situation is:

1. What will happen when Africa can no longer feed its growing population?
2. What will happen when the governments in Southeast Asia can no longer meet the challenges of doubling population growth rates?
3. What will be the consequences for industrial nations when the ecosphere can no longer sustain increasing energy consumption and the growing strain of waste and pollution?
4. What will be the consequences for the industrial nations when the Amazon's rain forest is burned down, or when the desert edges its way into formerly rich agricultural regions?

The survival of industrial nations is connected to ecological developments such as the ozone hole, the greenhouse effect, the expansion of the desert and the destruction of the rain forest, for they threaten nature as a whole—and therefore the Germans and the rest of the world. International solidarity of all people is the ethical foundation for development policy, and in the same measure, the population itself must begin to realize that events in the developing world are not isolated incidents but affect Germans too—both directly and indirectly—in the long term.

Despite the criticism it often receives, development policy has actually been remarkably successful, and this deserves to be mentioned. Life expectancy on the whole has been raised; there has been an increase in literacy, the elimination of certain epidemic diseases, less starvation, access to clean water and improved sanitary conditions for a greater number of people. Yet the population explosion has undermined many of these advances, and political and military conflicts—particularly in Africa—have destroyed much of the progress that has been achieved.

Faced with the challenges in some developing countries (and above all in Africa), many people have become more cautious about the prospects for development aid. Some even refer cynically to "fatal aid," because they claim that development aid itself is one of the main reasons for underdevelopment in many countries. What is often criticized is the fact that it seems to be the economic and political interests that drive donor nations, and that huge developmental bureaucracies have arisen whose own survival has become more important than the actual aid itself: a large share of development aid therefore gets wasted.

Aside from these sweeping claims, which eventually have to be addressed, there is truly the serious question whether development aid does to some degree corrupt the political elites in the individual countries and decrease their willingness to improve the economy through their own efforts. Sometimes, then, development aid does stem from the short-term economic interests of the donor nations and is not oriented to the needs of the receiver nations. Donor nations will therefore have to address the question whether development aid in its present form has truly resulted in effective support or whether perhaps the export of Western values and modernization proposals has in some ways precipitated their decline into poverty.

The debates in the 1970s and 1980s in particular required us to rethink our policy. In the meantime, many things have changed in development policy. Whereas before the goal was to satisfy the basic needs of the nations, today it is to encourage the poorer sectors of the population to participate in the process, to create conditions that will enhance development and to emphasize the important role of nongovernmental organizations. The "cross-sectional" dimension of environmental policy is now emphasized, that is, seeing environmental policy as a form of developmental responsibility as well as recognizing the importance of educating and training—in particular—women. But the actual motivation to "develop" must come from the affected nations themselves. What people today often criticize is the failure to promote generally accepted basic principles—such as in the field of human rights.

In the period between 1980 and 1991, the twenty-four member states of the Organization for Economic Cooperation and Development (OECD), to which the twelve EU states and twelve other western industrial nations at that time belonged (including the United States, Canada and Japan), contributed $450.6 billion in official developmental aid (ODA).[89] In relation to GNP, Norway pays the most; the least comes from the United States. Many countries have not even come close to giving the targeted 0.7 percent of their GNP to development aid (the United States, 0.2 percent; Japan, 0.3 percent; France, 0.63 percent; Germany, 0.39 percent; Great Britain, 0.31 percent; Canada, 0.46 percent; Denmark, 1.02 percent; Norway, 1.16 percent; Switzerland, 0.46 percent; and Austria, 0.30 percent).[90] Germany is in fourth position in what it gives in absolute terms (after the United States, Japan and France).

There has been a great deal of disappointment in many developing nations that not much has happened since the conference in Rio in 1992 (where the "Agenda 21" was signed by 140 heads of government and state). It was estimated then that the realization of "Agenda 21" would cost approximately $600 billion between the years 1993 and 2000.[91] The "Agenda 21" covers the entire spectrum of the world's environmental problems—from climate control to forest protection. It is also disappointing that in 1992, support from non-OECD members (i.e., the Arab states) decreased once again, to the low point of $1.5 billion, after it had already decreased by 50 percent from the year before (from $8.58 billion to $4.22 billion).[92]

There are examples of countries who have made the leap from the status of classical developing nation to economically viable democracy. But alongside these encouraging examples, there are countries and regions who do not instill such optimism. On the whole, environmental policy must be seen in a differentiated way, because the regions of the world have all evolved very differently. Without a doubt, Africa's problems are the most serious, whereas in Latin America and particularly in Asia, changes have taken place that have generally led to greater economic and political stability and to a higher level of modernization.

The end of the Cold War has, in some senses, led to a new stage in development policy. Whereas in the past economic support was based on political factors—such as, how could one reduce the sphere of influence of

Moscow and her satellite states—decisions can now be made according to different political criteria (such as, how can one promote democracy in the affected nations and to what extent are the individual governments willing to undertake reforms that will benefit the poorer sectors of the population).

Here is the situation in individual world regions:

Africa

The fact that the social, economic and ecological problems of Africa have multiplied and the number of brutal conflicts have increased has led to "Afropessimism," as some people in Germany have referred to it. Upon completion of this text, there were major crises and armed conflicts in eleven of the fifty-three countries in Africa, namely, Algeria, Angola, Burundi, the Congo Republic, Egypt, Liberia, Mozambique, Rwanda, Somalia, the Sudan and—until the recent elections—South Africa as well. The causes for this low level of progress—aside from the unfavorable geographic and climatic conditions—are rooted in internal and external factors. Internal factors include the repression of the people (particularly minorities), corruption and the state's involvement in the economy.

Some of the external factors include worsening export conditions, partially resulting from bureaucratic barriers and overvalued exchange rates, as well as low currency reserves and an extremely high deficit level. In the forty-seven nations south of the Sahara (excluding the Republic of South Africa), whose population of 525 million people make up about a tenth of the world's total, the 1991 level of GNP was about $350 per capita.[93] In comparison, the per capita total for the industrial countries within the OECD was $21,020. The sub-Saharan states' share of world trade was approximately 1 percent. The debt situation was just made worse by the low currency reserves resulting from this poor economic performance as well as the high level of imports and rising interest rates.

What is needed here, just as in the regions of Latin America and Asia, is a series of measures to combat poverty. These measures would include promoting democratic and market economic structures, social reforms and environmental protection, and investments in education, health and the infrastructure. But Africa also has economic regions that are less capable of developing themselves by their own initiative: they not only require a transfer of knowledge and technology but an internationally coordinated, long-term program that will help finance regular expenditures in the fields of education and health. But the goal must still be long-term self-sufficiency. This will require donor nations to participate in controlling the

public expenditures of these countries (a politically problematic proposition) so that they can justify their involvement to their own people.

Latin America

There are more grounds for optimism in the countries of Latin America,
though here too social reforms are necessary to eliminate—or at least
diminish—the dramatic gap between rich and poor. About one tenth of the
population of the developing world (approximately 445 million people)[94]
today live in Latin America. But about a third of the domestic product of
all developing countries comes from this region. And the average per capita
income—despite a decline in the 1980s—is still five to six times as high as
in South Asia or sub-Saharan Africa.[95] But since there has yet to be a
complete social reform, such as a land or tax reform, major social disparities
continue to exist in Latin America. Forty percent of the population lives in
poverty—half in extreme poverty (i.e., not capable of providing for their
basic needs)—though the economic potential of the region is so great that
its entire economic condition could be improved over the long term.

Social reforms are also needed if the democratization of the region that
started several years ago is to continue. Though many countries in Latin
America (except for Cuba and—to a certain degree—Peru) now have
governments in power that have been democratically elected (at least
officially), democratic ideals are far from being established, and legal
protection and freedom are still precarious. There continue to be substantial
human rights violations since the legal systems in these countries are
underdeveloped. And often the military is like a state within the state.

To be able to achieve its full potential, Latin America will need a
knowledge transfer so that it can improve its political, economic, social and
ecological framework; and it will need fairer chances on the world markets
for its products, particularly through the elimination of agricultural subsidies. Further, aid is needed to solve the problem of debt. Approximately 40
percent (i.e., $420 billion) of the developing world's foreign debt arises
from Latin America.[96]

But here too there are some hopeful signs. The proportion of debt to GNP
fell from 60–100 percent to 40 percent.[97] The dramatic flight of capital also
seems to be over. The flow of capital, which in 1993 reached a level of $65
billion (in 1992, $58.1 billion),[98] shows that the region has become more
attractive to both national and international investors alike, which has
benefited most of all the countries that have undertaken extensive economic
reforms—for example, by fighting inflation and by planning a solid financial policy and privatizing state industries.

Asia

The enormous ethnic, cultural, political and economic diversity of the Asian countries, where more than half the world's population lives, is reflected in their different rates of progress. Thus, the bustling economic centers of East Asia were able to expand their position on the world's markets, whereas there continued to be high levels of poverty in most other countries of Western and South Asia. Next to the economic powerhouse Japan, it is the so-called newly industrialized countries (NICs) that are setting the pace in the economic development of Asia: Taiwan, Singapore, Hong Kong, South Korea, and now also Thailand, Indonesia and Malaysia. The "Chinese economic region" (the People's Republic of China, Hong Kong, Taiwan) was able to increase its share of the developing countries' GNP from 10 to 25 percent over the past ten years.

In East Asia, the number of poor people—those with a per capita income of less than one dollar a day—was reduced by more than 100 million, particularly in China and Indonesia.[99] What contributed to this were substantial improvements in the agricultural sector, a lower level of population growth (with the exception of Malaysia) and extensive efforts to improve the levels of education, health and family planning. In the Central Asian republics of Kazakhstan, Kyrgyzstan, Tajikistan, Turkmenistan and Uzbekistan (all members of CIS), the average income is at the same level as medium-income countries.

In contrast, half of the world's 1.1 billion poor live in South Asia. What is needed here is a development policy directed at eliminating poverty; accordingly, the Federal Republic will begin to discontinue her development policy with the more dynamic Asian countries. Political decisions that improve trade fairness are more important for these countries than direct financial assistance. Moreover, they will also need qualified specialists— for example, to help with a system of taxation, in the establishment of a social security system or in the financial sector. Since the more advanced Asian states in the meantime also contribute to development aid, a "cooperation triangle" could eventually emerge. This would mean that Germany could help more prosperous Asian states with their development aid to poorer Asian nations.

As one of the world's most successful political associations, ASEAN (Association of Southeast Asian Nations) is also an extremely important factor. In the last ten years, the growth rates in the member states Thailand, Malaysia, Indonesia and Singapore have been on average three to four times as high as in the industrial states. The Philippines, Brunei and now Vietnam are also members of ASEAN. Though it was primarily political reasons that led to the original formation of ASEAN in 1967—namely, the Cold War and the conflict in Indochina—now the organization intends to expand to Laos and Cambodia, and eventually Burma.

AFTA (Asian Free Trade Area), on the other hand, is only progressing at a snail's pace. But ASEAN is not the only regional grouping in Asia. Since November 1993, there is also APEC (Asia-Pacific Economic Cooperation)—a consortium of almost twenty countries of the Pacific Rim, including the ASEAN countries, the United States, Japan, China and Australia. But there are many differences of opinion within this group. As a counterweight, Malaysia is supporting an East Asian Economic Caucus (EAEC), which would include ASEAN, Japan, South Korea, and China, but not the "Anglo-Saxon" countries. Then there is also the South Asian Association of Regional Cooperation (SAARC), which includes India, Pakistan, Bangladesh, Sri Lanka, Nepal, Bhutan and the Maldives.

Problems Confronting the Developing Countries

Economic Situation: The average growth rates in the developing countries fell from 8 percent in the 1960s to 6 percent in the 1970s and 3–4 percent in the 1980s. Their foreign debt rose from $100 billion in 1970, to $650 billion in 1980, to a level of $1,350 billion in 1990.[100] Though the developing countries did all they could to increase exports, the OECD's share of total world trade continued to increase: from 63 percent in 1980, to 70 percent by the end of the decade (see Chapter 6). This is partially due to a decline in oil prices and the prices of other natural resources, whereas several of the newly industrializing countries were able to increase their share of international trade by exporting manufactured goods.[101] Many developing nations are burdened with an enormous debt, and there are various causes for this situation. There have also been successful attempts to absolve the debt of extremely poor debtor nations.

Poverty and Starvation: The *World Development Report 1990* of the World Bank states: "The highest priority for political decision-makers in the world should be to lower the level of poverty."[102] About 1.1 billion people still suffer from hunger, and about 800 million of those are probably chronically underfed.[103] They have no means of sustaining themselves, because they have no jobs and cannot earn a living. In 1970, there were 3.7 billion people in the world; in 1990, it was already 5.3 billion; in 2010, it will be 7.2 billion.

Overpopulation: The population explosion is a serious global problem. According to estimates of the United Nations, the world's population will increase from 5.7 billion today to 6.2 billion in the year 2000. Three billion will live in cities. The global population is rising faster than at any time in history: about 3 people a second, and more than 255,000 a day. In the 1990s, global population will increase by 16 percent—a sixth of the world's present population. About 93 percent of this growth will be in the developing countries of Africa, Asia and Latin America. The United Nations discovered further that population in developing countries had doubled from 2.2 billion to 4.4 billion in the thirty-two years between 1962 and 1994. It will increase by another 7 billion by 2025. The total population will then reach 8.5 billion. On the other hand, the population level in industrial nations (Europe—including the former Soviet Union—North America, Japan, Australia and New Zealand) has increased from 832 million in 1950 to 1.2 billion in 1994. By 2025, these countries will have an estimated population of 1.4 billion. In 2025, the industrial nations will make up about a sixth of the world's population.[104]

One of the main reasons for the population explosion in the developing nations is poverty, for families see having many children as a form of financial security in old age. Another important reason for the high population growth is the socially inferior position of women in many of the societies. Even with a dramatic decline in the birth rate, demographic pressures will remain intense. Even now, half the people in the developing nations are younger than twenty!

Rising population rates have often undermined economic advances, and the competition for scarcer resources has increased. The UN Conference on Population and Development, which was inaugurated on September 7, 1994, in Cairo, exposed how controversial some aspects of population development could be. Numerous criticisms were voiced, particularly by the Vatican, which feared that abortion was being encouraged as a means of family planning. But abortion is also generally forbidden in Islam, being allowed only in emergencies—for example, when the mother's life is in danger, or when the pregnant woman has AIDS. Some Islamic holy men therefore rejected the goals of the world population conference, even though parts of the Islamic world often stressed the fact that Islam is not opposed to family planning as such.[105]

Environmental Problems: Both industrial nations, where until recently the majority of environmental pollution has taken place, and developing countries overexploit natural resources; but it has intensified in the latter due to the rise in population: this is, according to United Nations experts, the cause of 79 percent of the world's deforestation. Every year, 25 million tons of good soil are destroyed by erosion.[106] According to statistics from the Food and Agriculture Organization (FAO) of the United Nations, already by 1987 86 percent of the 1.7 billion cubic meters of the wood cleared from the tropics had been burned. Firewood is the most important energy source in most developing countries, because 70 percent of the population must use it to cook and heat. The death of the rain forests shows that population growth is closely linked to environmental problems.

Armed Conflicts and Mass Migration: In 1992, there were approximately twenty-nine conflicts with military repercussions: the majority of them involved developing countries. About 6 million people lost their lives—the highest number in seventeen years.[107] The hope that the end of the East-West conflict would relieve refugee pressures was not realized; instead, the number of refugees has increased since 1989—from 14.9 million to 18.2 million by the end of 1992. In the first ten months of 1993, the wave of refugees increased by another 700,000. Since October 1993, the civil war in Burundi has created another 800,000 refugees and has brought the number of refugees in the world to 19.7 million.

Since April 1994 this figure has risen dramatically once again. The civil war in Rwanda led to a massive flow of refugees into neighboring Zaire. Twenty years ago the United Nations High Commission for Refugees (UNHCR) recorded "only" 2.5 million refugees. In 1992, an average of 10,000 people a day were forced to leave their homes. Besides these refugees who leave their country, a further 24.2 million people were forced out of the towns and cities within their own borders due to domestic conflicts.[108] The 20 million or so people who flee their own countries are at least under the auspices of international law, but the 25 million or so exiles who remain in their own country go largely unnoticed.

Irresponsible Elites: Corruption in the developing countries (and not only there) has increased like wildfire. Many developing nations lack a political elite who are not only self-interested but who think primarily about their country's well-being. This situation is also revealed in the increasing tendency to take bribes ("commissions"). Whereas previously, according to specialists, about 5 percent of the order's value was expected as "commission," it can today be as high as 20 percent in some countries.

Further Aspects: Because more and more people are fleeing the countryside and settling in massive slum areas around major urban centers, large cities have become more unmanageable; diseases and starvation are widespread partly because waste and water disposal services do not function. Aside from that, developing countries are afflicted with some of the same serious problems that can be found in industrial countries. One of those is international organized crime: the revenues from the international drug trade for a one-year period totaled DM 400 billion—almost as much as the Federal Republic's total budget. Another one of the serious problems is the rise in epidemics, first and foremost AIDS. According to projections by the World Health Organization, by the year 2000, 10 million people will have been infected with the AIDS virus in Asia alone.[109]

What Can Be Done?

(1) The principle of "help to help oneself" is not pursued enough in development policy. Development policy is wrong if the developing nations see it as a structural policy imposed on them from the outside.[110] If this happens, the population often does not accept the policy. Many of these projects eventually deteriorate as soon as the development volunteers leave the country, because many of the projects are not in the real interest of the native population. Charitable aid can also lead to the opposite of what was intended—except in the cases of catastrophes and humanitarian aid in the narrow sense. For example, secondhand clothes from Europe can endanger the domestic production of textiles, affect the quality of textiles domestically and even cause crime, because people attempt to break into the warehouses where the clothes are stored.[111] Of course, the donation of clothes continues to be essential after major catastrophes.

But even food supplies can be controversial. Even though they are required in catastrophes, there is the danger that countries could become dependent on food supplies from abroad. This might mean that native farmers will no longer produce at the same levels, increasing the dependency on agricultural surpluses from the European Union or the United States. The European Union, for example, offers its subsidized surpluses on the world market; it even offers them to developing countries in the form of development aid. But this is not a meaningful development policy, because it destroys the native suppliers' incentive to produce. Donations of food supplies are a form of humanitarian support; but, on the other hand, they can create a permanent situation of dependency.

(2) There needs to be a clearer strategy toward the developing nations. That is why the German government has emphasized five criteria in its cooperation with them:

- The observance of human rights
- The populace's participation in the political process
- The guarantee of legal protection and the rule of law
- The creation of a market economic order

- The willingness of the governments in question to engage in social and economic reforms

These German criteria have in the meantime been adopted by the countries of the OECD. It is not a question of pressure or sanctions, but rather of encouraging developing countries through "positive measures" to create the right kind of conditions for development policy. The World Bank has similar criteria for "good governance."

However, Germany has been charged with trying to create its own conditions for distributing support and forcing a certain direction on developing countries. But considering the different functions of development aid, it must be linked to certain conditions. Since resources are getting scarcer, Germany cannot continue to try to help everyone equally. The country must set priorities (as well as time frames) whereby those nations should be helped most that show the clearest improvements in their political, social and economic situations and toward the realization of democracy. The goal of such a grand strategy would be to assist those countries that have begun to help themselves. Then these in turn can become role models for other developing countries.

Every country must create, strengthen and maintain its own form of democratic order according to its own value systems, its political traditions and social experiences. At the international level, democracy and the market economy now seem to have become models worthy of imitation. But of course, one cannot expect smooth transitions from authoritarian regimes to democratic systems or from state economies (particularly communist command economies) to a market economy. There will always be a lengthy period of instability.

On the other hand, many dictatorial regimes are now more open than ever to the ideas of democracy and the market economy. There will undoubtedly be periods of setbacks as democracy and market systems consolidate. That is why industrial nations must observe and support processes that will lead to the stabilization of democracy and market conditions. The goal is the worldwide promotion and maintenance of democracy and free markets. What is more important than the transfer of capital is the transfer of know-how to the developing countries, that is, the access to knowledge of how democracy functions, the significance of the basic principles of freedom, equality and justice, why independent courts are essential and which conditions must be realized before a market economy can flourish.

In advising these countries, it is important to stress the creation of regional communal structures, for democracy cannot be imposed from above but must evolve from below. One must make sure that functional elites can develop in the individual countries. East Asia was so successful in its attempts to catch up to the West because of its great efforts to invest in human capital, providing good schools for the broad masses, and educating females as well as males. In this sense, it is necessary to promote small and mid-size companies and to support a middle class, because it is the necessary precondition for any society. A well-functioning administration is equally important, so that training must be provided for members of the civil service.

In all these matters, nongovernmental organizations play a significant role, particularly the German political foundations,[112] for they promote the idea of democracy throughout the world. As experience has shown, wars between democracies are almost inconceivable. In that sense, a policy of democracy is in equal measure a policy for peace. Moreover, partnership programs can also be helpful: to help create decentralized structures and an effective communal administration, communities, associations, and chambers of commerce or trade chambers from industrial countries can put their experience to use within the framework of partnership programs. Of course, one must first ask if market systems can be successfully transplanted into societies where both the socioeconomic requirements and the "capitalist spirit" are lacking. The discussion, for example, on transferring the East Asian success story with its Confucian work ethic to the rest of Asia or Africa is not very realistic.[113]

(3) Poverty can only be controlled successfully by decisions made in the developing countries themselves. Here, the transfer of know-how is particularly important, that is, how the conditions for a national economic policy can be set up to help improve the economic situation (e.g., the protection of property, legal security for national and international investors, currency stability). The reduction in the national debt is also crucial in this regard. Though the industrial states cannot force a nation to accept a specific economic policy, they should favor nations who intend to combat poverty.

A policy that will combat poverty requires the right political conditions— democratic structures and the rule of law. Even without an effective administration, without an equitable tax structure or institutions for self-administration, there are still not enough reliable conditions in place to ensure success.[114] A social infrastructure is needed, as are measures to reduce population growth and an economic policy directed at the elimination of poverty. A policy to combat poverty that encourages countries to help themselves should not be understood as a form of social welfare.

Instead, it must be seen as a means of increasing the productive capacity of poor people. As several projects have clearly revealed, the masses of poor people in the developing nations can be put in a position to improve their situation through their own efforts, because the capacity for self-help is a lot stronger in extremely poor people than many people realize.

The example of the Grameen Bank in Bangladesh shows that even the poorest people can be successful small-scale businessmen if they receive the necessary loans. The bank lists 1.6 million loan holders, and there is a payback ratio of 98 percent. This bank is interesting because the majority of loan holders are women. What is important is that the projects to combat poverty are not projects from foreign organizations, but involve the affected people in the developing countries themselves. In fact, the significant role played by women is often underestimated. Integrating women in the process of development means enhancing their standing; and their higher education, health and legal equality will then help the family structure. In many societies, it is often the women who are the motivating force behind change.

According to the FAO, the situation of hunger can be combated best if the food is grown directly in the developing countries. In the meantime, even the FAO has recognized the need for a market-oriented development policy.[115] But to combat poverty it is also necessary to change the conditions of the world economy—for example, through the elimination of protectionism.

(4) It is now, at the end of the East-West conflict, that a democracy-oriented development policy has the best chances for success. For example, during the Cold War, human rights policy was often used as a political weapon. Even the West's development policy spared dictators if they appeared pro-Western or were strategically important or were economically interesting. Even during the Cold War, there were examples of trying to link foreign aid to the issue of human rights: Jimmy Carter made human rights one of the central themes of his presidency.[116] In the early 1980s, a handful of academics[117] in Germany also called for a "democracy-oriented" development policy. Of course, the question is whether the Western form of democracy can serve as a model for the entire world.

(5) Another important criterion for allocating development aid is the role of the military and the armaments policy in the country. Developing countries spend up to $200 billion a year for armaments: 4 percent of their GNP—or as much as for health and education combined. About 20–30 percent of their foreign debt is linked to weapons imports. On the average, 17 percent of their budgets went to the military.[118] The question that must be asked is if developing nations have actually used development aid to increase the size of their military beyond their true needs.

This arms buildup not only leads to military conflicts (and the misery of refugees), but it also forces industrial nations to make additional expenditures: in 1992 alone, the United Nations was forced to spend approximately $2.7 billion for peacekeeping and peace-making measures.[119] In 1990 and 1991, 10 percent of Germany's public aid expenditures—of which more than DM 1 billion came from the Ministry for Development Aid—went as special payments to individual developing nations to relieve the economic burdens of the Gulf War.[120] That is why one of the major criteria of "good governance" must be based on the armaments and security policies in these nations. But a policy linking development aid to the willingness of donor nations to disarm will only be credible if industrial nations themselves agree on a restrictive arms export policy.

(6) Industrial nations must be prepared to open their borders to goods from developing nations: it is the only way for these countries to obtain hard currency. But the industrial nations should also be interested in free trade: whereas their share of world trade was 63 percent in 1980, they were able to increase the ratio to 70 percent in 1988—while in the developing nations this percentage fell from 30 percent to 22 percent in the same time frame. This development was probably a result of protectionist measures, either through treaties that imposed self-restrictions or through regional trade blocs.[121]

The greater the economic potential of a country, the greater the advantages derived from regional economic blocs. That is why it is particularly important for developing nations to adhere to multilateral treaties and to maintain free access to the world's markets. A common study put out by the World Bank and the OECD concluded that a third of the social gains derived from the Uruguay round would flow to developing nations; that is a disproportionate amount in their favor measured against the number of countries and their share of international trade.[122]

All attempts to help developing nations through protectionist measures or through bilateral agreements—particularly with the United States and the former Soviet Union—did not fire up the economies as was expected. International free trade—the objective of the GATT agreement—offers developing nations the chance to put their competitive products on the world's markets according to (fair) market prices. This is the only way for these nations to obtain the hard currency needed to build up their economies and to achieve self-sufficiency. But it goes without saying that there must also be free capital markets and positive economic conditions in the countries themselves.

In general, developing nations should derive advantages from GATT. Past experience has shown that we need not expect worse trade conditions for developing nations, even though some have feared that this would be the result of free trade. Free trade in the spirit of the GATT means free and equal trade partners. But experience shows that this freedom is not guaranteed on a bilateral trade basis. Projections are that GATT will expand world trade considerably and will produce economic growth. Though the highest growth rates will probably be recorded in Japan, the United States and the most important trade partners of the European Union, the developing nations will certainly not fall short.[123]

The country that will probably benefit most from the agreement, some specialists say, is China—followed by the newly industrializing countries of East and Southeast Asia. Latin American countries are also hoping for advantages, primarily in the agricultural sector, less so in industrial production, where they are less competitive than their Asian rivals. On the other hand, the African-Caribbean-Pacific (ACP) countries, who have special ties to the European Union through the Lomé Agreement, are concerned that GATT will deprive them of their special privileges with the European Union.[124] On the whole, according to projections by the World Bank,[125] the benefits from the recent GATT agreement should be almost as high as the amount of development aid the developing countries received from industrial nations.

(7) The European Union's development policy could also assume greater importance, particularly since its direction has already been set in some ways by the Lomé Agreement and by other associative agreements. However, one should make sure that member states as much as possible discuss the planned actions among themselves, and that "smaller" member states receive equal chances within the EU. In the area of multilateral support, the role of the United Nations must be examined and evaluated.

Conclusion

One must reject development policy that merely supports the indigenous upper classes and that is not interested in bringing about reform. There can be little doubt that the reform forces in developing countries would like donor nations to show more self-assurance and resoluteness in their dealings with individual governments.[126] One also must realize that decisions from abroad cannot replace decisions made by native elites. The long-term success of development measures depend less on the actual volume of aid, even though some industrial nations, including Germany, will not be able to avoid contributing more to their development budgets: this was, moreover, the resolution of the 1992 United Nations Conference for Environment and Development in Rio.

Today, "development" should not only be understood as "economic development" or "modernization" but rather as "human development"— creating humane living conditions for everyone in an intact environment. The industrial nations should treat developing nations as partners in solving global problems and in creating an effective partnership within the world community. The majority of developing nations cannot solve the problems of hunger, population growth, debt and environmental damage on their own. It is a vicious circle, for poverty is also the cause for the destruction of the environment; it forces people to resort to overexploitation.

If industrial societies do not help these countries break through the vicious circle, then these problems will in turn catch up with the industrial societies—and not only through a rise in the number of refugees. In order for the industrial nations to survive, they will have to make development policy a central issue! "Global security" is being defined in different terms today. We must begin to realize that security and security policy can no longer be seen as individual nation-state security but as a way of securing man's basic requirements as well as those of the following generation. That is why the term "human security" was coined. If industrial nations are not willing to export stability, then down the line they will import instability. As Kennedy once told Americans: A society that cannot help the many poor can also not offer protection for the few rich.

7

In Lieu of a Conclusion: The Germans in Search of Security—Ten Theses

In the 1960s, there was a heated debate in the Federal Republic over the question "Is Bonn Weimar after all?"[1] Now, when many people are talking about "the end of the Bonn Republic,"[2] and are ringing in the new "Berlin Republic," the question about Germany's future must be raised once again—that is, how is her inner stability and what effect will German policy have on European and international constellations? How do the Germans see themselves? It is difficult to make predictions—especially about the future, Niels Bohr once joked. But there are a few insights that can tell us something about Germany's future course. The following ten theses are on this subject:

Thesis 1: With the collapse of the Berlin Wall and the iron curtain down the center of Germany, the Western world proved it was in theory superior; but what is now lacking is a "Western philosophy." The world has become more difficult and complex. The feeling of insecurity among people is growing, and not only in Germany.

As paradoxical as it may seem, the old bipolar order, which at times threatened to lead to a third world war, gave many people in Europe and Germany a solid foundation. The day of German reunification brought with it the end of the GDR as well as its polar opposite—the "old" Federal Republic. Some people in Germany were disappointed that the bipolar world ended, because they—both in the east and west—were integrated into a defined political system which felt threatened by its rival. The fear of foreign powers and ideologies creates a bond; it conveys a sense of security and orientation through a common enemy—an almost classic psychological mechanism.

Two thoroughly contradictory political systems are now expected to merge into one nation and to become unified. At the moment, the contrasts between east and west are still strong, but they will diminish the more that economic recovery removes the serious social gaps dividing the two regions. Won't this merging of two different societies also mean that west Germans will become more "eastern" and east Germans more "western"?

Abroad, one often asks whether Germany's western integration can last or whether Germany is returning to a tradition of "seesaw politics" between east and west. But right now, those fears can be allayed, particularly since East Central Europe has become more "western"—witness the triumph of western lifestyles and economic forms in many of the former socialist countries. Everywhere the "Western way of life" has become the model.

At the Cold War's end, Western societies must do more to define positive perspectives, for that is the only way that East Central Europe can be permanently Westernized. One of the main reasons we need a "Western philosophy" is that there is a large anti-Western, antimodern coalition of leftist intellectuals (often east German) as well as members of a "New Right." What is often forgotten is that Adenauer had to push through German policy's Western orientation—that is, the transatlantic partnership and integration into Europe—against hefty political opposition, including many intellectuals.

Doesn't reunification once again pose the danger of a renewed anti-Western movement? Might not the anti-Americanism of the nationalistic "right" combine explosively with anticapitalist cultural criticism such as inspires many east and west German "leftist" intellectuals? There has been a tradition of anti-Westernism among both the intellectual right and left. In a sense, the "Bonn Republic" was characterized by somewhat of a paradox: the "internationalist" left followed a national agenda, whereas the "conservative" position, represented by Adenauer, sided with Western integration—European integration.

For a long time, the majority of leftist intellectuals saw this as treason against Germany's traditional middleman role between East and West. As a result, the SPD vehemently opposed the Federal Republic's entry into NATO and the WEU. Instead, in a "German Manifesto" of January 1955, SPD politicians and unionists demanded that "an understanding on the four-power agreement concerning reunification take precedence over establishing a military bloc."[3] Their goal was to isolate Germany from the

East-West conflict, and to form an association of European nation-states that would act as a "third power" between East and West.

In the 1950s, there were repeated attempts to chart a "third course," for example, by authors such as Alfred Andersch: he supported a humanistic socialism for Germany, which could act as a mediator within a socialist Europe ("the free German Republic as a bridge").[4] Then there were politicians such as Kurt Schumacher (SPD), Karl Georg Pfleiderer (FDP) or the CDU politician Jakob Kaiser, who were also interested in Germany serving as a bridge. Kaiser's ideas synthesized elements from the East and West as well as Christian-socialist elements.[5]

These ideas of a "third course"[6] were reactivated in the 1970s and 1980s under the slogan "Middle Europe." For many intellectuals in Hungary or Czechoslovakia, this discussion can be seen as an attempt to free themselves from Moscow's influence—or at least to loosen their dependency. For many West German politicians the idea was attractive because it would have meant a "middle" position for Germany, that is, a third, independent course between East and West.

The "Middle Europe" discussion could have been dangerous, since it could have become a rallying call for new and old nationalists, for pacifists and neutralists—but also a forum for anti-Westerners dissatisfied with the trappings of modern pluralistic societies, with the Western Enlightenment and rationalism. It has been prognosticated that the future fault line in Germany will run between "supporters of the West and her enemies."[7] Even though this might be a little rigid, a rather diverse movement could easily develop against "the West"—a mixture of ideas from cultural pessimists of the "New Right," supporters of a "conservative revolution" and especially east German intellectuals.

According to Hans-Ulrich Wehler, intellectuals like Heiner Müller, Stefan Heym, Christa Wolf, Hermann Kant, Stefan Hermlin, Christoph Hein and Volker Braun are trying "hard to transform their personal anticapitalism into a traditional form of anti-Western resentment, which will help them in their peaceful search for the holy grail of true socialism—and this will, of course, have nothing to do with Honecker's goulash communism and the rule of the Stasi."[8] One of the representatives of the "New Right" declared that "Western integration was an ideological facade that has outlived its usefulness and had created a false consciousness":[9] "the raison d'être of the old Federal Republic is just as dead as the inventory of its antifascist converse."[10]

Momentarily, anticapitalist culture criticism has not yet become a traditional link between the intellectual left and right in Germany; the large majority of Germans take their Western orientation for granted, though they might not be able to give an intellectual justification for it. But in the medium term, one cannot rule out that some of the attacks against the "West," particularly from east German intellectuals, will resonate in the population.

At the same time, we are living in a television age in which the individual is constantly being bombarded by information, giving him the sense that the world's events are being transmitted directly into his living room. But this makes it more difficult to systematize random information, more difficult to find a sense of "orientation." Often, it is hard to distinguish between information and knowledge. Some have described the situation in the following way: We are information giants, but knowledge dwarfs. The talk show principle, based on the exchange of meaningless information, just promotes this loss of orientation.

What are "Western values," what is defensible about them? The present German society, merging into one, presently finds itself in a phase that is characterized by a search for orientation, and this results from the loss of the two ideological rivals. The dramatic events of 1989 led to the loss of the old negative stereotypes and the prevailing world perspectives. This crisis of orientation affects not only Germany, but the entire Western world—even the United States, which until recently offered orientation. The social pluralism of Western democracies fortunately precludes truth from being monopolized. Crises of orientation occur when no exclusive opinion exists because of social pluralism, when the social consensus has to be regained day after day.[11]

In that sense, the demand for a "Western philosophy" does not mean imposing a hermetic, exclusive ideology. Instead, what is needed is the theoretical framework for an open society where Western values—such as freedom, individuality, responsibility of the individual toward society and democracy, social responsibility, rule of law and justice—are practiced (and promoted worldwide). Moreover, if one sees important regions in the world grow in political self-confidence—for example, in Asia, where the terms "Eastern" or "Asian" can be heard more frequently—then it will become important for the West, in turn, to secure its intellectual and political-ethical foundations.

Thesis 2: With the decline in the old patterns of orientation there has been a crisis of modernity which has led people to look for new securities. Individualization and the pluralization of lifestyles have increased the insecurity of the individual.

The collapse of the bipolar world means the loss of clear patterns of orientation. In this century, inhumane utopian societies, based on such ideologies as National Socialism and communism, caused great devastation among the European peoples and their culture—and not only there. Joachim Fest refers to the "end of the utopian age."[12] In an age of pragmatism, it has become difficult for individual citizens to distinguish between the political philosophies underlying the parties that help run the society. But the longing for utopias continues on, most likely due to this pragmatism.

However, it would be premature to declare that all utopias and salvational political programs are dead, because extremist ideologies can have a long life, even if they have been disastrous, like communism. That can explain why many people in the east can be heard saying that socialism was not such a bad idea—it was only the politicians who failed. Salvational political doctrines such as communism—or National Socialism—have the advantage of being "one-dimensional." Whoever believes in some of the ideology's basic principles will not so easily waver from his faith.

Schumpeter was right in pointing out the religious nature of Marxism in a world that has become highly pragmatic and technological: "First of all, the faith offers a system of final principles; it contains the meaning of life and presents an absolute standard against which all actions and events can be measured. Secondly, it promises to lead to those goals, offering a sense of salvation and uncovering those evils from which mankind—or a small, select part of mankind—should be saved . . . Marxist socialism belongs to a creed that promises heaven even before the grave."[13]

Intellectual supporters of a modern liberal democracy—an open society—have a hard time convincing people, or being "fascinating," because of the multidimensionality of their political philosophy. That is why one can expect a revitalization of the socialism debate in Germany. After all, many West German intellectuals were also influenced by the idea of a socialist utopia. As for "the critical GDR intellegentsia," who are now beginning to speak up, they were "more strongly Marxist than the rest of the East Bloc," according to Günter de Bruyn.

Though the GDR's dogmatism "repulsed or suppressed many like-minded thinkers," many of these Marxist-influenced intellectuals have found a new home in the PDS or the SPD.[14] Since the present is characterized by a decline of ideologies and by the political spirit of pragmatism, there is a greater chance that a new ideological discussion will arise, and therefore a new discussion of Marxism due to the spiritual vacuum. But liberal politics in an open society cannot offer utopias, for they are often based on an unrealistic view of man and attempt to satisfy quasi-religious expectations of salvation. At the same time, the political parties and movements should develop and offer "concrete utopias" that can give individuals orientation and that can explain the principle of politics.

A crisis of modernity exists at the moment that seems to have produced an uneasiness with democracy. Modern democracies have created successful, though neutral structures—the market economy, a state ruled by law and order, and the social welfare system. Many citizens, however, find these structures too formalistic. They do not seem to understand that behind these formal structures stand the principles of a liberal democracy, of freedom, justice and solidarity. The sobriety of democracy and of an open society may not be able to satisfy the collective search for security. People who believe in God and in a life after death are less fixated on politics.

One can agree with Wolfgang Schäuble when he says, "By constantly undermining the religious dimension, we threaten to remove the anchor of a modern open society which has freed itself from political utopias."[15] The decline in church and religious ties can easily lead people to have exaggerated expectations toward politics, including the expectation that politics should offer "orientation." It is hard not to notice people's present need for orientation, particularly in this period of declining Christianity and secularization.[16]

This is confirmed by various surveys. When asked in 1991 "Do you believe in God?" 61 percent of surveyed west Germans said, "Yes, I believe that God exists," but only 21 percent of east Germans believed this. When asked the question "Do you believe in life after death?" 51 percent of west Germans said "yes," whereas only 14 percent of east Germans were of this opinion and 83 percent vehemently denied it.[17] The decline of ties to the church in both parts of Germany confirms this tendency toward secularization; on the other hand, there is also a search for new religious and spiritual experiences. So-called youth sects as well as some Islamic and religious movements from the Far East have become more popular, particularly among intellectuals.

How can a modern, pluralistic democracy convey a feeling of orientation? Though the basic consensus among people in a democracy is often greater than one might assume, it is the main characteristic of an open society that the idea of an "orientation" goes against the basic principles of a liberal democratic society. Of course, there must also be limits to liberality and openness—at times when political forces are active in trying to eliminate pluralism and liberalism. But even these forces have the right to free speech and to express their opinion. On the whole, it is very difficult today to convey a sense of orientation when television and the media are breaking the last remaining taboos. But this is not only a German phenomenon.

Secularization and the change in values stand in close connection. The answers to the questions about a change in values are so diverse because "values" are difficult to measure in social science categories. It is not even easy to determine if and to what degree the 1970s value shift continued into the 1980s. Thus Inglehart's "postmaterialism" is not a universal trend. Rather, there is a "value shift," according to Klages,[18] which combines the values of conformity and responsibility with the "postmaterial" values of self-realization. In Germany, one can even refer to a twofold value shift.

Martin and Sylvia Greiffenhagen have come to the following conclusion: "The personalities of many east Germans combine a mélange that includes traditionalist, modern, socialist and capitalist values, which rarely or never occurs in west Germany."[19] West Germans actually think that easteners "have a similar outlook toward so-called secondary virtues—obedience, order, industriousness, love of work, and discipline—that they as West Germans had in the 1950s."[20] German reunification and the deteriorating economic situation in west Germany have allowed the "material" aspects of the values discussion to become more prominent. Many do not see postmaterial values as an alternative to material values but rather as resulting from them: it was prosperity that first made the change in values possible.

Most observers (at least in west Germany) believe, however, that the trend to immaterial outlooks will dominate. Dieter E. Zimmer characterizes various psychological types:

The sensitive person is defined by three characteristics. He is spontaneous: he lives for the moment and does not plan for the long term. He is atheoretical: he values the moment more than any form of ideology. And he loves the world of imagination: he loves dreams, hopes, utopias, the leap out of an uninspired daily routine. His counterpart is the conscientious, responsible "political man," who strives after middle-class respectability—and even more, the "technical man," who praises performance and efficiency and who strives after social success through qualifications and competition.[21]

Many people, including politicians, theologians and academics, assume there has been a "decline in values." This suggests that the "good old days" are in some way desirable—the earlier decades, when social norms had a greater effect on the individual. A more realistic assessment, however, must take into account that the value change is highly ambivalent. The question must be, then, what values are actually mourned—or isn't it that every new generation must raise the value question for itself?[22] Klages comes to the conclusion that acceptance of authority and tradition has declined, whereas the need for "self-realization" has risen.

At the same time, however, the willingness to take on responsibility has grown. This means that people are not principally opposed to taking on responsibilities in organizations. People are willing to impose their own discipline, that is, to discipline themselves to reach certain goals. Klages also assumes that while traditional and formal authorities are accepted less, the general acceptance of norms has increased. So too has the willingness to perform under motivational conditions. What has also risen considerably since the 1950s is the willingness to respect and tolerate others.[23]

The change in values discussion cannot point to a single conclusion, because it is strongly influenced by individual opinion and perspectives. One should not be too pessimistic in evaluating the value shift in Germany, nor in any other modern industrial society for that matter. At the same time, however, one should be alerted to certain alarming tendencies, since a pluralism in lifestyles can blur norms that are important for society. Moreover, the call for greater "multiculturalism" does not facilitate binding rules without which an open society cannot function. In our modern condition— that is, in a polycentric society—values are not transmitted only by a handful of institutions. What has changed is the framework in which the value discussion takes place, for example, through the decline of the once influential milieus: the social classes and the familial ties. But because of the increasing anonymity of society, the individual citizen's need for security has grown, often despite improved material conditions.

It is not the state's function to transmit values. It must occur first and foremost in the family, in churches or in the various organizations that help give people a sense of purpose. If there are no attempts to offer purpose to young people, then they will risk going down dangerous roads while trying to find their own meaning. If democratic societies refuse to take on the question of values, the danger is that extreme organizations will satisfy their search for ideologies and utopias.

Moreover, traditional institutions can convey security as well. Whereas in some societies democratic traditions have existed for centuries, Germany does not have a similar democratic tradition. But it is particularly in moments of crisis that tradition can be highly stabilizing. On the other hand, in the nearly fifty years of its existence, the Federal Republic has become one of the best-functioning democracies in Europe, according to many foreign observers. It has shown itself to be a stable society with a successful economy—and this despite the challenges of German reunification. The federal structure of Germany also contributes to the society's political stability, since it respects the traditions of smaller states and prevents the predominance of a centralized state.

In summary, an increasing (at times exaggerated) trend toward individualization, a decline in the influence of social norms and greater secularization have led to a loss of orientation. Changes in Europe and Germany have also put an end to various certainties—some of them cherished, some of them merely tolerated. Dangerous alternatives present themselves, such as extremist parties and destructive sects. The search for security and orientation has become a central demand, and politics must confront it. Politics must go beyond the efficient solution of day-to-day problems and must start to offer orientation.

Of course, politics cannot take on too much: if politics wants to remain free, then it cannot answer all meaningful questions. But politics can support institutions that help transmit orientation—above all the family!—and help them in their efforts. Beyond that, politics should make sure that the rules of free discussion apply to everyone. Political education should convey that pluralism is not a threat but an opportunity to chart one's own course.

Thesis 3: A democracy requires community and civic spirit, not an elbow society. What we need is "the courage to educate" and "disarmament in the media."

In the old Federal Republic, it was relatively easy to appeal to "solidarity" because increases in the GNP would solve the political necessities of the moment and the problems of solidarity. But today, the distribution of resources is affected by the massive financial transfer from west to east, which is supposed to bring about the speedy social and economic integration of the two parts of Germany.

On top of that, Germany was hit by a worldwide economic recession. A large part of today's dissatisfaction with politics probably stems from the fact that the normal distribution mechanisms in Germany no longer function and that east Germans want to have the same standard of living as the west as soon as possible. They do not want to have the feeling that their "lives meant nothing" just because they lived on the "wrong side," and they demand unconditional solidarity from their west German compatriots.

Politics is called on to fight against the retreat into the private sphere and against exaggerated forms of individualism, and to instill a new community spirit.[24] Leaders need to face up to the fact that no society where the majority of citizens are on an "ego trip" can have a future. Of course, individualization and the pluralization of lifestyles have led to a greater amount of freedom. Some antiquated opinions, resulting from religious confessions or social barriers or a too rigid view of the sexes, have fortunately been overcome.

On the other hand, there has been a development toward "me-ism" and toward an "elbow" society which can burden the social order over the long term. Germans need more community spirit—an understanding for fellow citizens and for the nation as a whole. This appeal is not only directed at the individual, but at all of Germany. Germans must free themselves from their excessive, at times provincial, self-preoccupation and regain their sense of responsibility for others in the world.

Beyond that, politics must begin to take the concerns of young people seriously and to invite them to participate in society. Sensitivity and radicality, subjectivity and impatience are the "privileges" of youth. They must force politicians to constantly question their own actions. A look back at the long history of youth protest should prevent us from dramatizing the problem. Over the din of protest, we should be careful not to lose sight of those young people who are "normal" in the best sense of the word. Violent actions by small minorities should be stopped in their tracks, though one must try to find the reasons behind youthful violence so that precautions can be taken to prevent its occurrence. This would demand the "courage to educate"—even though this principle was undermined by the student revolts. And there must be a social consensus to "disarm the media" to combat the high level of violence in television programming.

Thesis 4: The integration of Germans into one nation after forty years of division will take time. But it will succeed, even if there are bound to be self-tormenting discussions. The Germans are struggling with many different identities—familial, local, regional, national and European. German and European identity are not opposed to each other but are complements.

The national is still what gives people their greatest sense of orientation, and it is the nation that gives them their political reference point. It is natural for man to derive orientation from his immediate surroundings. The old nation-state should not be nostalgically idealized as the highest form of identity, as the place of refuge and security. Karl Dietrich Bracher asks, "Is this not a backward-looking utopia—an ideal from the nineteenth century— but horribly refuted by the twentieth century?"[25]

Bracher warns against defining identity too broadly, even in association with the nation-state: "It would be pretty sad if we were to see the nation-state as our last form of identity. We must become part of a nation, but also a part of humanity, as Herder and Schiller already understood."[26] But one of the decisive questions in Germany's future will be this balance in Germany's identity, an identity that is equally rooted in familial, local, regional and European political structures. Just as there cannot be an opposition between Europe and one's identity as a German, there also should not be an opposition between the idea of democracy and the nation. For a long time to come, the nation-state will continue to be the point of reference—though in some ways, the nation-state model has become antiquated in practice.

For example, more than 35,000 transnational corporations crisscross the globe in a tightly interwoven transport and trade network. Billions of dollars can be transferred in seconds, since all financial capitals are connected by computer. It has been estimated that brokers can deal in up to a billion dollars a day in currency transactions—that is, four times the level of the German budget.[27] This clearly reveals Germany's dependence on decisions from abroad (also in threats to the environment, for example).

All the same, the discussion concerning German national identity is important because every society needs an emotional bond, an identity with a state. This form of discussion can be seen as an opportunity: for the first time in many decades democracy, state and nation are all one and the same. At the same time, history has taught Germans that Germany can only be conceived with and in Europe, and not against Europe. European integration should prevent destructive national interests from one day running rampant again in Europe. For that reason, Germany, as well as other states, must find its position in an overarching transnational structure: it must remain "integrated" in Europe and must live up to its European responsibility—particularly since European integration is also a question of survival.

Another aspect of German identity is its regional roots. Local regional integration continues to remain strong. For that reason, after the peaceful revolution, the federal state structure could quickly take the place of the former ahistorical district system of the GDR. The fact that Germany has sixteen individual—constitutionally protected—federal states, each with its own parliament, government, and so on, does not lead to separatism, but rather to regional pride. In that sense, there is not only an east-west division, but also—for example, in the case of Baden-Württemberg—a contrast between the people of Baden and the people of Württemberg; and in the eastern region, a contrast between Saxony and Brandenburg. Often, a person from Saxony will feel closer to a Bavarian or to a person from Baden-Württemberg than someone from Schleswig-Holstein or from Mecklenburg–West Pomerania. The influence of German regions continues to be strong—maybe it has even increased, now that the world has become "smaller."

Thinking in national terms (!) also requires confronting the nation's past and the fact that crimes (i.e., the Holocaust) were committed in the German name that have no parallel in history. It is understandable that Germans have difficulties with their national identity. The perversion of national thought through Hitler led to German division and to two separate societies. This caused many people to turn away from the idea of nation—particularly West Germans, and most of all youth, who associated their own western half with Germany as a whole. What Renan said about a nation being a "daily repeated plebiscite" can equally refer to Germany: approval for one's nation cannot be dictated but must be renewed daily.

Therefore, politics should contribute toward forming a common German identity. After all, reunification offers us the opportunity to rethink the need for a national consciousness. Without a common identity, the unified state would be artificial. As Richard Schröder expressed it, somewhat laconically: "To be a German is not something special, but something definite."[28] And it has to be based on something more than just acceptance of the Constitution. There also needs to be an emotional component, a feeling of belonging, that derives from the consciousness that we have become a *community of experience* through a common language, culture and history, that we can confront the future in common. Experience teaches the Germans that this kind of feeling can be misused, which should tell them that the act of reflecting on history should not be left to the nationalists. The national must be anchored to the ideals of democracy and human rights. Germany's common traditions and common future challenges will also require us to combine German national consciousness with the idea of European integration.

Thesis 5: A modern democracy cannot do without a functioning "elite." In Germany, due to the historic ruptures of the twentieth century, there is a "divided," not a homogeneous elite. Whereas in west Germany, the term "elite" for a long time seemed to contradict the egalitarian principle of modern democratic societies, in east Germany there was an extreme form of "elite," represented by the Communist Party, which had all the privileges of power.

For decades, the word "elite" was frowned on in West Germany, because it conflicted with the reigning egalitarian principles. At the most, people agreed that there could be a "functional elite," that is, one that could be defined by recognizable criteria such as grades, diplomas, exams or the position that one held.[29] As Wolfgang Schäuble remarked: "Our elites—to the extent that we still have them—have been weakened in their ability to function. This might possibly be attributed to our egalitarian tendencies, which are opposed to the idea of elites and authority."[30]

Though "elites" exist in all Western democratic societies, the influence that an "elite" exerts is probably smaller in Germany than anywhere else: one part of the elite—particularly the Jewish part—was forced to flee during the Nazi dictatorship or was exterminated. Another segment cooperated with the Nazi dictatorship and were stigmatized as they "began anew" in both parts of Germany. One part of East Germany's elite fled to West Germany during the SED dictatorship, whereas a "middle-class" elite was only able to survive through the protection of the Protestant or Catholic Churches.

The former GDR regime was unscrupulous in its use of an elite concept; it led to the SED's broad control over the entire higher educational system of the country ("the Workers' and Farmers' state"). A clever system of privileges and sanctions determined the formation of the communist elites. In concrete terms, this meant that only members of the old *nomenklatura* could pick up political experience, whereas oppositional forces and non-dogmatists were marginalized and could not take part in leadership functions. This also explains why so many former "comrades" after the turnover in east Germany were so flexible and quickly found positions in the newly developing market economy: oppositional forces did not even have the opportunity to experience political office or work within the economic sphere.

For this reason, we cannot speak of the German elite's broken relationship to its past and/or to a specific ethos, since even the concept of an elite itself is highly controversial. This is different from the American elite, for example, which lays claim to the country's tradition with almost zealous self-confidence and pride.[31] According to the political scientist Wilhelm Hennis, since the middle of the last century, Germany—of all the comparable large European states—is the "country with the weakest political leadership class."[32] Germany's political representatives were also less bold. The lack of a responsible elite in Germany that could help form opinion has had dramatic consequences. That is why it is of crucial importance for the future that Germany starts to recruit a political and intellectual leadership.

Moreover, seeing the loss of orientation that has been observed in Germany, it is regrettable that the country does not have an influential, responsible elite that could counter this trend. Of all Western European societies, Germany is probably the most egalitarian, which complicates the formation of an elite. A sign of this is that there are no elite schools or elite universities in Germany, such as is the case in many other modern societies.

But spiritual leadership can only exist in a country where an influential elite exists. It is wrong simply to blame "politics." It does not make sense to differentiate between an economic and political elite. On the contrary, what is needed in Germany is a stronger exchange of elites.

Instead, it is rare that members of a "power elite" (e.g., members of parliament, influential civil servants) take on important functions in the economy and vice versa. In contrast to other countries, there is no system in Germany to draw on "elder statesmen," that is, highly experienced and independent citizens who can engage in the political decision-making process or in public opinion discussions. Germany has neither an upper chamber nor a senate (aside from Bavaria) nor another type of system that can serve as a forum for experienced, competent and intellectually independent personalities who have retired from politics.

Thesis 6: In the future, the political parties will continue to play an important role in the selection of a political elite, a power elite. The more that a broad and active membership enlivens the party system, the more successful parties will be in projecting the political identity of the parties to the voters and in defining the all-important role of the national parties.

In the last several years, membership levels in the democratic parties and in youth organizations has declined. Only 3 percent of the eligible voting population is a member of a political party. If one assumes, moreover, that only a minority of party members are truly active in party organizations, then only a few people are truly involved in the selection process of leaders within the political parties. On the other hand, there is probably no other Western European country that has so many citizens belonging to political parties.

Whereas political parties in the German Empire and the Weimar Republic represented various thoroughly differentiated "sociocultural" or "socio-economic" milieus (the Catholic, the conservative, the middle-class/Protestant or the socialist), the relationship of today's voters to parties is much more pragmatic and instrumental. Citizens do not feel that parties address the question of meaning or give orientation. Individuals voted more on the basis of their own personal situation, their assessment of the problem-solving capabilities of the party and the persuasiveness of the political leadership. The more that political behavior is separated from sociostructural factors, the more that voters make tactical (vote-splitting), short-term, flexible decisions. As a result, it has become increasingly difficult for parties to bring together the political interests of the electorate.

The social changes in the Federal Republic have led to a substantial increase in the "new middle classes," who can no longer be classified according to their traditional class membership, religious confession or political oppositions. Particularly the younger generation—up to the age of forty-five—have grown out of the political patterns of the traditional milieus. This group includes, for example, well-educated employees and civil servants as well as business specialists. The parties must continue to care for the interests of their electoral bases, but if they only serve the needs of their traditional voters, then their political competitiveness will decline. The large national parties' balancing act between their traditional, milieu-based electoral bases and the new rising generation of voters will probably become even more difficult in a reunified Germany. With unification, the German electorate has surely not become more homogeneous, since the parties and electoral structures in the new states are less solidified than in the old Federal Republic.

The above-mentioned dissolution of party ties is connected to the rise of new lifestyles. Classical milieu-influenced lifestyles can only be found in 40 percent of the population. It is particularly the younger generation that has developed new lifestyles as a result of the shift in values. At the same time, a new form of alternative milieu has crystallized in parts of the population, a community of like-minded individuals—the Greens, a leftist-alternative milieu party with an aging political client base.[33] The SED successor party, the PDS, also has characteristics of a milieu party.

The widespread perception that the parties are all-powerful is a myth. Even in the political arena parties no longer have a power monopoly, but rather must compete regularly with other groups. They also no longer formulate the political agenda by themselves: though parties influence political themes and currents, they no longer control them; instead, they are acted out in other forums, above all the media. Various political and social groups and associations also accompany and influence the opinion-making process. Instead of referring to a monopolization of the political process through parties, one can speak of an actual polycentrism, which has made it difficult for parties and elected governments to develop concepts and to implement their own policies.

Therefore, a gap exists between what is expected of politics and its actual authority, which in turn just increases the people's disenchantment with parties and politics. That is why it is more difficult now than in earlier years to present ideas and normative standards. Moreover, as I have shown, the influence of the original value-instilling institutions such as the churches has also declined dramatically in the last years. If the forces of individualization and pluralization undermine the authority of values in German society, then that will affect the role of the parties and the large political parties in general.

Parties are indispensible if democracy is to function. The political will of a people in a democracy is expressed in the variety of individual and group interests. The function of parties is to consolidate the needs and interests that they find among the people and to translate them into competing political alternatives. Other social associations, institutions and movements cannot—as important as they may be—replace the important function of parties; they can merely complement it. Political scientists define the large national parties (CDU, CSU and SPD) as both member and electoral parties. The West German party system rapidly developed in the 1950s and 1960s from a multiparty system along Weimar lines to a more consolidated three-party system (though the "Union" is not only one party, as it is often characterized).

Since the early 1970s, however, there has been an ideological expansion of the party system. Moreover, the German system of party financing as well as the free television advertising time before elections assists in the formation of splinter parties, since they have access to the mass media as soon as they are admitted to the elections. Even minor electoral successes can result in major election cost reimbursements. However, the three-party system of the 1960s and 1970s, regarded for a long time as normal in Germany, has actually not been the rule in the Federal Republic's electoral history. One easily forgets that seventeen parties were up for election in the first German Bundestag and that representatives from eleven parties and two independents were elected in 1949. This parliament varied only slightly from the ideologically divided Reichstag of the late Weimar years. At that time, the question whether Bonn was Weimar was still unsettled. But thanks to the integrational force of Adenauer's politics, many of the small interest parties could not survive the early years.

German parties must critically reassess their role in the formation of political opinion. That is one of the reasons why Kohl consistently criticizes the threat of the "fat cats" in the party establishment. It has become difficult for parties to be responsible for everything—though parties often claim to be and people often expect it. They are expected to fulfill the endless demands and expectations of the population, which is of course impossible.[34] Their ability to influence opinion is not even enhanced by their presence in many public offices or in numerous sectors of society, such as in the media and the economy. On the whole, parties must learn more modesty. At the same time, the people's demands on parties must be scaled back and become more realistic. Parties are thought to be responsible for problems which actually lie in the personal domain.

One of the significant functions of a party is to recruit qualified political personnel, and to fill public offices efficiently with people of integrity. Another one of their jobs is to think about the political future, to develop new concepts, but above all to come up with concrete projects and to resolve concrete political problems. Parties must compete more than ever with civic groups, associations and organizations. They cannot view these as rivals, but rather must open themselves up to them, looking for ways to connect and to accept them as partners. That will also require making use of outside expertise as well as strengthening the participatory and decision-making rights of individual party members.

The dangers of a "career politician" can be avoided once the idea of a "temporary career politician" becomes more desirable. An important step in this direction would be to stop paying political representatives more. Members of parliament should have just enough personnel so that they can fulfill their political obligations. It should also be enough to enable the M.P. to maintain contact with his or her former profession.

In the future, forming political opinion and finding a consensus in a mass democracy will not be an academic exercise performed in a vacuum, but will demand a tedious process of consensus and compromise building within responsible committees. Moreover, because of the strong influence of regions as vouchsafed by the Constitution, Germany is already a form of "consensus democracy"—especially now, when the opposition holds the majority in the Bundesrat. It is difficult to make quick decisions on important political questions in the German governmental system, but this was also the intention of the founding fathers of the Republic.

Furthermore, Germany's form of governmental system does not make the executive branch more efficient, particularly since all governments until now (with one exception) have been coalition governments. The difficult process of consensus and compromise building is not possible against or alongside the parties, but only in and with them. In the end, it is the parties that must carry responsibility in parliamentary systems and that must convince voters. Thus, the national parties are called on to perform their integrative function—particularly now, with the strong pluralization of lifestyles and interests and with the weakened communal orientation of the population: "Basically we need more integration, not less. And for that reason the idea of the large national parties is now more relevant than ever."[35]

Plebiscitary, direct democratic elements are not the solution; they do not lead to more stability and trust. In a representative democracy, the balancing of interests occurs within the large national parties and not through the small client or interest parties.[36]

Thesis 7: The German state must become leaner. People's demands on the state must be reduced; the expectation that the state order all aspects of life must be scaled back to a reasonable level.

Politics has allowed, if not encouraged, itself to be taken as a regulator of all behavior and actions. Besides its essential functions, such as the maintenance of internal and external peace, the guarantee of basic necessities and security, the state has taken on a wide range of functions in the economic and social field and has developed into a caretaker state. During periods of growth, this led to a rise in the level of taxation, to a wider range of regulations and to heightened expectations. But now, in economically more trying times, we need to place limits on our demands for the state's all-inclusiveness. Heightened expectations have swung over to disappointment. At the same time, it has become nearly impossible to question entitlements:

The belief in the all-powerful state, on the state's sole responsibility in solving all problems, leads to passivity and to a transference of responsibility. A person who has not learned responsibility cannot develop an optimistic outlook on life. The state takes care of people, but it also patronizes them by doing so. It may take away some of life's risks, but it also takes away—particularly from young people—self-exertion and the courage to be self-sufficient.[37]

German unification will also affect the role the state plays. In the GDR, the identity of the Communist Party and the state were essentially the same. Both had the authority to regulate the lives of many individuals as protective and punitive state. Though the "punishment" factor has disappeared with reunification, the citizens of the GDR do not want to relinquish the protective factor or its overall influence in a period of radical change and high levels of unemployment. But in west Germany, the mentality has also arisen that state and politics are responsible for problems not within the primary competence of the state. Thus the danger is that, through the integration of the two German states, there will be a demand for greater state involvement.

How difficult it has become for the government to retreat from responsibilities it has assumed is revealed by the endless discussion on reforming the postal and railroad networks, as well as by the discussion of privatization at the communal level. It is necessary to change the nature of the discussion:

privatization should not have to justify itself; it is up to the state and communities to justify their continued involvement. By limiting itself to certain sectors, the state can help reduce overextended regulations that impede innovation. The many regulations have made the state untransparent, and it is precisely this lack of transparence that has led to the population's distance from politics.

The factor of transparence was further complicated by the growth of rapidly expanding technological areas that originally needed regulation. Moreover, as a result of the world coming closer together, national politics has become more dependent on a wide range of complex supranational and international compromise-seeking bodies. Though this holds true for all industrial nations, there are a series of specific German features that have intensified the complex nature of political processes in Germany.

Though the proportional electoral system enhances stability through good electoral representation, it almost always creates the need for coalitions. Coalitions tend to push decisions off onto informal committees. Federalism and communal self-administration can and should guarantee grassroots participation, but they also lengthen and slow down the voting process. One only need be reminded of the relationship between Bundestag and Bundesrat, of the way in which financial accounts are settled between the communes and the states, and of the many detailed and highly regulated sponsorship programs ("the golden reins"). Moreover, areas where finances have been combined have added to the inscrutability of the process. There is a great need to coordinate. All this means that political decision making takes a lot of time—to the dissatisfaction of citizens.

The tendency of Germans to see the state as legal mediator has further contributed to a diffuse sense of political responsibility. Increasingly, politics has hidden behind Supreme Court decisions. For example, the FDP could not distance itself on its own from Genscher, who felt that the Constitution needed to be changed for Germans to participate in UN actions. Instead, the FDP allowed itself to be overruled within the coalition and appealed to the Supreme Court against their own coalition government. But even individual citizens tend to take the smallest, most questionable demands (since they're protected by legal insurance) directly to the courts.

What will help to clarify the state's profile and political decisions is to roll back the state to its core responsibilities, to deregulate and to clearly separate sectors of competency and responsibility. A lean state means the state's organization must shed some of its fat. Smaller units and smaller parliaments, limiting themselves to fundamental political issues and the control of government action, can mean a more effective and transparent system of democratic control. Of course, there is always the risk that people will not know how to use their greater freedom: Germans have placed such a high value on egalitarianism that they will have difficulty adjusting.

Thesis 8: At the same time, we need a strong state that can meet the more intense security needs of the people in times of radical change. In every society, security is one of the top priorities, inner security most of all.

The crime statistics of the police confirm a process that exists in all Western industrial societies: the law and the state's function as peacekeeper are no longer taken for granted. Judicial clemency and suspended sentences are commonplace in the German legal system.[38] Many people are asking whether the German state can fulfill its fundamental responsibility of inner security.[39] It is essential to strengthen the individual citizen's faith that the state is guaranteeing his or her security—both externally and (most of all) internally.

Many Germans feel that crime has risen. All surveys indicate that the majority of the population are calling for the state to use all legal means at its disposal to ensure inner security and peaceful coexistence. According to a November 1993 survey, 53 percent of all citizens are very concerned that individuals can no longer be adequately defended against crime. A further 39 percent were somewhat concerned.[40]

According to 1993 criminal statistics for all of Germany, the police registered 6.75 million crimes.[41] The success rate in solving crimes was 43.8 percent; in cases involving murder or killings, the rate fell from 91.2 percent (1992) to 84.7 percent.[42] More than half of all crimes involve minor larceny. Politically significant is the fact that the percentage of foreigners involved in crimes has risen: in the old German states (including all of Berlin) it rose from 32.2 percent to 36.2 percent; in all of Germany, the rate is 33.6 percent.[43]

Moreover, political extremism should not be forgotten.[44] Aside from "inner German" right- and left-extremism there is also a considerable share of foreigner extremism. In 1993, there were fifty-nine organizations of foreign extremists and other associations considerably influenced by them. By the end of 1993, according to estimates by authorities, there were a total of 38,950 foreign extremists in Germany over the age of sixteen.[45]

In fact, the number of registered crimes has risen drastically in the west. Whereas the crime statistics revealed about 2,919,390 criminal cases in 1975 (4,722 cases per 100,000 inhabitants), in 1990 the number had risen to 4,455,333 cases (7,108 cases per 100,000). In the first statistic recorded for all Germany, that number had even risen to 8,337 per 100,000! But it is not only a quantitative problem: the statistical data cannot adequately take account of what the president of the Federal Criminal Police Office, Hans-Ludwig Zachert, calls the "development toward qualitatively more serious crimes."

Three central areas really stand out in particular, and they will preoccupy the society extensively: (1) violence and extremism, (2) everyday petty crimes and (3) organized crime. Of course, these phenomena are not limited to Germany; similar developments can be found all over Europe. The cooperation of the German intrastate and European transnational police is now more essential than ever. The serious transformation changes resulting from the end of the East-West conflict, the end of German and European division, and the dismantling of border controls within the European Union have enabled crime to spread throughout the European continent. The cross-border crime rate—drug smuggling, auto theft, the smuggling of illegal aliens and arms—has risen considerably. A new type of threat is nuclear crime. The Treaty of Maastricht set the foundation for cooperation between the security organs of the various member states. But that cooperation is still not satisfactory.

Due to its central geographic position, Germany has turned into a hub for international crime. One analysis has found that after the collapse of the USSR, 4,300 Mafia-style groups are causing trouble in the CIS countries; in the meantime, 300 of these groups are said to have been established in Germany, many of them in Berlin.[46] There is a long list of organizations operating in and out of Germany. Besides the "Red Mafia," Italian organizations such as "Cosa Nostra" and the "Camorra" or "N'drangheta" are as active in Germany as the Medellin or Cali cartels in Colombia or the Chinese Triads. There is also the danger that high sums of laundered drug money might be used for corruption in Germany.

In Germany, there is a discrepancy between media reportage and the opinions of the large majority of the population. For example, during a terrorist chase in Bad Kleinen, on June 27, 1993, the police made some mistakes that resulted in intense public opinion debates. The incident led to two deaths: a member of the Federal Border Guard (GSG-9) and a terrorist. In the media reports and commentary, what played the greatest role was the question whether the officials involved had engaged in a summary execution of the terrorist, while the death of the twenty-five-year-old GSG-9 member, Michael Newrzella, was hardly mentioned at all. All serious investigations have concluded that the claims of some members of the press cannot be substantiated. The discussion shows how sensitively the German media can react when there is the slightest suspicion of police error. The media's trust in the organs of the German state is a lot lower than that of the average citizen.

Apparently, all open societies have to come to terms with the phenomenon of rising crime; but it still should not be glossed over. Too few people recognize the law's function as peaceful arbiter. In Germany, political education needs to instill a greater constitutional and legal awareness, but so do families and schools.

Thesis 9: Germany is faced with a twofold challenge unlike that of any other country in the world: modernizing one section (the west) and transforming the other (the east) into a market economic system. The economic structures must become more effective. At the same time, Germany, like other Western nation-states, must pose the question about her future. The solution of these problems will greatly affect developments within the European Union and in all of Europe. Only by improving her economic performance will Germany be able to master competition from abroad.

Germany will only be able to face the challenges of the future if her economic situation improves. Many questions need to be asked: If west German union members demand western wages in the east—do they want to improve the conditions of east German workers or are they selfishly trying to prevent west German jobs from being transferred to the east? Can the state in this situation guarantee equality of living standards in a reunified Germany? In a divided German society, poor and rich can be found both in the various social classes and in the variously developed economic regions.

German society is divided at many different levels. Aside from the fact that wages in several East Central European states are one-twentieth to one-tenth as much as in east and west Germany, the question is how Germany will be able to accomplish this twofold process of modernizing the western economy while simultaneously creating an effective market economy in the east. Won't the fewer people who are employed have to carry the burden of the greater number of unemployed? Surveys indicate that many citizens are prepared to make sacrifices if they have the feeling of justice, of a just distribution of burdens, and if all citizens are affected equally. A communal spirit also means recognizing that the division of Germany can only be overcome by sharing. That requires a greater understanding of the larger economic connections and a willingness on the part of wage negotiators to agree on reasonable wage demands.

Even if some of Germany's European partners might secretly relish the fact that Germany is tied down with reunification and cannot assume an international leadership position, this situation cannot satisfy a true supporter of the European cause. When Germany's economy and political system are functioning well, it helps the European Union as a whole. In that sense, one should not underestimate Germany's capacity to promote economic prosperity for the rest of the European Union, since Germany has, in the meantime, become the strongest economy within the Union. What future questions will preoccupy Germany?[47] I will point out several:

Example 1: *Revitalization of the Social Market Economy*. The economic and social situation in reunifying Germany is presently affected by an intensely competitive world market; but it is also influenced to a large degree by the burdens that have resulted from the disastrous economic and ecological legacy of the SED. In that sense, the growing call for the state to intervene more directly in the economy is counterproductive. On the contrary, Germany must return again to the successful measures that had helped rebuild West Germany—the principles of the Social Market Economy.

Even with the Marshall Plan and the currency reform, it would have been much more difficult for the Federal Republic to have produced its economic miracles with today's high concentration of laws and regulations. Germany needs deregulation and a reduction in the level of taxation so as to make it easier to invest and innovate. A "state economy"—which is somewhat represented by the current tax rate of 54 percent—is not compatible with a Social Market Economy. It hinders economic competitiveness and the capacity to develop and impedes structural changes. One must combat the fallacy that today's level of state involvement is essential, that the Social Market Economy is more social if society distributes more.

Instead of arguing over distribution and prerogatives, we must again start to realize that we can only distribute what we actually produce. Through greater privatization we can relieve the public budget and speed up modernization, but most of all we can put a stop to the excessive rise of bureaucratic structures in areas where entrepreneurial action should develop. In a Social Market Economy, it is not the state's job to be active in the economy if a private business can offer these same services just as well or better. Subsidies that are directed at preserving noncompetitive structures only serve to prevent modernizing measures.

If, for political reasons, one decides to maintain certain industries despite inefficiency, then those decisions must be constantly reevaluated and must be compared to the costs that they produce. On the whole, subsidies should be structurally degressive and should be phased out over time; their existence should only be extended if their continued usefulness can be proven. Long-term subsidies are useless because they cannot help protected businesses retain their standing on international markets. They are also antisocial, because they make the employees in the affected business think they have job security, though this does not actually reflect the true conditions on the job market. Flexibility and deregulation are necessary on the job market. If various (well-intentioned) measures cancel out market mechanisms, then the markets will never be able to fulfill their true functions.

Example 2: *The Promotion of New Technologies.* Another problem for Germany's future is the public's animosity toward technology, particularly among people involved in public life and in the field of education. Germans have an ambivalent attitude toward modern technologies: on the one hand, they reject large-scale technologies; and on the other, they use high-tech equipment in all aspects of daily life. Examples of the latter are the use of Teflon pans; audiovisual equipment, which can now be found in almost every German household; automobile electronics; and vaccines created from gene technology, protecting against diseases on tropical vacations.

A major gap exists between the acceptance of high technology in the abstract and the use of high-tech products—a gap that cannot be explained rationally. Many Germans, for example, use insulin from neighboring countries, whereas the production in Germany proceeds only gradually because of the supposed risks involved. Why is it that Japan and America are the leaders in the field of information and communications technologies even though the first computer was built sixty years ago in Germany by Conrad Zuse? Of approximately 2,000 experiments involving gene technology that have been carried out in the world until 1993, only 6 took place in Germany.

Germany was once considered the "apothecary of the world," because it was the home of the most modern medical supplies and medical research. Today, on the other hand, researchers are emigrating to other countries. That does not mean uncontrolled experiments should be encouraged or research should exclude ethical questions. But in Germany, criticism of modernity, progress and technology—the kind that hinders progress—is more influential than in other countries.

On the whole, trust in science and technology has decreased since the 1960s. According to a 1966 survey by the Allensbach Institute, 72 percent of people surveyed thought that technology was a blessing for mankind; in 1987, only 36 percent did.[48] A survey carried out by the Konrad Adenauer Foundation also reveals that many Germans have a critical attitude toward technological progress. In 1993, 43 percent of all Germans agreed "completely and fully" (or "somewhat") with the statement that "technology threatens man today more than it helps him"; 56 percent "generally" did not agree with this or "not at all."[49] East Germans are 4 percent more tolerant of technology than west Germans. There are ominous signs that Germany will lose her leading position. If one takes registration of international patents as an indicator of a nation's innovativeness, then the regressive development becomes apparent. For many years, Germany was in second position after the United States. In the 1980s, however, the situation got worse, and Germany's position in international comparison declined. The number of patent registrations stagnated, while those of the United States almost doubled. Japan was also able to improve its technological competitiveness.

Germany is particularly falling behind in future technologies. In the fields of biotechnology and gene technology, American firms own the most important patents. The situation is similar in the computer, communications and office machines sectors. In Germany, almost every tenth person now owns a computer, but they are mostly manufactured in the United States or Japan. In 1991, the United States exported $19.1 billion worth of computers and other communication technology; Japan and Southeast Asian countries exported $41.6 billion worth of equipment to Western Europe; whereas Western Europe in the same time period was only able to export $13.7 billion to these countries.

Example 3: *The Problem of Social Aging*. Another challenge stems from demographic developments.[50] A rising number of old people is coupled with a diminishing number of young people. Today, 20 percent of Germany's total population is made up of people over sixty. In the year 2030, the percentage will be over a third. This development of "demographic over-aging" is a phenomenon that can be observed in all developing industrial societies but is particularly pronounced in Germany. It is caused by a considerable decline in the birthrate, by a decline in early fatalities and the rising life expectancy of older people.

This demographic development will also have various economic repercussions, since the population of people in the prime working ages between twenty and sixty will clearly decrease. Whereas in 1990 58 percent of the population belonged to this age group, in the year 2030 not even half of the population will be in their working prime. Whereas in 1989 there were 100 working-age people for every 73 people younger than twenty or older than sixty, it is predicted that by 2030 100 working-age people will exist for 109 people in the dependent age groups. This means the middle generation will increasingly have to support the needs of a growing number of older people. Moreover, it is hard to predict the psychological effect this societal overaging will have on the future younger generation.

Even though there are no short-term measures that can be taken to halt this serious demographic development, it must be admitted that—despite reservations about "population policy" arising from German history—a society with fewer and fewer children is a society without a future. Politics is called on to intercede when a desire for children cannot be fulfilled for material reasons—particularly in the difficult search for affordable housing for young families. Therefore, along with improving the status of families, there should also be a redistribution to their advantage. People who complain that this is not affordable should be reminded that a social system that allows children to become more unaffordable will itself become unaffordable over the long term through demographical pressures.

Example 4: *Improvement of the Educational System.* Since Germany is relatively poor in natural resources, it is very dependent on a functioning educational system. This has become the biggest challenge for Germany's federal system. The sixteen states have authority in cultural matters, and their ability and willingness to enact reforms on structural core elements of the German educational system is very limited. The German educational system used to be considered one of the best in the world, but it now reveals a series of deficiencies reducing its level of efficiency. These include the erosion of the structured school system, the declining status of the junior high school, longer studies, the decline in the Humboldt-style university model, the overpopulation and strain on the universities, the lower appeal of a vocational education, the growing need for continued education, the declining interest in education and employment for women, the greater need to integrate children of foreigners and the need to standardize general and vocational education.[51]

As the long-standing president of the German Research Community, Hubert Markl, says:

To summarize: our educational system suffers from bloating at the upper levels, from the lack of differentiation in terms of talent and performance, from making career entry too dependent on the educational examination process, from placing too much emphasis on academic qualifications and too little emphasis on (and therefore undervaluing) career-oriented qualifications and from the unwillingness or inability to promote high performance through a differentiated selection of talent. The latter has partially ideological motives, partially political-economic ones.[52]

What needs to be done is to tighten the curricula and the system of training, whereby it is the states' responsibility to guarantee a comparable level of educational qualifications. There must be adequate foreign language training, and further overpopulation of universities must be prevented. Too many students attend universities, even if they are not intellectually equipped. About 16 percent of all employed Germans with a university diploma (about 720,000 people) do not have adequate jobs—that is, jobs that require university level qualifications. About 115,000 university graduates are presently unemployed, and about a fourth of all people who start out at the university (75,000 students)[53] break off their studies at one point. At the same time, German universities have become less attractive for foreign students. Not all scholarship positions offered at German universities are filled. German universities are no longer the prime choice for students to attend.[54] On the whole, students from developing countries now have their eyes on the American educational system, but not on Germany, which used to have (in the Weimar Republic) the highest reputation as a nation of science.

Example 5: *Control of the Migration and Refugee Problem.* The worldwide phenomenon of migration is an additional future problem. It affects all economically prosperous countries, but Germany most of all, because of her geographically central position.[55] In Eastern Europe alone, approximately 20 million people are seriously considering moving to Western Europe, according to a survey by the European Commission.[56] Whereas France has to cope with refugees, immigrants and people looking for political asylum from Arab and French-speaking countries, Germany is the gateway for people from Eastern Europe. That is why it is so important to assist these countries in their political and economic development.

Yet, the migration pressures from the Southern Hemisphere will eventually be far more pressing than from East Central Europe. Whereas the migrants from that latter region can more easily be integrated into Germany because of their primarily Christian cultural background, the population growth in North Africa, with its predominantly Islamic culture, represents a ticking time bomb. In 1950, 140 million people lived north of the Mediterranean, and 70 million south. Now, the ratio has been inverted: In North Africa, there are already more than 150 million people; and according to estimates, by 2025 there will be approximately 300 million.

In Algeria alone, the population will double in the next twenty-five years. The Mediterranean used to represent a barrier between two very different levels of prosperity; but over the long term, it will no longer serve this function if population growth and poverty continue to increase at the present dramatic rate. The Mediterranean can be crossed by ship in a matter of hours. The number of people seeking political refuge increased in almost all European countries. But before the change in the political asylum law, on July 1, 1993, which was highly controversial, 80 percent of the people looking for political asylum within the European Community wanted to come to Germany.[57]

Germany distinguishes more or less between five different categories of immigrants:

- People looking for political asylum
- Family members coming to live with foreigners who are legal residents of Germany
- Germans from Eastern European countries
- Citizens of the European Union
- Illegal immigrants or foreigners who have gone underground since they can no longer legally stay in Germany

At the end of 1992, 6.496 million foreigners were living in Germany, that is, 614,000, or 10 percent, more than at the end of December 1991 (5.882 million). They represented about 8 percent of the total population; at the same time, many foreigners also left the country. Of the approximately 6.5 million foreigners living in Germany by the end of 1992, the Turks made up the largest share, with 1.855 million, or 29 percent.[58] The number of naturalizations in Germany is higher than generally assumed. In 1991, 141,636 people were naturalized, though 114,335 were people with the right of naturalization (i.e., exiles of German ancestry) and 27,295 were discretionary naturalizations. In the period between 1977 and 1990, 615,041 people were naturalized in the Federal Republic.[59] Before it was changed, the extremely liberal law governing asylum suited many European nations because it helped to channel the flow of refugees to Germany.

Germany has one of the highest population concentrations in Europe, and some Germans are demanding a concrete immigration policy—in view of the fact that the wave of immigrants actually relieved the job market and the public budget, according to some economists. On the whole, immigration works against the aging of the native population and takes a burden off of future social security payments. Often, there is even a demand for more immigrants. But it is doubtful that the demands for a European immigration plan[60] are realistic, considering the selfishness of EU member states.

Many Germans do not mind the increased naturalization of foreigners with a similar cultural background. In that sense, living together with people from other EU member states does not pose many problems. But problems arise when the foreigners come from non-Christian societies. Other Western industrial societies are asking themselves as well if a society is capable of integrating immigrants from other cultures which are highly different from their own culture. There are already about 12 million Muslims living in Europe and the United States today.

Thesis 10: The world has not become safer after the end of the bipolar world. It will be hard for Germany to resist the pressure from many of her foreign partners to participate more forcefully in the international arena. It will also be in her own interest—if she really wants to guarantee the foreign security of the country. NATO and the WEU will continue to establish the framework for Germany's security policy. It will be detrimental to Europe's future if Russia cannot find a cure for her social ailments. At the same time, the Europeans must be prepared—as in the tragic situation in former Yugoslavia—to take on more responsibility. The world has become "smaller," problems more global and the nation-states' maneuverability more limited. Germany is fatefully linked to developments in other countries and regions in the world.

Germany will do all she can in the future to remain a loyal alliance partner; and she will fulfill the demands expected of her to the same degree that other partners in the European Union are ready to assume their own increased share of responsibility for the fate of Europe. The cooperation agreed on in the Treaty of Maastricht in the form of the "Common Foreign and Security Policy" is progressing slowly. For many East Central European countries, Germany is considered to be the most important European partner nation. But Germany cannot fulfill all their expectations. The Germans must try to involve their European partners in a cooperative foreign policy toward East Central Europe. In Germany, more than in other Western European societies, people have begun to realize that the region of East Central Europe will probably be chronically unstable. Since it will be years before a common European peacekeeping system can be successfully implemented, Germany's foreign policy interests will be to reduce instabilities in the region.

It is also in Germany's interest that the United States maintain a military presence in Europe and Germany in particular. Its stabilizing influence should not be underestimated. But Russia too continues to be an influential global actor. It will affect all of Europe if Russia does not attain political and economic stability. Russia continues to be a nuclear power, and there are growing signs that Russia's foreign policy is returning to the basic principles of traditional czarist diplomacy. On the whole, Germany and the West must be interested in incorporating the East Central European countries into the European integration process.

There are three crucial questions: How can the European Union be intensified in the period after the Treaty of Maastricht? How will the Atlantic alliance's partnership continue with the United States[61] under the changing circumstances? How will life be breathed into the German-Russian treaty? Germany's Western integration cannot suffer as a result of this, even if Europe's balance will shift more toward the East due to changing geopolitical circumstances and to what the Germans consider the necessary eastern expansion of the European Union. The art of German foreign policy must be to harmonize her growing interests in the East and her position of Western integration (represented by the European Union, NATO and the Western European Union).

A Germany reunified must find a new role in Europe and in the world. This will take time—after years of being "weaned away" from power. Because of Germany's geographic location and her strong economy, it will be impossible for her to go her own way. She can also no longer hide from problems. The Germans cannot disappoint their friends and partners or the world community. That is why Germany in the future will have to participate in military activities with other members of the world community to create peace. A stable and lasting integration into a transnational framework does not preclude an awareness of one's own national interests; in fact, that integration is the prerequisite for those interests. The most important foreign policy goal of Germany will be to avoid foreign pressures to her stability. That is why she will need to support measures that will help the economic recovery of the former East Bloc, but particularly Russia and the democratic reformers there.

From the very beginning, Western European integration was linked to the question of national sovereignty. Some people were afraid of this at the time, but those fears could be assuaged. Germans must be aware that Europe will only be able to master the challenges of her future if she truly develops into a political Union. The goal must be both to solidify the European Union and to expand it to those countries that fulfill the economic and political requirements of membership and who participate in strengthening the Union.

Moreover, aside from European integration, foreign policy must start to be understood as "world domestic policy." A very important priority must be to fight poverty in the countries of Africa, Asia and Latin America by helping them to help themselves. They need fair trade conditions, but also a "know-how" transfer to help them establish functioning democratic structures and social reforms. It is morally imperative to help these countries in light of their terrible suffering and starvation. Equally, it is in the German interest. Overexploitation due to poverty affects the international climate. Migration resulting from poverty can undermine the social stability of rich countries. Religious fundamentalism, furthered by poverty, can become a worldwide threat to peace.

In the opinion of many specialists, Germany is one of the best-functioning democracies in Europe, with a social stability that is envied by many foreigners. An Italian journalist described the situation somewhat hyperbolically: "Even if a German continually fears the social state will be watered down or become soft—in the eyes of a foreigner, it still remains a great miracle: the unattainable German model."[62] At the same time, the foreign media sometimes continue to have doubts about Germany—understandable in light of historical experience, but does it reflect reality?

On June 6, 1993, for example, in the influential *Sunday Times* of London, the following appeared under the headline "Kaput!": "Suddenly, gripped by economic recession as well as political and social paralysis, Germany is foundering in unprecedented gloom."[63] Certainly, German politics is affected by a degree of paralysis, and a rich society like west Germany is especially not very keen on sacrificing its wealth for the cause of unity. But isn't this less a sign of how "national" Germany is, and more an indication of her materialism?

The shift in values that occurred in all industrial nations particularly affected reunifying Germany—though here it is a two-sided value change. If one considers that German election laws give smaller parties opportunities, then Germany's present political stability is even more remarkable. Without trying to downplay extremist activities—particularly against foreigners—or to relativize them by mentioning similar occurrences in other European countries, it must be said in all fairness that Germany's elite has learned the lessons of history. Just as little as Bonn was Weimar, so Berlin will not become Weimar in the future.

The Germans are in search of security, both domestically and internationally. "Security" cannot only mean the nonexistence of foreign perils; it must also be based on a degree of self-reflection, on the self-assurance of liberal Western democracies. After the political changes of 1989, the Germans, more than other nations, must start to become "aware" of themselves. This self-awareness should be seen by the Germans as a chance to reevaluate their position in Europe and the world.

This does not mean that Germany should get rid of old certainties, ones that have given her security. Free and open democracies are in a better position to reform themselves than ossified societies. Germans must get used to the fact that irritations and insecurities are a normal part of fast-paced times. In fact, there will not be easy answers to the many challenges facing Germany after reunification, and this will be a consolation to many foreign countries. A country that resorts to quick answers neglects experience and becomes an unpredictable and unreliable power. Government cannot achieve "security" by pushing a button. Yet Germans, in coming to understand their new identity, will have to be aware of Germany's new significance for the rest of Europe and for the international balance of power.

Notes

YOUTH AND THE CHANGE IN VALUES

1. For more on the term "individualization," see Ulrich Beck, *Risikogesell-schaft: Auf dem Wege in eine andere Moderne* (Frankfurt am Main 1986), in particular p. 121. Beck also refers to an "individualization and diversification of lifestyles" and to a "political privatization." See also Gerhard Schulze, *Die Er-lebnisgesellschaft: Kultursoziologie der Gegenwart* (Frankfurt am Main/New York 1992); Peter Gluchowski, "Lebensstile und Wählerverhalten," in Hans-Joachim Veen and Elisabeth Noelle-Neumann, *Wählerverhalten im Wandel* (Paderborn 1991).

2. Hans Bertram, "Die Stadt, das Individuum und das Verschwinden der Familie," *Aus Politik und Zeitgeschichte*, B 29–30/94, July 22, 1994, p. 22.

3. Ibid., p. 22.

4. Ibid.

5. Ibid., p. 23.

6. Ibid., p. 32.

7. Elisabeth Beck-Gernsheim, "Auf dem Weg in die postfamiliale Familie: Von der Notgemeinschaft zur Wahlverwandtschaft," *Aus Politik und Zeit-geschichte*, B 29–30/94, July 22, 1994, p. 11. See also: *BIB-Mitteilungen* (1993) 3, p. 13. For the divorce rate in the United States, see Andrew J. Cherlin, *Marriage, Divorce, Remarriage* (Cambridge, MA 1992), pp. 7 and 24.

8. Bernhard Nauck, "Familien und Betreuungssituationen im Lebenslauf von Kindern," in Hans Bertram (ed.), *Die Familie in Westdeutschland* (Opladen 1991), p. 427, quoted in Beck-Gernsheim, p. 11.

9. Christian Geyer, "In der Mitte bleibt ein Hohlraum—die neue Jugend-weihe," *Frankfurter Allgemeine Zeitung,* June 18, 1994. See also *Frankfurter Allgemeine Zeitung*, April 13, 1994.

10. See also Martin Merz, "Ein Walzer für die Weihlinge," *Die Zeit*, April 22, 1994.

11. Quoted in *Die Welt*, March 8, 1994. For more poll results, see "Thesis 2" in Chapter 7 of this book.

12. *KAS-Umfrage*, Archive-No. 9305.

13. Bundesministerium für Bildung und Wissenschaft, *Grund- und Struktur-daten*, Ausgabe 1993/1994 (Bonn, December 1993), pp. 72–73. The figures up to 1980 refer to former West German territory; the 1992 figures include East Berlin as well as the former West German territory.

14. See Ronald Inglehart, *The Silent Revolution: Changing Values and Political Styles among Western Publics* (Princeton, NJ 1977).

15. See Peter Kmieciak, *Wertstrukturen und Wertewandel in der Bundesre-publik Deutschland* (Göttingen 1976); Helmut Klages and Peter Kmieciak (eds.), *Wertewandel und gesellschaftlicher Wandel* (Frankfurt am Main 1979); Elisabeth Noelle-Neumann, *Werden wir alle Proletarier? Wertewandel in unserer Gesell-schaft* (Zurich 1978); Günther Rüther (ed.), *Werteverzicht in der Industriegesell-schaft?* (Bonn 1976). See also Gerd Langguth, *Jugend ist anders: Porträt einer jungen Generation* (Freiburg Basel, Vienna 1983), pp. 25–26; Wolfgang Zapf, Sigrid Breuer, Jürgen Hampel, Peter Krause, Hans-Michael Mohr and Erich Wiegand, *Individualisierung und Sicherheit—Untersuchungen zur Lebensqualität in der Bundesrepublik Deutschland* (Munich 1987).

16. Hans-Joachim Veen, Walter Jaide, Barbara Hille, Walter Friedrich and Peter Förster, *Eine Jugend in Deutschland* (Opladen 1994), pp. 46–47.

17. See Hans-Joachim Veen and Peter Gluchowski, "Die Anhängerschaften der Parteien vor und nach der Einheit—eine Langfristbetrachtung von 1953 bis 1993," *Zeitschrift für Parlamentsfragen*, Heft 2, 1994.

18. These are results from a study carried out by the Cologne Institute for Empirical Psychology and sponsored by the German Association of Unions (DGB). The poll responses were described in the *Frankfurter Allgemeine Zeitung*, July 27, 1994. According to a study by the management-oriented Institute of the German Economy, the percentage of youth in the DGB had gone down even further; even German reunification hadn't improved union prospects. This study reports that there were 987,000 young people in the DGB in 1993—184,000 less than the year before. ("Die deutschen Gewerkschaften verlieren die Gunst der Arbeitnehmer," *Frankfurter Allgemeine Zeitung*, July 27, 1994.)

19. Veen et al., *Eine Jugend in Deutschland*, pp. 46–47.

20. Imbke Behnken, *Schülerstudie '90, Jugendliche im Prozess der Ver-einigung* (Weinheim/Munich 1991), p. 125.

21. Shell-Jugendwerk (ed.), *Jugend '92, Lebenslagen, Orientierungen, und Entwicklungsperspektiven im vereinigten Deutschland* (Opladen 1992), Vol. 1, p. 265.

22. Bundestagsdrucksache 12/6836, *Antwort der Bundesregierung auf die Grosse Anfrage der CDU/CSU- und FDP-Fraktion zur Situation der Jugend in Deutschland*, p. 30.

23. Ibid., p. 31.

24. Shell-Jugendwerk, *Jugend '92*, Vol. 1, p. 216.

25. Ipos-Studie, March 1993, quoted in Bundestagsdrucksache 12/6836, p. 35.

26. Deutsches Jugendinstitut, *Jugend-Umfrage 1992*.

27. Shell-Jugendwerk, *Jugend '92*, Vol. 1, p. 61.

28. See also Ulrich Hermann, "Wandel der Lebensformen, politische Umbrüche und die Aufgaben der Erwachsenenbildung. Mit zwei Denkschriften von Reinhard Buchwald aus dem Jahre 1945," in Martha Friedenthal-Haase, Jost Reischmann, Hans Tietgens, and Norbert Vogel (eds.), *Erwachsenenbildung im Kontext* (Bad Heilbrunn/Obb. 1991), p. 191.

29. See Michael Brake, *Comparative Youth Culture: The Sociology of Youth Cultures and Youth Subcultures in America, Britain and Canada* (London 1985).

30. More on this in Gerd Langguth, *Protestbewegung—Entwicklung, Niedergang, Renaissance: Die Neue Linke seit 1968* (Cologne, 1983).

31. Ernst Fraenkel, *Deutschland und die westlichen Demokratien* (Frankfurt am Main 1991), p. 68.

32. Richard Löwenthal, *Der romantische Rückfall* (Stuttgart/Berlin/Cologne/Mainz 1970), p. 9.

33. Herbert Marcuse, *Das Ende der Utopie* (Berlin 1967), p. 66.

34. See Veen et al., *Eine Jugend in Deutschland*, p. 99.

35. Ibid.

36. *KAS-Archive*, No. 9104.

37. Arnold Gehlen, *Die Seele im technischen Zeitalter* (Hamburg 1957), p. 109.

38. Janucz Korczak, in *Begegnungen und Erfahrungen* (Göttingen 1972).

39. More on this in Langguth, *Jugend ist anders*, p. 71.

40. Veen et al., *Eine Jugend in Deutschland*, p. 95.

41. See "With a Firm View to the Past: PDS—The Party with the Janus Face," in Chapter 3.

42. Federal Ministry of the Interior (ed.), *Report for Constitutional Protection 1993* (Bonn, June 1994), p. 22.

43. Ibid., p. 76.

44. Ibid., p. 79.

45. Ibid., p. 94.

46. Ibid.

47. Federal Ministry for Youth and Women, *Press Report* of June 9, 1993, No. 32, with reference to an Ipos Study.

48. See Peter Struck, *Erziehung gegen Gewalt* (Neuwied-Kriftel/Berlin 1994).

49. Peter Schneider, "Es will dich hier niemand ausgrenzen, Arno!" *Frankfurter Allgemeine Zeitung*, September 7, 1993, p. 37.

50. Federal Interior Ministry (ed.), *Report for Constitutional Protection 1992* (Bonn 1993), p. 70.

51. Ibid., p. 81.

52. This was the conclusion of the report "Violence against Foreigners: An Analysis of Perpetrator Structures and Escalation Processes from the Scientific Group Helmut Willems, Stefanie Würtz and Roland Eckert, commissioned by the Federal Ministry for Youth and Women"; cited in the Press Report of the Federal Ministry for Women and Youth, No. 35, June 29, 1993.

53. Hans-Joachim Maaz, "Gewalt in Deutschland—Eine psychologische Analyse," *Aus Politik und Zeitgeschichte*, B2–3/93, January 8, 1993, p. 29.

54. Stephan Wehowsky, "Lust an der Randale," *Süddeutsche Zeitung*, November 21–22, 1992.

55. Ibid.

56. Institute of Jewish Affairs, *Antisemitism. World Report 1994* (London 1994); see also *Neue Zürcher Zeitung*, July 23, 1994.

57. *Die Welt*, May 28, 1994.

58. Werner Bergmann of the Institute for Anti-Semitism Research at the Technical University of Berlin, refers to this in *Der Tagesspiegel*, January 30, 1993.

59. Ibid.

60. According to this survey of November–December, 1992, 77 percent of the German population do not want to have right-wing extremists as neighbors; 67 percent do not want drug addicts; 64 percent do not want gypsies; and 61 percent do not want left-wing extremists (*Allensbacher Archive*, IfD Surveys 5074). A survey commissioned by the American Jewish Committee concluded that 22 percent "would prefer not" to have Jews as neighbors (59 percent said "they didn't care," 12 percent said "they would like to have them as neighbors"). This survey also shows that 11 percent of west Germans would not want east Germans as neighbors and 11 percent of east Germans would not want west Germans as neighbors; 68 percent reject gypsies as neighbors; 47 percent Arabs; 32 percent Vietnamese; 36 percent Turks; 39 percent Poles; and 37 percent Africans (Emnid Institute Bielefeld, "The Present Attitude of Germans Toward Jews and Other Minorities," commissioned by the Emnid Institute January 12–31, 1994). This survey, however, concluded that a high percentage of Germans are well informed about the Holocaust: 87 percent of Germans are able to say with a certain degree of accuracy what is meant by the word "Holocaust"; 91 percent recognize the golden Star of David that Hitler forced the Jews to wear. Twenty percent of Germans think that Jews have too much influence on German society. Eleven percent of the German population (12 percent in the West, 5 percent in the East) agree "strongly" with the statement that the Nazi Holocaust no longer has significance today since it happened fifty years ago (26 percent agree "somewhat"—28 percent in west Germany, 17 percent in east Germany). Still, 18 percent of the Germans consider it "essential" and 50 percent "very important" that Germans are informed about the Holocaust (19 percent find it "less significant," 7 percent "unimportant," 7 percent did not respond).

61. Konrad Brendler, "Die Holocaustrezeption der Enkelgeneration im Spannungsfeld von Abwehr und Traumatisierung," in Wolfgang Benz (ed.), *Jahrbuch für Antisemitismusforschung 3* (Frankfurt/New York 1994), p. 337.

62. See Hans-Dieter Schwind, "Die Empfehlungen der (Anti-) Gewaltkommission—und was aus ihnen geworden ist," *DVJJ-Journal*, 2/1994, No. 146, p. 114.

63. *Mut zur Erziehung: Beiträge zu einem Forum am 9./10. Januar 1978 im Wissenschaftszentrum Bonn–Bad Godesberg* (Stuttgart 1979), pp. 163–65.

64. *Der Spiegel*, January 25, 1993, p. 41.

65. Peter König, "Wir Voodookinder," *Kursbuch 113* (September 1993), p. 3.

66. Jo Groebel and Uli Gleich, *Gewaltprofil des deutschen Fernsehprogramms* (Opladen 1993), p. 72.

67. Ibid., p. 32.

68. See Langguth, *Jugend ist anders*, p. 166.

69. Ibid., p. 172.

THE GERMANS' VIEW OF POLITICS

1. See Hans-Joachim Veen, "Radikaler Veränderungsschub: Wählergesellschaft und Parteienentwicklung nach der Vereinigung," in Peter Haungs, Karl Martin Grass, Hans Maier and Hans-Joachim Veen (eds.), *Civitas: Widmung für Bernhard Vogel zum 60. Geburtstag* (Paderborn 1992).

2. *KAS-Archive*, Nos. 9101, 9102.

3. See Michael Eilfort, *Die Nichtwähler: Wahlenthaltung als Form des Wahlverhaltens* (Paderborn/Munich/Vienna/Zurich 1994).

4. For more on the development of the parties, see Chapter 7, "Thesis 6."

5. See Gerd Langguth, *The Green Factor in German Politics* (Boulder, CO/London 1986). Also see Gerd Langguth, "Bündnis 90/Die Grünen nach ihrer zweiten Parteigründung: Vier Thesen," *Politische Studien*, No. 334, March/April 1994, pp. 36–51.

6. Kai Schnabel, Jürgen Baumert and Peter-Martin Roeder, "Wertewandel in Ost und West: Ein Vergleich von Jugendlichen und Erwachsenen in den neuen und alten Bundesländern," in Gisela Trommsdorff, *Psychologische Aspekte des sozio-politischen Wandels in Ostdeutschland* (Berlin/New York 1994), pp. 91–92. See also Hans-Joachim Veen, Walter Jaide, Barbara Hille, Walter Friedrich and Peter Förster, *Eine Jugend in Deutschland* (Opladen 1994).

7. Ipos, *Zusammenhalt in Deutschland* (September 1993).

8. *Allensbacher Archiv*, IfD Surveys 5094.

9. *KAS-Archive*, No. 9104.

10. Survey from June 1991, *KAS-Archive*, No. 9104.

11. See Chapter 6.

12. *Allensbacher Archiv,* IfD Surveys 4194/E, 9002, 4197/II, 4197/III; see also Renate Köcher, "Die Ostdeutschen frösteln in der Freiheit," *Frankfurter Allgemeine Zeitung,* September 9, 1992; see also *Handelsblatt,* December 27, 1991.

13. Ipos, *Wirtschaftsstandort in Deutschland,* May 1994, published in June 1994.

14. Ibid.

15. *Allensbacher Archiv,* IfD Survey 5092.

16. *Allensbacher Archiv,* IfD Surveys 5054, 5076, 5088.

17. See Kurt Reumann, "Kohls Optimismus steckt die Wähler an—Er ist seine stärkste Waffe," *Frankfurter Allgemeine Zeitung,* October 18, 1994.

18. David Gow (*The Guardian*), in ARD television program *Presseclub,* October 16, 1994.

19. See Veen, "Radikaler Veränderungsschub," p. 507.

20. Infas Election Analysis, *Dpa Report* of October 17, 1994.

21. Infratest Burke, Berlin, commissioned by Die Zeit, in *Die Zeit,* No. 41, October 7, 1994.

22. *Dpa Report,* October 17, 1994.

23. Forschungsgruppe Wahlen, *Dpa Report,* October 17, 1994.

24. See also results of the Forschungsgruppe Wahlen, "Wer wie gewählt hat," in *Die Zeit,* October 21, 1994, p. 6.

25. Infratest Burke, Berlin, in *Die Zeit,* October 7, 1994; see also Elisabeth Noelle-Neumann, "Eine Richtungswahl," *Frankfurter Allgemeine Zeitung,* September 7, 1994.

26. The *Stuttgarter Zeitung* described the situation in the following way: "Scharping started brilliantly, but serious mistakes followed—such as his offended reaction when Herzog was elected president, his unfortunate comment on income tax and above all his fateful decision to make the PDS politically acceptable in Saxony-Anhalt. This shifted the balance between incumbent and challenger." (Thomas Löffelholz, *Stuttgarter Zeitung,* October 17, 1994). The *Süddeutsche Zeitung* criticized the fact that Scharping as challenger had not developed a plan for the transition to power: "Scharping not only didn't present such a plan—he didn't have one. That is why he avoided any mention of a coalition. By dodging a stance on the issue of a red-green partnership, as he did, Scharping wasn't credible in his commitment to change" (Heribert Prantl, *Süddeutsche Zeitung,* October 18, 1994).

27. For more detailed information, see Patrick Moreau and Viola New, *Die PDS zwischen Linksextremismus und Linkspopulismus,* Konrad-Adenauer-Stiftung, Interne Studien No. 76/1994, Sankt Augustin bei Bonn.

28. Heinrich August Winkler, *Frankfurter Allgemeine Zeitung,* July 28, 1994.

29. *Frankfurter Allgemeine Zeitung,* July 30, 1994.

30. Compare Table 3.1.

31. These figures come from an analysis by the Mannheimer sociologists Matthias Jung and Dieter Roth, Forschungsgruppen Wahlen, and they can be

found in the *Informationsdienst INTER ESSE, Wirtschaft und Politik in Daten und Zusammenhängen*, 9/94, p. 1.

32. RTL Television, June 29, 1994.

33. For example: Paglia Giuseppina, Rifondazione Communista, fifth place; Georgias Koukoulas, Communist Party of Greece, eighth place. Source: Documents of the PDS Election Congress in March 1994.

34. Results of the Federal Congress of ARD Television, Young Comrades, January 22–23, 1994.

35. On "The Communist Platform: The Statutes of the Communist Platform of the PDS," see *Statements of the KPF*, Heft 1/1993, Vol. 4, No. 35, p. 15; KPF, Political Statement, Draft of October 29, 1993, manuscript; Eberhard Czichon and Hein Marohn, *Marxismus und Dogmatismus: Zur Verteidigung des revolutionären Marxismus* (Berlin 1994).

36. Federal Interior Ministry (ed.), *Report for Constitutional Protection 1993* (Bonn 1994), p. 55.

37. *Der Spiegel*, No. 31, August 1, 1994, p. 27.

38. Infas, *Deutschland Politogramm*, July 1994.

39. This discussion paper is dated September 20, 1993.

40. *Der Spiegel*, Interview, No. 30, July 25, 1994.

41. See in particular Ernst Topitsch, *Die Freiheit der Wissenschaft und der politische Auftrag der Universität* (Neuwied/Berlin 1969).

42. Karl Dietrich Bracher, *Zeit der Ideologien: Eine Geschichte politischen Denkens im 20. Jahrhundert* (Stuttgart 1982), p. 170.

THE GERMANS AND THEIR NATION

1. See Wolfgang Herles, *Nationalrausch: Szenen aus dem gesamtdeutschen Machtkampf* (Munich 1990).

2. Also see M. Rainer Lepsius, *Demokratie in Deutschland* (Göttingen 1993), p. 219.

3. Peter Longerich (ed.), *Was ist des Deutschen Vaterland? Dokumente zur Frage der deutschen Einheit 1800–1990* (Munich 1990), Introduction, pp. 13–53.

4. Also see Gerd Langguth, "Nation und Demokratie," in Gerd Langguth (ed.), *Offensive Demokratie: Versuch einer rationalen Orientierung* (Stuttgart 1972), p. 128.

5. For the SED's failure to create a unique socialist German nation, see Gerd Langguth, "Neuer Kurs in der nationalen Frage? Die Haltung der SED zu der deutschen Haltung," *Die Politische Meinung*, No. 33, 1988.

6. Radio Berlin International, January 16, 1990.

7. *Supreme Court Decision*, 36 (1974, p. 1).

8. An in-depth analysis of this can be found in Jens Hacker, *Deutsche Irrtümer: Schönfärber and Helfershelfer der SED-Diktatur im Westen* (Berlin/Frankfurt am Main 1992).

9. Karl Jaspers, *Wohin treibt die Bundesrepublik?* (Munich 1966), p. 241.

10. "For decades now, the center-right parties have been babbling on about this possibility, which will never be realized—neither in the foreseeable future nor perhaps at any time. . . ." In Günter Gaus, *Wo Deutschland liegt—Eine Ortsbestimmung* (Munich 1986), paperback first edition (Hamburg 1983), p. 21.

11. Ibid., p. 29.

12. Ibid., p. 174.

13. More on this in Gerd Langguth, "Die deutsche Frage und die europäische Gemeinschaft," in Karl Dietrich Bracher, Manfred Funke and Hans-Peter Schwarz (eds.), *Deutschland zwischen Krieg und Frieden—Beiträge zur Politik und Kultur im 20. Jahrhundert* (Düsseldorf 1990), p. 246.

14. See Jürgen Schmude, "Deutsch-deutsches Verhältnis—aus der Geschichte lernen!," Informationen der Sozialdemokratischen Bundestagsfraktion, *Tagesdienst* No. 931, May 17, 1985, p. 9. See also *Bundestagsdrucksache* zur aktuellen Stunde, "Die Äusserungen des stellvertretenden Vorsitzenden der SPD-Fraktion, Schmude, zum Wiedervereinigungsgebot des Grundgesetzes," 140th session, May 23, 1985, p. 1036. The position of the former deputy director of the SPD, Jürgen Schmude, created intense political controversies at the time. In comparing the preamble of the Constitution with Article 6 of the Basic Treaty, Schmude thought the call for reunification had become obsolete.

15. This idea of identity expresses the difficulty Germans have with their nation and with establishing a common historical level of experience. More on this in Werner Weidenfeld (ed.), *Die Identität der Deutschen* (Munich/Vienna 1983).

16. Released in *Bulletin of the Press and Information Office of the Federal Government*, No. 134, p. 1147, November, 29, 1989.

17. Marion Gräfin Dönhoff, in *Die Zeit*, January 20, 1989.

18. Willy Brandt, "Deutsche Wegmarken," *Der Tagesspiegel*, September 13, 1988. See also Hacker, *Deutsche Irrtümer*, p. 237.

19. Egon Bahr, "Das Gebot staatlicher Einheit und das Ziel Europa im Widerspruch," *Frankfurter Rundschau*, December 13, 1988.

20. Ulrich Schacht, "Ländchen oder Vaterland," *Die Welt*, March 5, 1994.

21. For parliament's involvement with questions of recent German history, see "Bericht der Enquete Kommission: Aufarbeitung von Geschichte und Folgen der SED Diktatur in Deutschland," *Bundestagsdrucksache 12/7820*, May 31, 1994.

22. Young intellectuals in the former GDR showed great aversion to the thought of German unification, which is revealed by a survey of students at the University of Leipzig in 1991: "The questionnaire assumes that I can identify with Germany. But I can't" (a student of Arabic studies in Leipzig, twenty); and "I can't integrate socially and intellectually into an exploitative state" (student of Chinese studies, Leipzig, nineteen); and "I'd like to make it known that I didn't agree and still don't agree with the FRG's annexation of the GDR" (student of Arabic studies, Leipzig, twenty). See Paul-Ludwig Weinacht and G. Sara Nathir, " 'Deutschland

sollte . . . .': Opinions of Students in East and West on Germany Today,"
Deutschland Archiv, No. 10, October 1991, p. 1065.

23. Interview with Karl Dietrich Bracher in *Die Welt*, April 26, 1993.

24. Interview with Bracher in *Die Welt*, August 15, 1994.

25. Ibid. The legal philosopher Sibylle Tönnies also points to the fact that "the closer that right and left get to their ideological core, the closer they become: Both movements were antiideal, antiliberal, anti–rule of law, partisan and based on the masses. The great repression mechanism of the left stems from their blindness to this very obvious fact." See Sibylle Tönnies, "Der Rest von Marx—Rechts und Links: Über die totalitäre Vergangenheit der Linken und ihre Verdrängungsleistung," *Die Zeit*, May 20, 1994.

26. Hans-Joachim Maaz, *Der Gefühlsstau: Ein Psychogramm der DDR* (Berlin 1990), p. 25.

27. Ibid., p. 31.

28. Interview with Joachim Gauck,"Die Arroganz der Macht war grösser als ich es vermutet hätte," *Die Welt*, August 15, 1994.

29. Ibid. See also Gerd Langguth, *Protestbewegung—Entwicklung, Niedergang, Renaissance: Die Neue Linke seit 1968* (Cologne 1983), p. 256; and Langguth, "Die Friedensbewegung in der Bundesrepublik Deutschland zu Beginn der achtziger Jahre," Stellungnahme aus Anlass der Anhörung der Enquete-Kommission, Aufarbeitung und Folgen der SED-Diktatur in Deutschland, November 2, 1993.

30. Heribert Prantl, in *Süddeutsche Zeitung*, October 1, 1994.

31. Ulrich Schacht, "Ländchen oder Vaterland."

32. Cora Stephan, *Der Betroffenheitskult: Eine politische Sittengeschichte* (Berlin 1993), p. 17.

33. Ibid., p. 116.

34. See the comments by Jens Reich, "Da sind wir, Figuren federwerkgetrieben. Das verhinderte Kultbuch einer Generation in der DDR: Eine neue Lektüre von Uwe Johnsons Mutmassungen über Jakob," in *Frankfurter Allgemeine Zeitung*, May 18, 1994.

35. See Martin Walser, *Vormittag eines Schriftstellers* (Frankfurt am Main 1994).

36. See Helmut Peitsch, "Antipoden im 'Gewissen der Nation?' Günter Grass und Martin Walsers deutsche Fragen," in Helmut Scheuer (ed.), *Dichter und ihre Nation* (Frankfurt am Main 1993), pp. 459–89.

37. Günter Grass, *Kopfgeburten oder Die Deutschen sterben aus* (Darmstadt, Neuwied 1980), pp. 153–54.

38. Günter Grass, "Deutscher Lastenausgleich: Wider das dumpfe Einheitsgebot," in *Reden und Gespräche* (Frankfurt am Main 1990), p. 11. Here, Grass' decisive argument was the connection between a unified nation-state on German soil and Auschwitz. See Rudolf Augstein and Günter Grass, *Deutschland, einig Vaterland? Ein Streitgespräch* (Göttingen 1990), p. 55.

39. *Der Spiegel*, No. 47, November 20, 1989.

40. The quotes are from a speech Martin Walser held in Bergen-Enkheim on August 8, 1977. Walser quotes them again himself, in *Reden über das eigene Land* (Munich 1988), p. 22, and in *Über Deutschland reden* (Frankfurt am Main 1989), p. 89.

41. Walser, *Über Deutschland reden*, p. 30.

42. *Frankfurter Allgemeine Zeitung*, February 11, 1994.

43. Ibid.

44. Günter de Bruyn,"So viele Länder, Ströme, Sitten: Gedanken über die deutsche Kulturnation," in *Jubelschreie, Trauergesänge—Deutsche Befindlichkeiten* (Frankfurt am Main 1991), p. 21.

45. Heiner Müller, *Zur Lage der Nation: Interview mit Frank M. Raddatz* (Berlin 1990), p. 56.

46. Hans Magnus Enzensberger, "Gangarten—Ein Nachtrag zur Utopie," *Frankfurter Allgemeine Zeitung*, May 19, 1990.

47. See Bernhard Giesen et al., "Vom Patriotismus zum Nationalismus: Zur Evolution und der Deutschen Kulturnation," in *Nationale und kulturelle Identität: Studienentwicklung des kollektiven Bewusstseins der Neuzeit* (Frankfurt am Main 1991), pp. 253–303.

48. Günter Kunert, *Der Sturz vom Sockel: Feststellungen und Widersprüche* (Munich 1992), p. 32.

49. Ibid., pp. 32 and 57.

50. Thomas Rietzschel, *Über Deutschland: Schriftsteller geben Auskunft* (Leipzig 1993), Introduction, pp. 9–10.

51. Ibid., p. 11.

52. Ibid.

53. Peter Schneider, *Vom Ende der Gewissheit* (Berlin 1994), p. 115.

54. For a definition of this term, see Werner Weidenfeld (ed.), *Die Identität der Deutschen* (Munich 1983); Hermann Lübbe et al., *Der Mensch als Orientierungswesen? Ein interdisziplinärer Erkundungsgang* (Freiburg/Munich 1982).

55. *Der Spiegel*, September 19, 1994, p. 65.

56. See also Langguth, *Offensive Demokratie*, p. 135.

THE ECONOMIC CHALLENGES OF A REUNIFIED GERMANY

1. Government statement of July 8, 1994.

2. Hans Herrmann Hertle, "Das reale Bild war eben katastrophal!" Discussion with Gerhard Schürer, former chairman of the State Planning Commission and Member of the Politburo, in *Deutschland Archiv*, No. 10, October, 1992, p. 1031.

3. More detailed information on these figures in Karl-Rudolf Korte, *Die Chance genutzt? Die Politik zur Einheit Deutschlands* (Frankfurt/New York 1994).

4. See Roland Stimpel, Henning Krumrey and Hans-Peter Canibol, "DDR: Die Kosten der Modernisierung einer modernen Wirtschaft," *Wirtschaftswoche*, January 12, 1990, No. 3.

5. *Die Zeit*, October 8, 1993.

6. See Herbert Henzler, "Kritische Würdigung der Debatte um den Wirtschaftsstandort Deutschland," *Zeitschrift für Betriebswirtschaft*, Vol. 63 (1993), p. 5.

7. See *Monatshefte der Deutschen Bundesbank*, February 1994, p. 6.

8. See Michael Heise, "Die deutsche Wirtschaft im internationalen Standortwettbewerb," *Wirtschaftsdienst*, Vol. 73, (1993), p. 348.

9. See Herbert Giersch, *Risiken und Chancen für Ostdeutschland*, Volkswirtschaftliche Korrespondenz der Adolf-Weber-Stiftung, No. 4/1991.

10. See Norbert Walter (ed.), "Standort D—Zeit zum Handeln," *Deutsche Bank Research*, Bulletin from October 7, 1993.

11. See Heinz Gert Preusse, *Ist die Frage nach der internationalen Wettbewerbsfähigkeit überholt?* (Göttingen 1988), p. 2.

12. See Jörg Beyfuss and Bernd H.-J. Kitterer, *Deutsche Direktinvestionen im Ausland: Bestandsaufnahme und Ergebnisse einer Unternehmensbefragung* (Beiträge zur Wirtschafts-und Sozialpolitik, Institut der deutschen Wirtschaft Köln, No. 181) (Cologne 1990).

13. See Reinhard Büscher and Jochen Hermann, "Standort Diskussion: Altes Thema mit neuer Brisanz," *Wirtschaftsdienst*, Vol. 89 (1989), p. 237.

14. See for example, Erhard Kantzenbach, *Der Wirtschaftsstandort Deutschland im internationalen Wettebewerb*, HWWA-Diskussionspapier No. 11 (Hamburg 1993), p. 14.

15. See Franz Thoma, "Warum Deutschland zurückgefallen ist," *Süddeutsche Zeitung*, January 25, 1994.

16. See Heise, "Die deutsche Wirtschaft im internationalen Standortwettbewerb," p. 349.

17. *Monatsberichte der Deutschen Bundesbank*, March 1993, p. 21.

18. See Lester Thurow: *Kopf an Kopf* (Düsseldorf/Vienna/New York/Moscow 1993), p. 283.

19. See Bolke Behrens and Hans-Peter Canibol, "Einäugiger König," *Wirtschaftswoche*, No. 53, December 24, 1992, pp. 36–41.

20. "Irenic" refers to the attempt to engage in a peaceful, interconfessional debate with the goal of reconciliation.

21. See Walter Eucken, *Grundsätze der Wirtschaftspolitik* (Tübingen 1952), p. 14.

22. See Walter Eucken, "Die Wettbewerbsordnung und ihre Verwirklichung," *ORDO*, Vol. II (1949), p. 32; and Jörg M. Winterberg, *Religion und Marktwirtschaft* (Baden-Baden 1994), p. 44.

23. See Karlheinz Kleps, *Staatliche Preispolitik* (Munich 1984), p. 145.

24. This is the normal term in recent macroeconomic literature for young industries that (according to protectionist policy makers) need to be protected by native tariffs while they grow to a level where they can compete successfully.

25. "If it is correct that one can only distribute what has already been produced, then the focus of social reformers should be on the economic system that will be the most economically productive" (Eucken, *Grundsätze der Wirtschaftspolitik*, p. 315).

26. See Sachverständigenrat zur Begutachtung der gesamtwirtschaftlichen Entwicklung, *Jahresgutachten 1992/93*, p. 184. and *Jahresgutachten 1993/94*, p. 249.

27. See Manfred E. Streit, *Am Beginn einer europäischen Industriepolitik*, Volkswirtschaftliche Korrespondenz der Adolf-Weber-Stiftung, No. 3/1992.

GERMANY'S INTERNATIONAL ROLE

1. For more detailed information, see Gerd Langguth (ed.), *Berlin: Vom Brennpunkt der Teilung zur Brücke der Einheit* (Cologne 1990). See in particular Hans-Heinrich Mahnke, *Vom Londoner Protokoll zum Viermächte-Abkommen*, p. 88; Peter Füsslein, *Ausgestaltung und Entwicklung des Viermächte-Abkommens bis zum Herbst 1989*, p. 107; Roger Morgan, *Die Berlinpolitik der Westmächte*, p. 126., and Gerd Langguth, *Die Berlinpolitik der DDR und der Sowjetunion*, p. 142.

2. See Bundesminister für innerdeutsche Beziehungen (ed.), *Texte zur Deutschlandpolitik*, Vol. II/3 (Bonn 1976), p. 440.

3. For more detail, see Gerd Langguth, "Die deutsche Frage und die Europäische Gemeinschaft," in Karl Dietrich Bracher, Manfred Funke and Hans-Peter Schwarz (eds.), *Deutschland zwischen Krieg und Frieden: Beiträge zur Politik und Kultur im 20. Jahrhundert* (Cologne 1990), p. 251.

4. Gerd Langguth, "Innerdeutsche und internationale Aspekte der Berlin-Politik," *Aus Politik und Zeitgeschichte*, B 33–34/86, August 16, 1986.

5. For more detail, see Langguth, *Die deutsche Frage*, p. 259–60. See also Vernon A. Walters, *Die Vereinigung war voraussehbar—Hinter den Kulissen eines entscheidenden Jahres* (Berlin 1994).

6. See Karl Kaiser, *Deutschlands Vereinigung: Die internationalen Aspekte* (Bergisch Gladbach 1991).

7. See Horst Teltschik, *329 Tage: Innenaussichten der Einigung* (Berlin 1991), p. 313.

8. See *Die Welt*, August 31, 1994.

9. Gregor Schölgen, *Stationen deutscher Aussenpolitik—Von Friedrich dem Grossen bis zur Gegenwart* (Munich 1992), p. 169.

10. Christian Hacke, *Weltmacht wider Willen: Die Aussenpolitik der Bundes-republik Deutschland* (Frankfurt/Berlin 1993). (The first edition of this book in 1988 already had this title.)

11. Hans-Peter Schwarz, "Deutsche Aussenpolitik nach der Vereinigung," in Peter Haungs, Karl Martin Grass, Hans Maier and Hans-Joachim Veen (eds.), *Civitas: Widmung für Bernhard Vogel zum 60. Geburtstag* (Paderborn 1992), p. 500.

12 Ibid., p. 484.

13. Hans-Peter Schwarz, *Die Zentralmacht Europas: Deutschlands Rückkehr auf die Weltbühne* (Berlin 1994).

14. David Marsh, *Der zaudernde Riese: Deutschland in Europa* (Munich 1994).

15. See, for example, Francis Fukuyama, *Das Ende der Geschichte* (Munich 1992).

16. Hans-Peter Schwarz, "Auf dem Weg zum post-kommunistischen Europa," *Europa Archiv*, Vol. 44, No. 11 (1989), p. 319.

17. Ibid.

18. Samuel Huntington, "The Clash of Civilizations?" *Foreign Affairs*, Vol. 72, No. 3, 1993.

19. Schwarz, "Deutsche Aussenpolitik," p. 485.

20. See Helmut Kohl, "Die Sicherheitsinteressen Deutschlands," *Bulletin of the Press and Information Office of the Federal Government*, No. 13, p. 101, February 10, 1993.

21. See Gerd Langguth, "Konrad Adenauer: 'Vater' der Wiedervereinigung oder 'Spalter' Deutschlands?" in Gerd Langguth, *Macht bedeutet Verantwortung* (Cologne 1994), p. 75.

22. Klaus Kinkel, "Die Rolle Deutschlands in der Weltpolitik," *Bulletin of the Press and Information Office of the Federal Government*, No. 18, March 3, 1993, p. 142.

23. Spiegel Interview, *Der Spiegel*, No. 3 (1993), January 18, 1993, p. 22.

24. See Alain Minc, *Die deutsche Herausforderung: Wird die Bundesrepublik den Europäischen Binnenmarkt beherrschen?* (Hamburg 1989).

25. See also *OECD-Wirtschaftsausblick*, No. 54, December 1933, p. 133.

26. *Neue Zürcher Zeitung*, June 9, 1994, based on analyses by the Vienna Institute of International Economic Comparisons (WIIW).

27. Norbert Wagner, "Zur Lage in Russland nach den Wahlen," *KAS-Auslandsinformationen*, No. 2 (1994), p. 55.

28. Allen Lynch, "Die politische Zukunft Russlands nach den Wahlen vom Dezember 1993," No. 3, January 1994, an up-to-date brief analysis by the Forschungsinstituts der Deutschen Gesellschaft für Auswärtige Politik, Bonn, January, 1994.

29. *Neue Zürcher Zeitung*, August 29–30, 1993.

30. *Neue Zürcher Zeitung*, March 4, 1994.

31. Quote from Marc Champirn, *Moscow Times*, February 3, 1994.

32. Zbigniew Brzezinski, "Die übereilte Partnerschaft—die Vereinigten Staaten und Russland," *Europa Archiv*, No. 5, March 10, 1994, p. 130.

33. Jürgen Nötzold, "Wie die Ukraine zu retten wäre," *Neue Zürcher Zeitung*, April 24–25, 1994.

34. *Neue Zürcher Zeitung*, August 5, 1994.

35. Theo Sommer, "Jetzt erst der Krieg zu Ende," *Die Zeit*, No. 36, September 2, 1994.

36. See *Frankfurter Allgemeine Zeitung*, September 10, 1994.

37. Compare Lothar Rühl, "Bedürfnis nach Sicherheit," *Die Welt*, December 9, 1993.

38. See *Europa Archiv*, No. 17, September 10, 1994, p. 500.

39. *Neue Zürcher Zeitung*, June 11, 1994.

40. Richard Nixon, *Beyond Peace* (New York 1994).

41. *Bulletin of the Press and Information Office of the Federal Government*, No. 128, November 13, 1991, p. 1041.

42. See *Europa Archiv*, No. 3, February 1994, p. 127.

43. See Andras Inotai, "Die Beziehungen zwischen der EU und den assoziierten Staaten Mittel- und Osteuropas," *Europäische Rundschau*, No. 3/94, p. 19.

44. See, among other things, *Neue Zürcher Zeitung*, May 11, 1994; *Frankfurter Allgemeine Zeitung*, May 9, 1994.

45. See Karl-Heinz Kamp, *Die Frage einer "Osterweiterung der NATO,"* Interne Studien und Berichte der Konrad-Adenauer-Stiftung, No. 47/93 (Sankt Augustin bei Bonn 1993).

46. *Bulletin of the Press and Information Office of the Federal Government*, No. 3, January 17, 1994.

47. By the end of phase I, seven years after start of the treaty, each side will have to have reduced the total number of their stationed strategic nuclear warheads by about 3,800 to 4,250. There should then be no more than 1,200 land-based intercontinental missiles with multiple warheads, 2,160 sea-based missiles, and 650 on heavy intercontinental missiles. By the end of phase II, which should be completed by the year 2003, or as early as the year 2000, each side should have reduced the total amount of its stationed strategic nuclear warheads by 3,000 to 3,500. All land-based intercontinental missiles from then on can only carry a single warhead. The total number of warheads allowed for sea-based missiles will be 1,700 to 1,750; but here multiple warheads will be allowed. Whereas the United States will give up two thirds of her sea-based strategic warheads, Russia will mostly give up her heavy land-based intercontinental missiles of the type SS-18, SS-19 and SS-24.

48. See Volker Rühe, *Deutschlands Verantwortung: Perspektiven für das neue Europa* (Frankfurt/Berlin 1994), p. 93.

49. See excerpts from an evaluation by the president of the Federal Intelligence Service, in *Die Zeit*, No. 34, August 19, 1994.

50. Karl-Heinz Kamp, *Probleme nuklearer Abrüstung: Die Vernichtung von Kernwaffen in der GUS*, Interne Studien und Berichte der Konrad-Adenauer-Stiftung, No. 45/93 (Sankt Augustin bei Bonn 1993).

51. *Die Welt*, June 25, 1994.

52. *Frankfurter Allgemeine Zeitung*, April 8, 1993.

53. See here Günter Burghardt, "Die Erweiterung der Europäischen Union um die Länder Mittel- und Osteuropas," *KAS-Auslandsinformationen*, No. 5 (1994), p. 85.

54. *Frankfurter Allgemeine Zeitung*, June 21, 1993.

55. See Michael Wolffsohn, *Frieden jetzt? Nahost im Umbruch* (Munich 1994).

56. See Michael J. Inacker, *Unter Auschluss der Öffentlichkeit, Die Deutschen in der Golfallianz* (Bonn 1991).

57. See Gebhard Schweigler, *Supermacht mit Führungsschwächen*, Forschungsbericht der Stiftung Wissenschaft und Politik Ebenhausen (Ebenhausen 1993); Gebhard Schweigler (ed.), *Zur weltpolitischen Rolle der USA*, Forschungsbericht der Stiftung Wissenschaft und Politik, Ebenhausen (Ebenhausen 1994).

58. Economic Strategy Institute, *Shrinking the Atlantic: Europe and the American Economy* (Washington, DC 1994). See also Josef Joffe, "Die Wiederentdeckung Europas," *Süddeutsche Zeitung*, June 24, 1994.

59. Figures come from Werner Weidenfeld, "Jenseits des Selbstverständlichen: Europa und USA brauchen einen Neubeginn," *Europa Archiv*, No. 13/14, July 25, 1994, p. 371.

60. Ibid. For the economic aspect, see also Daniel Hamilton, *Beyond Bonn: America and the Berlin Republic* (Washington, DC 1994), particularly pp. 54–57.

61. For more on this, see Weidenfeld, "Jenseits," p. 369.

62. *Neue Zürcher Zeitung*, April 17–18, 1994.

63. See Günther Nonnenmacher, "Prinzipien internationalistisch: Nachdenken über die Zukunft der deutschen Aussenpolitik," *Frankfurter Allgemeine Zeitung*, October 22, 1992.

64. *1992 World Bank Report*, quoted from Dieter Senghaas, in *DGAP-Arbeitspapiere*, No. 72 (Bonn 1993).

65. Paragraph 301 of American trade law, introduced by President Bush to combat unfair trade practices. According to Paragraph 301, the U.S. government can unilaterally, without consulting trade partners or GATT, impose punitive measures against countries that engage in dumping in attempts to gain a competitive advantage, or that do not open their markets enough to American imports. "Super 301" is America's most important device to threaten Japan in her supposedly unfair trade practices. Paragraph 301 goes against the spirit of the GATT agreement in principle. The World Trade Organization, which is supposed to supersede GATT according to its resolutions, will hopefully motivate the U.S. Congress to revoke 301—or at least make it superfluous.

66. See the section "Democracy as a Policy for Peace" in this chapter.

67. *Der Spiegel*, No. 14, April 4, 1994. This multinational survey was jointly conducted by the *New York Times* (United States), *The Guardian* (Great Britain) and *Asaki Shinbun* (Japan).

68. Hans-Peter Schwarz, *Die gezähmten Deutschen: Von der Machtbesessenheit zur Machtvergessenheit* (Stuttgart 1985).

69. Survey conducted by the German Armed Forces, *Frankfurter Allgemeine Zeitung*, August 17, 1993.

70. *KAS-Umfrage*, Archive No. 9301.

71. *Der Spiegel*, survey, No. 14, April 4, 1994.

72. *Frankfurter Allgemeine Zeitung*, August 17, 1993.

73. United States Information Agency, *USIA Opinion Research Memorandum* (M-146–94), June 16, 1994, p. 3.

74. Schwarz, "Deutsche Aussenpolitik nach der Vereinigung," in Haungs et al. (ed.), *Civitas*, p. 486.

75. See also Günter Rinsche, "Grundfragen einer neuen politischen Ordnung in Europa," *KAS Auslandsinformationen*, 1/1994, p. 26; and Peter R. Weilemann, "Zwischen nationalem Interesse und europäischen Engagement," *KAS-Auslandsinformationen*, 1/94, p. 127.

76. Jacques Delors, "Entwicklungsperspektiven der Europäischen Gemeinschaft," *Aus Politik und Zeitgeschichte*, B 1/93, January 1, 1993, p. 4.

77. Ibid.

78. *KAS-Umfrage*, December 1993.

79. See Gerd Langguth, "Die Einstellung der Deutschen zu Europa," *Die Sonde*, No. 1/2, 1989, pp. 21–31.

80. At the same time, 77 percent agreed that a "firm integration of a more powerful Germany into the EU" is in the interest of Germany and her neighbors (15 percent did not agree on the whole, 8 percent did not have an opinion). Survey in *Die Zeit*, June 3, 1994, conducted by Infratest-Burke, Berlin, May 13–20, 1994. In another survey, 66 percent of Germans felt that Germany's membership in the EU was a "good thing," 23 percent thought it was "neither good, nor bad," and 8 percent thought it "bad" (3 percent did not respond). Sixty-six percent of the surveyed Germans were "fundamentally for a unified Europe," 18 percent were "neither for nor against," 12 percent were "against a unified Europe" (4 percent no response). *Focus*, No. 23/94, survey by Basis research, May 16–20, 1994.

81. *Eurobarometer* No. 41, Spring 1994, Early Release, p. 10.

82. See Gerd Langguth, "Memorandum zur Demokratieentwicklung in der EG," *EG-Informationen*, published by the Representation of the EC Commission Bonn, No. 5 (1994), p. 13.

83. See Carl Otto Lenz (ed.), *EG-Vertrag-Kommentar* (Cologne/Basel/Vienna 1994).

84. Comments on how to reform the European Union were presented by a study group from the Bertelsmann Foundation, called the "European Structural Commission," which was headed by the political scientist Werner Weidenfeld from Mainz. See "Wider die Erosion von innen: Ein Reformkonzept für die Europäische Union/Strategien und Optionen," *Frankfurter Allgemeine Zeitung*, July 14, 1994.

85. See Gerd Langguth, commentary on Article 3b (subsidiarity principle) of the EC treaty, in Lenz, *EG-Vertrag-Kommentar*.

86. I already referred to the conditions of membership in the European Union in the section "Historic Changes and Open Questions" in this chapter.

87. Quoted in Chancellor Helmut Kohl's government statement to the Bundestag, September 25, 1992.

88. See Carl-Dieter Spranger, *Verantwortung für die Eine Welt: Deutsche Entwicklungszusammenarbeit* (Berlin and Frankfurt/Main 1994).

89. See the *World Development Report* of the World Bank, 1993. Quoted from Werner Lachmann, "Grenzen und Chancen der Entwicklungshilfe," *Aus Politik und Zeitgeschichte*, B 20/94, May 20, 1994, p. 11.

90. *Focus*, No. 21, May 21, 1994, p. 44. Based on 1992 data provided by the Federal Ministry for Economic Cooperation and Development.

91. *Frankfurter Allgemeine Zeitung*, May 13, 1994.

92. *Neue Zürcher Zeitung*, March 25, 1994.

93. *World Development Report 1993*, published by the World Bank, August 1993, Bonn, p. 247.

94. Ibid.

95. Federal Ministry for Economic Cooperation and Development, *Concept for Developmental Cooperation with Latin America*, December 1992, p. 2.

96. Ibid., p. 4.

97. Alfred Zänker, "In Lateinamerika geht es bergauf," *Die Welt*, January 6, 1994.

98. "In Lateinamerika richtet sich das Augenmark auf die sozialen Reformen," *Frankfurter Allgemeine Zeitung*, April 11, 1994.

99. Federal Ministry for Economic Cooperation and Development, *Concept for Developmental Cooperation with the Countries of Asia*, July 1993.

100. Lothar Brock, "Die Dritte Welt in ihrem 5. Jahrzent," *Aus Politik und Zeitgeschichte*, December 4, 1992, p. 17.

101. Ibid.

102. Quoted from the *Ninth Report of the Federal Government's Development Policy*, Federal Ministry for Economic Cooperation and Development, BT-Drucksache 12/4096, January 13, 1993.

103. See *Neue Zürcher Zeitung*, November 21/22, 1993.

104. Population Fund of the United Nations (UNFPA)/German Society for the United Nations (DGVN) (ed.), *World Population Report 1994* (Bonn 1994). See also *Kurzinformationen 1994*.

105. *Frankfurter Allgemeine Zeitung*, August 2, 1994.

106. See Joachim Schöps, "In jeder Sekunde 3 Menschen mehr," *Der Spiegel*, March 8, 1993.

107. *Frankfurter Allgemeine Zeitung*, November 11, 1993.

108. Ibid.

109. *Frankfurter Allgemeine Zeitung*, August 3, 1994.

110. See Lachmann, "Grenzen und Chancen der Entwicklungshilfe," p. 12.

111. Ibid., p. 13.

112. See Klemens van de Sand, "Gemeinsamkeit trotz unterschiedlicher Wege? Plädoyer für mehr Zusammenarbeit der Entwicklungsorganisationen," *Der Überblick*, 4/93, p. 92.

113. See Franz Nuscheler, "Learning from Experience or Preaching Ideologies? Rethinking Development Theory," *Law and State*, Vol. 38, 1988, pp. 104–25.

114. See suggestions from the Konrad Adenauer Foundation for the World Conference for Social Development in Copenhagen 1995: "Für Demokratie und soziale Gerechtigkeit: Vorbereitungskonferenz," Sankt Augustin bei Bonn, April 28, 1994.

115. *Neue Zürcher Zeitung*, November 21/22, 1993.

116. See Friedbert Pflüger, *Die Menschenrechtspolitik der USA: Amerikanische Aussenpolitik zwischen Idealismus und Realismus 1972–1982* (Munich/Vienna 1983).

117. Theodor Hanf, "Nach Afghanistan: Überlegungen zu einer Demokratieorientierten Dritten-Welt-Politik, in Helmut Kohl (ed.), *Der neue Realismus— Aussenpolitik nach Iran und Afghanistan* (Düsseldorf 1980), p. 168. Dieter Oberndörfer, "Politik und Verwaltung in der Dritten Welt: Überlegungen zu einer neuen Orientierung," in Joachim Jens-Hesse (ed.), *Politikwissenschaft und Verwaltungswissenschaft*, PVS-Sonderheft 13 (Opladen 1982), pp. 447–57.

118. Carl-Dieter Spranger, "Vortrag vor der Führungsakademie der Bundeswehr am 22. Februar in Hamburg," *Bulletin of the Press and Information Office of the Federal Government*, February 25, 1994, p. 165.

119. Ibid.

120. Ibid.

121. See Gerd Langguth, "Wird das GATT-System überleben?" *Aussenpolitik*, No. 3/92, p. 220.

122. See "Auch Entwicklungsländer sind Gewinner," *Frankfurter Allgemeine Zeitung*, December 16, 1993, p. 17.

123. Compare Thomas Oppermann and Marc Beise, "Die neue Welthandelsorganisation: Ein stabiles Regelwerk für weltweiten Freihandel?" *Europa Archiv*, No.7/94, p. 195.

124. Hans-Helmut Taake, "Die Integration der Entwicklungsländer in die Weltwirtschaft," *Europa Archiv*, No. 8/94, p. 227.

125. Ibid.

126. Wolfgang Nieländer, "Vorsicht vor zu viel Caritas," *Frankfurter Allgemeine Zeitung*, May 28, 1994.

IN LIEU OF A CONCLUSION: THE GERMANS IN SEARCH OF SECURITY—TEN THESES

1. At the time, there were major discussions about the book by Fritz René Allemann, *Bonn ist nicht Weimar* (Cologne 1956). There was concern as the right-radical party "National Democratic Party of Germany" was elected into several state parliaments between 1966 and 1968.

2. Margareta Mathiopoulos, *Das Ende der Bonner Republik* (Stuttgart 1993).

3. Werner Weidenfeld, *Der deutsche Weg* (Berlin 1990), p. 150.

4. Ibid., p. 151.

5. Jakob Kaiser, *Wir haben Brücke zu sein: Reden, Äusserungen und Aufsätze zur Deutschlandpolitik*, edited by Christian Hacke (Cologne 1988).

6. See Rainer Dohse, *Der dritte Weg: Neutralitätsbestrebungen in Westdeutschland zwischen 1945–1955* (Hamburg 1974).

7. Dan Diner, "Feinde des Westens," *Frankfurter Allgemeine Zeitung*, May 11, 1994.

8. Hans-Ulrich Wehler, "Gurus und Irrlichter: Die neuen Träume der Intellektuellen," *Frankfurter Allgemeine Zeitung*, May 6, 1994.

9. Karlheinz Weissmann, "Die Nation denkt: Wir sind keine Verschwörer," *Frankfurter Allgemeine Zeitung*, April 22, 1994. See also Rainer Zitelmann, Karlheinz Weissmann und Michael Grossmann (eds.), *Westbindung—Chancen und Risiken für Deutschland* (Frankfurt/Main 1993).

10. Weissmann, "Die Nation denkt: Wir sind keine Verschwörer."

11. See Gerd Langguth, "Was ist Politik?" in Günther Rüther, *Politik und Gesellschaft in Deutschland* (Cologne 1994).

12. Joachim Fest, *Der zerstörte Traum: Vom Ende des utopischen Zeitalters* (Berlin 1991).

13. Joseph A. Schumpeter, *Kapitalismus, Sozialismus und Demokratie* (Bern 1950), p. 19.

14. Interview with *Der Spiegel*, No. 30/94, July 25, 1994.

15. Wolfgang Schäuble, *Und der Zukunft zugewandt* (Berlin 1994), p. 51.

16. For more on this, see the surveys cited in Chapter 2 of this book.

17. *Spiegel* Spezial, "Das Profil der Deutschen: Was sie vereint, was sie trennt," January 1991, pp. 72–76.

18. See Helmut Klages, *Traditionsbruch als Herausforderung: Perspektiven der Wertewandelgesellschaft* (Frankfurt/New York 1993).

19. Martin and Sylvia Greiffenhagen, *Ein schwieriges Vaterland: Zur politischen Kultur im vereinigten Deutschland* (Munich/Leipzig 1993), p. 172.

20. Ibid., p. 32.

21. Dieter E. Zimmer, "Expedition zu den wahren Gefühlen," *Die Zeit*, July 3, 1981.

22. See Kurt Sontheimer, *Zeitenwende* (Hamburg 1983).

23. See Bergedorfer Gesprächskreis, *Wieviel Gemeinsinn braucht die liberale Gesellschaft?* (Hamburg 1993), p. 68.

24. See the American communitarianism discussion, in Konrad Adam, "Was von den Richtungskämpfen bleibt," *Frankfurter Allgemeine Zeitung*, March 12, 1994. See also "Manifest der amerikanischen Kommunitarier: Die Stimme der Gesellschaft hörbar machen," *Frankfurter Allgemeine Zeitung*, March 8, 1994; and Walter Reese Schäfer, *Was ist Kommunismus?* (Frankfurt/New York 1994).

25. Interview with Karl Dietrich Bracher, *Die Welt*, April 26, 1993.

26. Ibid.

27. Hans-Peter Martin/Harald Schumann, " 'Der Feind sind wir selbst.': Die Menschheit auf der Suche nach einem neuen Zivilisationsmodell," *Der Spiegel*, No. 2, January 11, 1993, p. 102.

28. Richard Schröder, *Deutschland schwierig Vaterland: Für eine neue politische Kultur* (Freiburg/Basel/Vienna 1993), p. 19.

29. Aside from a "functional elite," there has to be a distinction made between "value elites" and "power elites."

30. Schäuble, *Und der Zukunft zugewandt*, p. 25.

31. See Klaus Mehnert, *Der deutsche Standort* (Stuttgart 1967).

32. *Die Zeit*, December 31, 1993.

33. See Gerd Langguth, *Der grüne Faktor: Von der Bewegung zur Partei?* (Osnabrück/Zurich 1984).

34. See Jürgen Rüttgers, *Dinosaurier der Demokratie: Wege aus der Parteienkrise und Politikverdrossenheit* (Hamburg 1993).

35. Wolfgang Schäuble, in *Süddeutsche Zeitung*, May 15–16, 1993.

36. Ibid.

37. Gerd Langguth, *Jugend ist anders: Porträt einer jungen Generation* (Freiburg/Basel/Vienna), p. 171.

38. The public was made aware of this situation when a Hamburg court gave a suspended arrest in October 1993 to the man who had stabbed Monica Seles, the world's best tennis player, in the neck from behind.

39. See Martina Fietz and Michael Jach (eds.), *Zündstoff Kriminalität—Innere Sicherheit auf dem Prüfstand* (Munich/Landsberg am Lech 1994).

40. Konrad-Adenauer-Stiftung, *Forschung und Beratung*, Archive No. 930540.

41. "Die Kriminalität in Deutschland." Polizeiliche Kriminalstatistik für das Jahr 1993, in *Bulletin des Presse- und Informationsamtes der Bundesregierung*, No. 50, May 30, 1994.

42. The quota of solved crimes for murder and killings applies to the old states, including Berlin as a whole.

43. As a rule, these are foreigners who lived in Germany for a short period. Thirty-seven percent of all crimes by foreigners are committed by applicants for political asylum.

44. Look for the appropriate figures in Chapter 2.

45. *Verfassungsschutzbericht 1993*, p. 162.

46. See the information of the Association of German Criminal Investigators, November, 1993.

47. See Peter Hintze, "Politik für die Zukunft," *Die politische Meinung*, No. 298, September 1994, p. 71.

48. Institut für Demoskopie Allensbach, Archive No. 2019, 4087.

49. KAS-Archive No. 9303X0.

50. See Meinhard Miegel and Stefanie Wahl, *Das Ende der Individualität: Die Kultur des Westens zerstört sich selbst* (Munich/Lansberg am Lech 1993); the study "The Aged of the Future," presented by the Minister of Family Hannelore Rönsch in August 1994; and Ursula Lehr and Konrad Repgen (eds.), *Älterwerden: Chance für Mensch und Gesellschaft* (Munich 1994).

51. See Norbert Lammert, *Königswege und Trampelwege: Zur Modernisierung des deutschen Bildungssystems* (Bochum 1994), p. 11.

52. Quoted from Lammert, *Königswege und Trampelwege*, p. 19.

53. Statistics from Dieter Timmermann, Universität Bielefeld, in *Frankfurter Allgemeine Zeitung*, May 7, 1994.

54. According to the president of the German Academic Exchange Program, Berchem. Of 800 Turks who had received government scholarships, 770 decided for the United States and Great Britain; only 12 opted for Germany.

55. In the section "Democracy as a Policy for Peace" in Chapter 6 there are more extensive references to worldwide immigration movements.

56. See the statements by the Commission on the topic "Immigration" SEK (91) 185 E and the topic "Asylum" SEK (91) 1857 E, also the statements by the Commissions on Immigration and Asylum Policy, COM (94) 23 ENDG, February 23, 1994.

57. See Werner Weidenfeld and Olaf Hillenbrand, in *Europa Archiv*, No. 1/94. In 1992, 559,829 people sought asylum in countries of the European Community. Whereas Great Britain recorded 24,000 applicants for asylum in 1992, the Federal Republic was confronted with 438,000. Alongside the applicants for asylum, there were 230,000 emigrants of German heritage from the former Soviet Union, Poland and Romania. It is known that about 3.2 million Germans still live in the countries of the former East Bloc, the majority of whom would like to move to Germany, and who have a legal right to enter Germany and to be naturalized, as they are not technically considered "foreigners."

58. Followed by 916,000 (14 percent) from former Yugoslavia, 286,000 (4 percent) from Poland; from countries of the EU, 558,000 came from Italy (9 percent) and 346,000 (5 percent) from Greece. (See *Süddeutsche Zeitung*, June 3, 1994.)

59. Of these cases, 404,747 were naturalizations by right, 210,294 were discretionary naturalizations. Of the latter, 28,985 were Yugoslavians, 17,755 Czechoslovakians, 16,165 Poles, 13,133 Turks and 12,826 Austrians (ibid.).

60. See Weidenfeld and Hillenbrand, in *Europa Archiv*, No. 1/94.

61. See Lothar Rühl, "Partner Russland," *Die Welt*, September 7, 1994.

62. Vanna Vannuccini, in *Die Zeit*, No. 37, September 9, 1994.

63. "Kaput," *Sunday Times*, June 6, 1993.

Selected Bibliography

Allensbacher Jahrbuch für Demoskopie 1984–1992 (Munich 1993).

Alten, Jürgen von. *Die ganz normale Anarchie: Jetzt erst beginnt die Nachkriegszeit* (Berlin 1994).

Ardagh, John. *Germany and the Germans: An Anatomy of Society Today* (New York 1987).

Backes, Uwe. "Extremismus und Populismus von rechts." *Aus Politik und Zeitgeschichte*, B 6–47/1990.

Baring, Arnulf. *Deutschland, was nun?* (Berlin 1991).

——— . *Machtwechsel: Die Ära Brandt-Scheel* (Stuttgart 1982).

Bark, Dennis L. and Gress, David R. *Democracy and Its Discontents 1963–1988* (Oxford/Cambridge 1989).

——— . *From Shadow to Substance 1945–1963* (Oxford/Cambridge 1989).

Beck, Ulrich. *Risikogesellschaft: Auf dem Weg in eine andere Moderne* (Frankfurt am Main 1986).

Beck, Ulrich and Beck-Gernsheim, Elisabeth (eds.). *Riskante Freiheiten. Individualisierung in modernen Gesellschaften* (Frankfurt am Main 1994).

Bergsdorf, Wolfgang. *Deutschland im Stress: Politische und gesellschaftliche Herausforderungen nach der Wende* (Munich/Landsberg am Lech 1993).

Biedenkopf, Kurt H. *Einheit und Erneuerung: Deutschland nach dem Umbruch in Europa* (Stuttgart 1994).

Biedenkopf, Kurt and Miegel, Meinhard. *Investieren in Deutschland: Die Bundesrepublik als Wirtschaftsstandort* (Landsberg am Lech 1989).

Bracher, Karl Dietrich. *Zeit der Ideologien: Eine Geschichte politischen Denkens im 20. Jahrhundert* (Stuttgart 1982).

——— (ed.). *Geschichte der Bundesrepublik Deutschland*, 5 vols. (Stuttgart 1986).

Bracher, Karl Dietrich; Funke, Manfred; and Schwarz, Hans-Peter (eds.). *Deutschland zwischen Krieg und Frieden: Beiträge zur Politik und Kultur im 20. Jahrhundert* (Düsseldorf 1990).

Brzezinski, Zbigniew. *Macht und Moral: Neue Werte für die Weltpolitik* (Hamburg 1994).

Bundesministerium des Innern (ed.). *Verfassungsschutzbericht 1993* (Bonn 1994).

Conradt, David P. *The German Policy* (New York and London 1993).

Cooney, James A.; Friedrich, Wolfgang-Uwe; Kleinfeld, Gerald R.; and Lindemann, Beate. *Deutsch-Amerikanische Beziehungen: Jahrbuch 2/German-American Relations Yearbook 2* (Frankfurt am Main/New York 1994).

Dahrendorf, Ralf. *Gesellschaft und Demokratie in Deutschland* (Munich 1965).

Delors, Jacques. "Entwicklungsperspektiven der Europäischen Gemeinschaft." *Aus Politik und Zeitgeschichte*, B 1/93, January 1, 1993.

Economic Strategy Institute. *Shrinking the Atlantic: Europe and the American Economy* (Washington, DC, June 1994).

Eilfort, Michael. *Die Nichtwähler. Wahlenthaltung als Form des Wahlverhaltens* (Paderborn/Munich/Vienna/Zurich 1994).

Elias, Norbert. *Studien über die Deutschen* (Frankfurt am Main 1989).

Erhard, Ludwig. *Wohlstand für Alle* (Düsseldorf 1964).

Evans, Gareth. *Cooperating for Peace: The Global Agenda for the 1990s and Beyond* (St. Leonards, Australia 1993).

Falter, J. W. and Schumann S. "Politische Konflikte, Wählerverhalten und die Struktur des Parteienwettbewerbs." In Gabriel, Oscar W. and Brettschneider, Frank (eds.), *Die EG-Staaten im Vergleich: Strukturen, Prozesse, Politikinhalte* (Opladen 1994).

Fest, Joachim. *Der zerstörte Traum: Vom Ende des utopischen Zeitalters* (Berlin 1991).

Fietz, Martina and Jach, Michael (eds.). *Zündstoff Kriminalität: Innere Sicherheit auf dem Prüfstand* (Munich/Landsberg am Lech 1994).

Fraenkel, Ernst. *Deutschland und die westlichen Demokratien* (Frankfurt am Main 1990).

Fricke, K. W. "Politische Strafjustiz im SED-Staat." *Aus Politik und Zeitgeschichte* 4/1993.

Fukuyama, Francis. *Das Ende der Geschichte* (Munich 1992).

Gabriel, Oscar W. and Brettschneider, Frank (eds.). *Die EG-Staaten im Vergleich: Strukturen, Prozesse, Politikinhalte* (Opladen 1994).

Gaddum, Eckart. *Die deutsche Europapolitik in den 80er Jahren: Interessen, Konflikte und Entscheidungen der Regierung Kohl* (Paderborn/Munich/Vienna/Zurich 1994.

Garton Ash, Timothy. *Ein Jahrhundert wird abgewählt* (Munich/Vienna 1990).

―――. "Germany's Choice." *Foreign Affairs*, July/August 1994.

―――. *Im Namen Europas: Deutschland und der geteilte Kontinent* (Munich/Vienna 1993).

Gaus, Günter. *Wo Deutschland liegt: Eine Ortsbestimmung* (Munich 1986).

Giesen, Bernhard. *Die Intellektuellen und die Nation: Eine deutsche Achsenzeit* (Frankfurt am Main 1993).

Gluchowski, P. "Lebensstile und Wandel der Wähler." *Aus Politik und Zeitgeschichte* 12/1987.

Goff, Jacques Le. *Das alte Europa und die Welt der Moderne* (Munich 1994).

Greiffenhagen, Martin and Sylvia. *Ein schwieriges Vaterland: Zur politischen Kultur im vereinigten Deutschland* (Munich/Leipzig 1993).

Grimm, Thomas. *Was von den Träumen blieb. Eine Bilanz der sozialistischen Utopie* (Preface by Heiner Müller) (Berlin 1993).

Grosser, Alfred. *Der schmale Grat der Freiheit* (Munich/Vienna 1981).

Hacke, Christian. *Weltmacht wider Willen: Die Aussenpolitik der Bundesrepublik Deutschland* (Preface by Gordon A. Craig) (Frankfurt am Main/Berlin 1993).

Hacker, Jens. *Deutsche Irrtümer: Schönfärber und Helfershelfer der SED-Diktatur im Westen* (Berlin/Frankfurt am Main 1992).

Hamilton, Daniel. *Jenseits von Bonn* (Frankfurt am Main/Berlin 1994).

Henzler, Herbert. "Kritische Würdigung der Debatte um den Wirtschaftsstandort Deutschland." *Zeitschrift für Betriebswirtschaft*, Vol. 63 (1993).

Hintze, Peter. "Politik für die Zukunft." *Die politische Meinung*, No. 298, September 1994.

Huntington, Samuel P. "The Clash of Civilizations?" *Foreign Affairs*, Vol. 72, No. 3, 1993.

Inacker, Michael. *Unter Ausschluss der Öffentlichkeit? Die Deutschen in der Golfallianz* (Bonn 1991).

Inglehart, Ronald. *Kultureller Umbruch: Wertwandel in der westlichen Welt* (Frankfurt am Main/New York 1989).

———. *The Silent Revolution: Changing Values and Political Styles among Western Publics* (Princeton 1977).

Inotaí, András. "Die Beziehungen zwischen der EU und den assoziierten Staaten Mittel- und Osteuropas." *Europäische Rundschau*, 94/3.

Jäger, Wolfgang. *Wer regiert die Deutschen? Innenansichten der Parteiendemokratie* (Zurich 1994).

Jugendwerk der Deutschen Shell (ed.). Jugend '92. *Lebenslagen, Orientierungen und Entwicklungsperspektiven im Vereinigten Deutschland*, Vols. 1–4 (Opladen 1992).

Kaiser, Karl. *Deutschlands Vereinigung: Die internationalen Aspekte* (Bergisch Gladbach 1991).

Kaiser, Karl and Maull, Hanns W. (eds.). *Deutschlands neue Aussenpolitik.* (Munich 1994).

Kamp, Karl-Heinz. *Die Frage einer "Osterweiterung der NATO."* Interne Studien und Berichte der Konrad-Adenauer-Stiftung, No. 47/93, November 1993.

Kantzenbach, Erhard. *Der Wirtschaftsstandort Deutschland im internationalen Wettbewerb.* HWWA-Diskussionspapier No. 11, 1993.

Kissinger, Henry A. *Die Vernunft der Nationen. Über das Wesen der Aussenpolitik* (Berlin 1994).

Klages, Helmut. *Häutungen der Demokratie* (Zurich 1993).

————. *Traditionsbruch als Herausforderung: Perspektiven der Wertewandelsgesellschaft* (Frankfurt am Main/New York 1993).

————. *Wertedynamik. Über die Wandelbarkeit des Selbstverständlichen* (Zurich 1988).

Klages, Helmut and Kmieciak, Peter (eds.). *Wertewandel und gesellschaftlicher Wandel* (Frankfurt am Main 1979).

Klingemann, Hans Dieter and Kaase, Max (eds.). *Wahlen und Wähler: Analysen aus Anlass der Bundestagswahl 1990* (Opladen 1994).

Kmieciak, Peter. *Wertstrukturen und Wertewandel in der Bundesrepublik Deutschland* (Göttingen 1976).

Knütter, Hans-Helmuth. *Die Faschismus-Keule* (Frankfurt am Main/Berlin 1993).

Kohl, Helmut (ed.). *Der neue Realismus: Aussenpolitik nach Iran und Afghanistan* (Düsseldorf 1980).

Kohler, Georg (ed.). *Die Folgen von 1989* (Munich/Vienna 1994).

Körber-Stiftung (ed.). *Wieviel Gemeinsinn braucht die liberale Gesellschaft?* 100th Bergedorfer Gesprächskreis in Dresden and Hamburg, November 13 and 14, 1993.

Korte, Karl-Rudolf. "Auf der Suche nach dem verlorenen Selbst: Schriftsteller und das historisch-politische Bewusstsein." In *Bundesrepublik Deutschland 1989.*

————. *Die Chance genutzt: Die Politik zur Einheit Deutschlands* (Frankfurt am Main/New York 1994).

————. *Über Deutschland schreiben: Schriftsteller sehen ihren Staat* (Munich 1992).

————. "Von Thomas Mann bis Martin Walser: Schreiben über Deutschland—Leiden an Deutschland." In Gerd Langguth, *Autor, Macht, Staat: Literatur und Politik in Deutschland* (Düsseldorf 1994).

Koslowski, Peter. *Die postmoderne Kultur: Gesellschaftlich-kulturelle Konsequenzen der technischen Entwicklung* (Munich 1987).

————. *Gesellschaft und Staat: Ein unvermeidlicher Dualismus* (Stuttgart 1982).

————(ed.). *Die religiöse Dimension der Gesellschaft: Religionen und ihre Theorien* (Tübingen 1985).

Krockow, Christian Graf von. *Die Deutschen in ihrem Jahrhundert 1890–1990* (Hamburg 1990).

Lammert, Norbert. *Königswege und Trampelpfade: Zur Modernisierung des deutschen Bildungssystems* (Bochum 1994).

Langguth, Gerd. *Berlin: Vom Brennpunkt der Teilung zur Brücke der Einheit* (Cologne 1990).

————. *Der grüne Faktor: Von der Bewegung zur Partei?* (Zurich 1984). English extended edition: *The Green Factor in German Politics* (Boulder, CO and London 1986).

————. "Innerdeutsche und internationale Aspekte der Berlin-Politik." *Aus Politik und Zeitgeschichte*, B 33–34/86, August 16, 1986.

————. *Jugend ist anders: Porträt einer jungen Generation* (Freiburg/Basel/Vienna 1983).

————. *Protestbewegung: Entwicklung, Niedergang, Renaissance. Die Neue Linke seit 1968* (Cologne 1983).

————. "Was ist Politik?" In Günther Rüther, *Politik und Gesellschaft in Deutschland* (Cologne 1994).

———— (ed.). *Autor, Macht, Staat: Literatur und Politik in Deutschland. Ein notwendiger Dialog* (Düsseldorf 1994).

———— (ed.). *Macht bedeutet Verantwortung: Adenauers Weichenstellungen für die heutige Politik* (Cologne 1994).

———— (ed.). *Offensive Demokratie: Versuch einer rationalen Orientierung* (Stuttgart 1972).

Lehr, Ursula and Repgen, Konrad (eds.). *Älterwerden: Chance für Mensch und Gesellschaft* (Munich 1994).

Lepsius, M. Rainer. *Demokratie in Deutschland: Soziologisch-historische Konstellationsanalysen* (Göttingen 1993).

Lepszy, Norbert. "Die Republikaner." *Aus Politik und Zeitgeschichte*, B 41–42/1989.

Longerich, Peter. *"Was ist des Deutschen Vaterland?" Dokumente zur Frage der deutschen Einheit 1800–1990* (Munich/Zurich 1990).

Maaz, Hans-Joachim. *Der Gefühlsstau: Ein Psychogramm der DDR* (Berlin 1990).

————. "Gewalt in Deutschland: Eine psychologische Analyse." *Aus Politik und Zeitgeschichte*, B 2–3/1993.

Marsh, David. *Der zaudernde Riese: Deutschland in Europa* (Munich 1994).

————. *The New Germany at the Crossroads* (London/Sydney/Auckland/Johannesburg 1990).

Mathiopoulos, Margarita. *Das Ende der Bonner Republik* (Stuttgart 1993).

Maull, Hanns W. (ed.). *Japan und Europa: Getrennte Welten?* (Frankfurt am Main/New York 1993).

McAdams, A. James. *Germany Divided: From the Wall to Reunification* (Princeton 1993).

Meier, Christian. *Deutsche Einheit als Herausforderung* (Munich/Vienna 1990).

Meissner, Doris M.; Hormats, Robert D.; Garrigues Walker, Antonio; and Ogata, Shiguro. *International Migration: Challenges in a New Era. A Report to the Trilateral Commission* (New York/Paris/Tokyo 1993).

Miegel, Bernhard and Wahl, Stefanie. *Das Ende der Individualität: Die Kultur des Westens zerstört sich selbst* (Munich/Landsberg am Lech 1993).

Minc, Alain. *Die deutsche Herausforderung: Wird die Bundesrepublik den europäischen Binnenmarkt beherrschen?* (Hamburg 1989).

Morsey, Rudolf. *Die Deutschlandpolitik Adenauers: Alte Thesen und neue Fakten* (Opladen 1991).

Muller, Steven. "Democracy in Germany." *Daedalus*, Journal of the American Academy of Arts and Sciences, Winter 1994, Vol. 123, No. 1.

Niclauss, Karlheinz. *Kanzlerdemokratie: Bonner Regierungspraxis von Konrad Adenauer bis Helmut Kohl* (Stuttgart 1988).

Nixon, Richard. *Beyond Peace* (New York 1994).

Noelle-Neumann, Elisabeth. *Demoskopische Deutschstunde: Vom Wartesaal der Geschichte zur deutschen Einheit* (Zurich 1991).

Oberndörfer, Dieter et al. (eds.). *Wirtschaftlicher Wandel, religiöser Wandel und Wertwandel* (Berlin 1985).

Pflüger, Friedbert and Lipscher, Winfried (eds.). *Feinde werden Freunde: Von den Schwierigkeiten der deutsch-polnischen Nachbarschaft* (Bonn 1993).

Plessner, Helmut. *Die verspätete Nation: Über die politische Verführbarkeit bürgerlichen Geistes* (Stuttgart 1959).

Pond, Elisabeth. *Beyond the Wall: Germany's Road to Unification* (Washington, DC 1993).

Preusse, Heinz Gert. *Ist die Frage nach der internationalen Wettbewerbsfähigkeit überholt?* Diskussionsbeiträge des Ibero-Amerikanischen Instituts für Wirtschaftsforschung der Universität Göttingen No. 46, 1988.

Rietzschel, Thomas. *Über Deutschland: Schriftsteller geben Auskunft* (Leipzig 1993).

Rinsche, Günter. *Grundfragen einer neuen politischen Ordnung in Europa. KAS-Auslandsinformationen*, 1/1994.

Rühe, Volker. *Deutschlands Verantwortung: Perspektiven für das neue Europa* (Frankfurt am Main/Berlin 1994).

Rühl, Lothar. *Zeitenwende in Europa: Der Wandel der Staatenwelt und der Bündnisse* (Stuttgart 1990).

Rüther, Günther (ed.). *Werteverzicht in der Industriegesellschaft?* (Bonn 1976).

Rüttgers, Jürgen. *Dinosaurier der Demokratie: Wege aus der Parteienkrise und Politikverdrossenheit* (Hamburg 1993).

Sachverständigenrat zur Begutachtung der gesamtwirtschaftlichen Entwicklung. *Für Wachstumsorientierung: Gegen lähmenden Verteilungsstreit. Jahresgutachten 1992/93* (Stuttgart 1992).

————. *Zeit zum Handeln-Antriebskräfte stärken. Jahresgutachten 1993/94* (Stuttgart 1993).

Schäuble, Wolfgang. *Und der Zukunft zugewandt* (Berlin 1994).

Scheuch, Erwin K. *Wie deutsch sind die Deutschen? Eine Nation wandelt ihr Gesicht* (Bergisch Gladbach 1991).

Scheuer, Helmut. "Nation und Europa:Stellungnahmen deutscher Schriftsteller im 20. Jahrhundert." In Gerd Langguth, *Autor, Macht, Staat: Literatur und Politik in Deutschland* (Düsseldorf 1994).

Schneider, Peter. *Vom Ende der Gewissheit* (Berlin 1994).

Schöllgen, Gregor. *Stationen deutscher Aussenpolitik: Von Friedrich dem Grossen bis zur Gegenwart* (Munich 1992).

Schröder, Richard. *Deutschland schwierig Vaterland. Für eine neue politische Kultur* (Freiburg/Basel/Vienna 1993).

Schulze, Gerhard. *Die Erlebnisgesellschaft: Kultursoziologie der Gegenwart* (Frankfurt am Main/New York 1992).

Schulze, Hagen. *Staat und Nation in der europäischen Geschichte* (Munich 1994).

Schumpeter, Joseph A. *Sozialismus und Demokratie* (Bern 1950).

Schwarz, Hans-Peter. "Deutsche Aussenpolitik nach der Vereinigung." In Haungs, Peter; Grass, Karl Martin; Maier, Hans; and Veen, Hans-Joachim (eds.), *Civitas: Widmungen für Bernhard Vogel zum 60. Geburtstag* (Paderborn/Munich/Vienna/Zurich 1992).

————. Entscheidung für den Westen. In Funke, Manfred (ed.), *Entscheidung für den Westen: Vom Besatzungsstatut zur Souveränität der Bundesrepublik 1949–1955* (Bonn 1988).

————. *Die gezähmten Deutschen: Von der Machtbesessenheit zur Machtvergessenheit* (Stuttgart 1985).

————. *Die Zentralmacht Europas: Deutschlands Rückkehr auf die Weltbühne* (Berlin 1994).

Sontheimer, Kurt. *Deutschlands politische Kultur* (Munich 1990).

————. *Zeitenwende? Die Bundesrepublik Deutschland zwischen alter und alternativer Politik* (Hamburg 1983).

Spranger, Carl-Dieter. *Verantwortung für die Eine Welt* (Berlin/Frankfurt am Main 1994).

Stephan, Cora. *Der Betroffenheitskult: Eine politische Sittengeschichte* (Berlin 1993).

Stoltenberg, Gerhard. "Plädoyer für innovatives Denken. Aufgaben der internationalen Wirtschafts- und Währungspolitik." *Europa Archiv*, No. 7, 1994.

Stöss, Richard. "Rechtsextremismus und Wahlen in der Bundesrepublik." *Aus Politik und Zeitgeschichte*, B 11/1993.

Struck, Peter. *Erziehung gegen Gewalt* (Neuwied/Kriftel/Berlin 1994).

Szabo, Stephen F. *The Diplomacy of German Unification* (New York 1992).

Teltschik, Horst. *329 Tage: Innenansichten der Einigung* (Berlin 1991).

Thomas, Rüdiger, "Aufklärung statt Abrechnung: Anmerkungen zum Umgang mit der DDR-Geschichte." In Weidenfeld, Werner (ed.), *Deutschland: Eine Nation—Doppelte Geschichte. Materialien zum deutschen Selbstverständnis* (Cologne 1993).

Thurow, Lester. *Kopf an Kopf: Wer siegt im Wirtschaftskrieg zwischen Europa, Japan und den USA?* (Düsseldorf 1993).

Treverton, Gregory F. *America, Germany and the Future of Europe* (Princeton, NJ 1992).

Veen, Hans-Joachim. "Zwei Identitäten in Deutschland? Nationale Zugehörigkeit, politische Prioritäten und Wertorientierungen der West- und Ostdeutschen." In Jäger, Wolfgang; Mühleisen, Hans-Otto; and Veen, Hans-

Joachim (eds.), *Republik und Dritte Welt: Festschrift für Dieter Oberndörfer zum 65. Geburtstag* (Paderborn/Munich/Vienna/Zurich 1994).

Veen, Hans-Joachim and Gluchowski, Peter. "Die Anhängerschaften der Parteien vor und nach der Einheit—eine Langfristbetrachtung von 1953 bis 1993." *Zeitschrift für Parlamentsfragen*, No. 2, 1994.

Veen, Hans-Joachim; Jaide, Walter; Hille, Barbara; Friedrich, Walter; and Förster, Peter. *Eine Jugend in Deutschland? Orientierungen und Verhaltensweisen der Jugend in Ost und West* (Opladen 1994).

Vernet, Daniel. *Was wird aus Deutschland?* (Bergisch Gladbach 1993).

Wagner, Norbert. "Zur Lage in Russland nach den Wahlen." *KAS-Auslandsinformationen* 2/1994.

Watson, Alan. *Die Deutschen—wer sind sie heute?* (Berlin 1993).

Weber, Hermann. *DDR: Grundriss der Geschichte 1945–1990* (Hannover 1991).

Weidenfeld, Werner. *Der deutsche Weg* (Berlin 1990).

Weidenfeld, Werner (ed.). *Deutschland: Eine Nation—Doppelte Geschichte. Materialien zum deutschen Selbstverständnis* (Cologne 1993).

———— (ed.). *Die Identität der Deutschen* (Munich 1983).

———— (ed.). *Maastricht in der Analyse—Materialien zur Europäischen Union* (Gütersloh 1994).

Weidenfeld, Werner and Korte, Karl-Rudolf. *Die Deutschen: Profil einer Nation* (Stuttgart 1991).

Wickert, Ulrich (ed.). *Angst vor Deutschland* (Hamburg 1990).

Wolffsohn, Michael. *Frieden jetzt? Nahost im Umbruch* (Munich 1994).

Zapf, Wolfgang; Breuer, Sigrid; Hampel, Jürgen; Krause, Peter; Mohr, Hans-Michael; and Wiegand, Erich. *Individualisierung und Sicherheit: Untersuchungen zur Lebensqualität in der Bundesrepublik Deutschland* (Munich 1987).

Index

Abkrhazia, 125
Afropessimism, 167
AFTA (Asian Free Trade Area), 145, 170
Agenda 21, 166
AIDS, 171, 173
Antifascism, 31, 73, 84, 88, 183
Anti-Semitism, 3, 34–35, 124
Antitotalitarianism, 72, 84
APEC (Asia-Pacific Economic Cooperation), 145, 170
Arms export policy, 177
ASEAN (Association of Southeast Asian Nations), 145, 169
Associations, 12, 195–97, 300
Asylum law, 207–8
Austria, 132, 145, 161, 166
Autonomous units, 29

Basic Law/German Constitution, 13, 70, 78, 80, 192, 197, 199
Belarus, 125–26, 135–36
Belgium, 132, 154
Blue helmets, 140, 149
Brutality, 31, 35–37
Bulgaria, 121, 133
Bundeswehr (German Armed Forces), 4, 45, 140–42, 148–49

Bureaucracy, 27, 102–3, 108, 203

Canada, 34, 130, 145, 147, 166
Career politician, 197
Caretaker state, 198
Chechnya, 123
China, 143–44, 148, 169–70, 178
Church statistics, 14
Churches, 12–14, 39, 186, 188, 195
CNN factor, 9, 118
Coalition governments, 54–59
COMECON, 4, 79
Committees for Justice, 70
Common European Currency/Single European Currency, 158–59
Common Foreign and Security Policy, 120, 131–32, 139, 152, 209
Communal self-administration, 175, 198
Communal spirit, 83, 91, 190, 202
Communist Platform, 29, 67–69
Competitive ability, 95, 97, 99–101, 103–4, 107, 203
Concerns and fears, 45, 50
Conference of Rio, 166, 179
Confession, membership in a religious, 13–15
Corporate tax, 103, 109

Corruption, 167, 172, 201
Crime, 30–32, 34–35, 82–83, 90, 172–73, 200–202
CSCE (Conference on Security and Cooperation in Europe), 5, 130. *See also* OCSE
Culture nation, 76, 87–88
Currency speculation, 118
Cyprus, 161
Czech Republic, 111, 115, 121, 126, 131, 133–34, 161

Debt crisis, debt situation, 167–68, 170, 175, 179
Deindustrialization, 97
Democracy, 9, 23, 36–38, 43, 76–77, 87–91, 106, 166–67, 174, 184–86, 188, 191, 196–98
Democracy, level of satisfaction with, 19–21, 43–45
Democracy, support of, 9, 49, 53, 82, 167, 175
Deregulation, 109, 199, 203–4
Developing countries, 27, 94, 145–46, 148, 207
Development policy, 163–79
Drug addiction, 20
Drug trade, international, 172–73, 201

EAEC (East Asian Economic Caucus), 170
East-west conflict, 1, 6, 75, 114, 116–17, 140, 172, 176, 183, 201
Ecological situation, in the former GDR (German Democratic Republic), 71, 203
Economic and Currency Union, 98–99
Economic situation, 48, 51, 59, 93–112, 154, 170, 174–79, 187, 202
Educate, courage to, 36–37, 189–90
Education, 7, 16, 22, 25, 97, 143, 148, 165, 167, 176, 204

Education, antiauthoritarian, 22, 25, 36
Educational system, 14, 84, 104, 206–7
Electoral participation, 40, 58
Elites, 172, 192–94
Environment, 90, 95, 171–72, 179, 191
Environmental movements, 16–17, 26, 67
Environmental protection, 26, 91, 102, 118, 163, 166–67
Estonia, 115, 124, 133
EURATOM (European Atomic Energy Community), 119
European Central Bank, 152, 158–59
European Commission, 73, 119, 132, 137, 152–53, 155–57, 159–61, 207
European Community (EC)/European Union (EU), 2, 4, 43–44, 79–80, 93, 103, 114, 116–20, 130–34, 137–39, 142–45, 147–48, 151–63, 173, 178, 201–3, 207–9
European Economic Area (EEA), 103, 143–45, 147–48
European elections, 40, 61, 64, 153, 157
European integration, 4–5, 9, 79, 87, 142, 144, 149, 151–54, 157–58, 161–63, 182, 191, 209–10
European Parliament, 40, 61, 131, 153, 157, 160
Everyday and petty crimes, 201. *See also* Crime
Extraparliamentary Opposition (APO), 16, 24, 26

Families, 12, 16, 27, 35, 176, 188–89, 202, 206
Federalism, 199
Finland, 132–33, 145, 161
Five percent clause, 40, 62–63, 71
Floating voters, 39

Food supplies, 173
Foreign debt, of the GDR (German Democratic Republic), 94
Foreign trade, 98–99, 143
Foreigner extremism, 30
Foreigner hatred, 30–33, 35–36
France, 14, 22, 34, 72, 103, 114, 116, 119, 126, 128, 132, 137, 142, 144, 147, 154, 158, 161–63, 166, 207
Functional elite, 192

GATT (General Agreement on Tariffs and Trade), 108, 127, 145–47, 177–78. *See also* World Trade Organization
Gene technology, 102, 118, 204–5
Generational conflict, 3, 19–21, 23
German citizenship, 80
German Democratic Republic (GDR), 2, 4, 7, 34, 41, 65–66, 71, 77–78, 80, 83–89, 91, 94–96, 113–15, 157, 181, 185, 191, 193, 198
German question, 81, 113–15
German treaties, 80
German unity, 40–48, 73–79, 81
Great Britain, 14, 34, 114, 116, 119, 126, 128, 132, 137, 142, 144, 147–48, 154, 158, 162, 166
Greece, 131–32, 154, 161
Greenhouse effect, 164

Help to help oneself, 173, 175–76, 210
Hitler dictatorship/Nazi dictatorship, 93, 193
Holocaust, 3, 33, 35, 77, 148, 192
Human rights, 7, 70, 88, 91, 96, 131, 144–45, 152, 166, 168, 173, 176, 192
Hunger, 164, 170, 176, 179
Hungary, 75, 111, 115, 121, 126, 131, 133–34, 161

Identity, 3–5, 9, 40–41, 75, 77–82, 85–90, 190–92, 212
Ideology, 26, 64, 66
IMF (International Monetary Fund), 127
Immigration, 118, 207–8
Individualization, 11–12, 17–18, 184, 189, 195–96
Inflation rate, 98, 104, 125, 158
Information technology, 102, 104, 204–5
Infrastructure, 69, 95, 104
Innovation, 102, 199, 203, 205
Innovative weakness, 102
Intellectuals, 24–25, 85–89
Ireland, 131–33, 154, 161
Islamic fundamentalism, 117, 139
Italy, 72, 119, 132, 144, 147, 154

Japan, 100–103, 137, 142–44, 147–48, 166, 169–71, 178, 204–5
Job performance, 17, 20, 154

Korea, Republic of, 111, 144, 170

Large organizations, 8, 12, 18–19, 27–28
Latvia, 75, 115, 133
Left and right radicalism, 29, 35, 43
Left radicals, 29
Liechtenstein, 145
Lithuania, 75, 115, 133
Luxembourg, 132–33, 154

Maastricht, Treaty of, 90, 110, 131–32, 151–53, 157–60, 162, 201, 209
Machine operating times, 101
Malta, 161
Market economy, 45, 71, 94, 99, 105–7, 173–75, 186, 193
Marriage, 12, 17
Marriage-like partnerships, 12
Marshall Plan, 93, 203

Mass unemployment, 112, 121
Media, 17, 20, 22, 25, 28, 33, 37–38,
    196, 202, 211
Migration, 8, 18, 90, 139, 164, 172,
    207, 210. *See also* Refugees
Milieus, changes in, 18–19, 24, 188,
    195
Montan Union, 4, 119

NAFTA, 145
Nation, 5, 73–91, 181, 190–91
National parties, 12, 18, 39–40, 61,
    71, 194–97
National Socialism, 21, 34, 72, 77,
    82, 84, 93, 157, 185
NATO/Atlantic alliance, 2, 4–5, 117–
    20, 126–27, 130–35, 138, 140–41,
    144–45, 148–51, 182, 209
Naturalization, 208
Netherlands, the, 132, 154
New Left, 22
New social movements, 22
Newly industrialized countries, 137,
    169–70, 178
1968 rebellion, 11, 16, 23–26, 72, 89
Nonvoters, 21
North-south problem, 27
Norway, 132–33, 145, 166
Nuclear power plants, 20, 118, 137
Nuclear proliferation, 136–37, 139

OECD (Organization for Economic
    Cooperation and Development),
    127, 138, 166–67, 170, 174, 177
Organizations, 29, 32, 68, 145, 194,
    197
Orientation, 9, 12, 17–18, 184–86,
    189–90, 194
Orientational crisis/loss of orienta-
    tion, 2, 8, 184–85, 189, 197
OSCE (Organization for Security and
    Cooperation in Europe), 130. *See
    also* CSCE

Ostpolitik, 114
Out-of-area deployments, of the Ger-
    man army, 140
Overaging, 205–6
Overpopulation, 164–65, 170–71, 206
Ozone hole, 164

Parties, 18–20, 194–97
Parties, dissatisfaction with, 195
Partnership for Peace, 127, 130, 133–
    35
Peace movement, 85
Peaceful revolution, 7, 91, 191
Peacekeeping, 6, 118, 140, 142, 149,
    176, 209
Pluralization, 184, 189, 196–97
Poland, 75, 115, 121, 126, 131–34,
    144, 161
Political education, 7, 35, 189, 202
Political foundations, 137, 175
Politicians/politics, dissatisfaction
    with, 19–21, 189, 195, 199
Population policy, 164, 169, 175,
    206. *See also* Overpopulation
Portugal, 131–32, 154, 161
Postadolescence, 16
Postmaterialism/postmaterial, 16–17,
    22, 41, 187
Poverty, fight against, 164, 168–70,
    175–76, 210
Pricing mechanism, 106–7
Private property, 107
Privatization, 96–97, 104, 107–8,
    168, 198–99, 203
Production costs, 98–99, 101–2, 203
Proportional representation, system
    of, 40, 55, 199
Protest voters, 71
Punks, 29–30

Rain forests, 164, 172
Rapallo, 128
Red Army Faction (RAF), 24

Refugees, 118, 172, 176, 179, 207–8. *See also* Migration
Regionalization, 76, 145–47
Religious fundamentalism, 210
Republikaner, 40, 55–59, 63, 71, 157
Reunification/call to reunify, 1, 6, 18, 42, 73–75, 78–79, 81, 85–87, 152, 154, 158, 162–63, 181–82, 187–88
Right-wing radicalism/right-wing radicals, 29–34, 36, 88
Romania, 121, 126, 133
Rome, Treaty of, 4
Russia, 6, 115, 121–28, 132–38, 209–10. *See also* Soviet Union

School education, 14, 35–37, 206
Secularization, 13, 186–87, 189
SED (Socialist Unity Party) dictatorship/SED leadershp/SED regime, 39, 58, 65, 68, 70–71, 78–79, 82–84, 86, 193
Service economy, 18, 22–24
Single households, 12
Skinheads, 29–30
Slovakian Republic, 121, 126, 131, 134
Slovenia, 121
Social Market Economy, 7, 74, 96, 105–7, 109, 203–4
Social reforms, 174
Social security, 66, 88, 93, 104, 106–7, 148, 169, 208
Social system, 23, 106–7, 175, 203, 206
Socialism, 1, 40–43, 65, 67, 69, 72, 78, 84, 86, 89, 183, 185
Sovereignty, 4, 6, 80, 113–15, 126, 163, 210
Soviet Union, 2, 4, 115, 124, 128, 136–37, 177, 201. *See also* Russia
Spain, 72, 131–32, 144, 154, 158, 161
Squatting, 29

State, role of the, 24, 97, 188, 198–99, 203
State security system/Stasi, 67–68, 82–85
Strategic nuclear weapons, 135–36
Student revolts, 3, 22, 190
Studies, 14, 206–7
Subsidies, 99, 107–8, 125, 146, 168, 203
Sweden, 34, 161
System, trust in the, 43–47

Taiwan, 111, 169
Tax hikes, 103, 112
Tax rate, 102–3, 109–10, 198, 203
Totalitarianism, 82, 84, 88
Trade conditions, 210
Transformation processes, 1–2, 9, 12, 16, 18, 22, 48
Turkey, 117, 132–33, 138, 141, 161
Two-Plus-Four Negotiations, 114–15

Ukraine, 121, 125–26, 135–36, 138
Unemployment, 32, 66, 71, 87, 95, 98–99, 103–4, 164, 198, 202
Unions, 19, 27, 68, 202
United Nations, 6, 114, 127–28, 130, 139–42, 149, 170–72, 176, 178, 199
United States, 4–5, 12, 22, 34, 100–103, 114, 117, 127, 130, 132–33, 137–38, 142–48, 150, 165, 170, 173, 177–78, 184, 204–5, 208–9

Value shift/values, 11–38, 41, 187–88, 195, 211
Violence, 22, 24–26, 29–35, 70
Voluntary Ecological Year/Voluntary Social Year, 20

Wage structure, 101–2, 202
Wages, incurred costs of, 101
Wandervogelbewegung, 21

Warsaw Pact, 4, 114, 121, 127
Weimar Republic, 34, 76, 82, 112,
    181, 194, 196, 207, 211
West, ties to the, 115, 118
Western European Union (WEU),
    132–33, 141, 151, 182,
    209
Western orientation, 4, 119, 182–84
World domestic policy, 164, 210
World trade, 103, 145–46, 148, 170,
    177–78

World Trade Organization (WTO),
    127, 145–46. *See also* GATT
World War II, 3, 18, 22, 93, 105,
    114, 140, 142, 148, 163

Youth culture, 19–22, 28
Youth movement, 21–22
Youth ordination (*Jugendweihe*), 13
Youth protest, 21, 24–27, 190
Yugoslavia, 27, 75, 117, 128, 141,
    209

About the Author

GERD LANGGUTH is Executive Chairman of the Konrad Adenauer Foundation in Germany, as well as Visiting Professor of Political Science at the University of Bonn. He has served as a member of the German Bundestag, as a representative of Germany to the EC Commission, and has authored numerous books on Germany.

ISBN 0-275-95231-2

HARDCOVER BAR CODE